The European Family

The European Family

Patriarchy to Partnership
from the Middle Ages to the Present

MICHAEL MITTERAUER
AND
REINHARD SIEDER

Translated by
Karla Oosterveen and Manfred Hörzinger

The University of Chicago Press

First published in German as
Vom Patriarchat zur Partnerschaft: Zum Strukturwandel der
Familie
© C. H. Beck'sche Verlagsbuchhandlung (Oscar Beck),
München, 1977,
and revised for this edition

The University of Chicago Press, Chicago 60637
Basil Blackwell Ltd, Oxford OX4 1JF
© 1982 by Basil Blackwell Ltd
All rights reserved. Published 1982. Reprinted 1983, 1988
Printed in the USA

89 88 87 86 85 84 83 82   54321

Library of Congress Cataloging in Publication Data

Mitterauer, Michael.
  The european family.

  Translation of: Vom Patriarchat zur Partnerschaft.
  1. Family – History.   2. Family – Europe – History.
I. Title
HQ503.M513   306.8′ 094   81-21954
ISBN 0-226-53240-2   AACR2

Contents

Foreword

PETER LASLETT

No better origin for a book on the history of the European family can be imagined than Vienna, and no better authorship than that of the two Viennese scholars who have collaborated to produce the work in front of us. Originally published as a beginner's guide five years ago, unburdened either with footnotes or with references, it has undergone that happy evolution which on rare occasions takes author and publisher by surprise. It has established itself as the authoritative preliminary statement on the history of the family, in German-speaking countries.

Suggestions which were put forward as provisional hypotheses are fast turning into working principles of enquiry. Bold, original, interesting, fast in pace, intellectually penetrating yet easy to read, it would be strange in my view if its career in the English reading world did not follow a similar course. For our benefit it has been revised as well as translated, and equipped, as will be seen, with a formidable series of references, though still without footnotes.

Since his election as Professor of Economic and Social History at the University of Vienna early in his career, Michael Mitterauer has devoted his time and effort to historical sociology, and particularly to what might be called the micro social structure in the past. With the research funds attached to his chair, and with the help of Austrian and German foundations, he has set up a group to investigate that topic over a great deal of the vast region of which Vienna is the historic cultural and communications centre or point of interchange, in succession to Austrian political overlordship. Areas now incorporated into Hungary, Czechoslovakia, Yugoslavia and reaching as far as Italy, Poland and even into the Soviet Union, have been surveyed for this purpose, and copies of the relevant documents assembled in Vienna. Reinhard Sieder has been a leading figure in the research and in the analysis. For the last two or three years the Cambridge Group for the History of Population and Social Structure has enjoyed a regular relationship of interchange with them.

It is the structure of the family as a production unit in pre-industrial times which has been the predominant interest of the Viennese. The change to a position in which reproduction and consumption have come to dominate its workings at the expense of production, now done elsewhere, is a leading theme of their book.

Mitterauer and Sieder will be found in fact to qualify the familial concept in interesting and important ways, emphasizing that the family as the unit of man, wife and child did not exist as a single expression in the German language before the eighteenth century. Without being able even to name the concept of the 'nuclear' family as we think of it in our day, how can the men and women of that era have thought of it as we do?

Our two authors make it clear in fact that any attempt to understand familial groups exclusively or even predominantly in terms of kinship, reproduction and biology, is liable to serious error. Contemporary sociologists of the family, they imply, misunderstand the subject because of such preconceptions, and because of their too easy acceptance of the family as a final social unit, the building blocks of society. Views such as these have tended to imprison our own generation in the assumptions and dogmas of our vanished pre-industrial past, preventing us from adapting familial institutions to our own contemporary purposes, preventing us in fact from replacing patriarchalism with partnership.

No better illustration of the effectiveness of historical sociology can be found than in chapter 3 of this volume. There they tackle the well-established theory of the developmental cycle of the domestic group and demonstrate its historical inadequacy. It is a delicious irony that in this way Viennese historians should have demonstrated that the Oedipus phenomenon cannot be called a human universal, but belongs historically to the imperial Vienna where Sigmund Freud himself resided. It is both inadequate and inappropriate, in their view, to apply such dogmas unmodified to the family life of the peasants and artisans of former times.

The psychiatrist and social worker may find equally arresting their confident assertion about the durability of emotional bonding within the family. It is not in our day, but it was in that of our peasant predecessors, that the family membership was evanescent, familial relationships brief, intermittent and presumably unstable. Our trouble, they seem to imply, may be that the same restricted set of emotional relationships within the family group continues for such an inordinate length of time, lacking both variety and relief.

It would be an injustice to our two authors, however, to represent them as basing their bold suggestions on a systematic, numerical analysis from all over the vast European region in which they interest themselves, or as claiming universality for their statements. The word 'European' in their title may be thought of as roughly covering what is conveyed by the vague expression 'Central Europe', as contrasted with the European East, which must mean Russia, and rather less definitely distinguished from the European West, where we in Britain equally clearly belong. Their detailed information seems to come for the most part from the splendid sources which they have uncovered and worked upon in their own Austrian countryside and its urban areas, Vienna and Salzburg in particular, sources which make the English historian of such subjects sigh with envy.

They intend in fact to attach their generalizations to a complex which they name 'Central and Western' Europe, an expression which, I must confess, makes the historical sociologist working on British and North-West European evidence slightly uneasy. They themselves point out that adoption, which plays no insignificant part in their modification of the reproductive and kin-based familial theories which they associate with contemporary sociology, was absent in England until the twentieth century. They comment that this shows how much variation in social practices there must have been within their nominated 'European' area. The whole subject of our continent as an arena of variation in familial structure and social structure generally, on the large scale and the small, is at present being actively pursued in many places. Hypotheses and fresh results have made their appearance even since Mitterauer and Sieder completed their refurbished text.

Because the differences which are being unearthed are so interesting in themselves and because it is vital that the reader in Britain, the United States, or elsewhere amongst English speakers, should not make the mistake of supposing that the statements on the European family necessarily apply unmodified to their own ancestry in pre-industrial times, I venture to complete this preface in the following way. I append a list of some of the salient differences in what we now know of the history of the family and kinship in England, from those set out so economically and persuasively for 'Europe' by our two Viennese scholars.

First, and most important, the comparative remoteness in Britain of the onset of industrialization and hence of the fading of the 'traditional' social order. In our own particular European region, the Great Industrial Revolution began its course in the middle to later eighteenth century; in Central Europe a hundred years or more after this. Which means that there were still people alive until quite recently who remembered the Austria of almost entirely pre-industrial times, and that areas of small scale, family farming on the traditional peasant mould still exist in that country, to be visited and commented upon. With us neither of these things is true.

Second, the considerable extent of economic and social individualism in England, even in medieval times, and especially of a market in labour. Because of this there were always more family groups in our country than elsewhere which were not production groups, where the wages of the household head made up the important, often the only source of income, and were earned from work done outside the household. Work group and kin group were related differently in Austria and Central Europe than they were in England.

Third, the failure of agrarian social organization in our country even in pre-industrial times to conform at all precisely to the peasant model, where a family line was identified with a house and a plot of land handed down from generation to generation. There are scholars who even deny that a peasantry of this type, traditionally supposed to be present all over Europe, or even all over the world, in succession to the hunter gatherers, ever existed at all in England.

Fourth, and as a corollary to this, the prevalence in some parts of Austria and elswhere in Central Europe of the famous stem family form of domestic group, a form rather narrowly defined by Mitterauer somewhat as follows:

Such a group existed when a married heir was dwelling with his wife and their children, if any, in the family of the household head, the holder of the family plot, and under his authority. When succession occurred, that heir took over the family house and plot and the stem was carried on. In such circumstances, which cannot of course have been universal even under undisturbed peasant agrarian conditions, the same household can be said to continue in being from generation to generation.

It is very difficult indeed to uncover evidence for the prevalence of arrangements of this kind in England at any time in our past. With us, therefore, every marriage seemed to have meant a *new* household, even if the couple inherited the house and land of the previous holder. In the earliest years of marriage, especially in the towns, an occasional couple might live for a little while in one or other of their parental families, but this was in the way of waiting time until their own, fresh household establishment could begin its career.

Fifth, the tendency in Austria and Central Europe for servants to be related to the head of the household in which they worked, and to be entitled *servants* rather than cousin, niece, or even son or daughter. In England, where servants may have been even more common than in Austria, this did occur but very much less often. Kin titles within the family group over-rode work titles, under the exceedingly rare circumstances when both could be used of the same person. Only a difference of phraseology perhaps but an interesting one.

Sixth, the greater insistence which seems to have been laid on retirement arrangements in Austria and in many parts of Europe than was the case in England. This is implied by what has been said about the stem family and means that agreements with retiring farmers, parts of houses and premises set aside for their final years, formal agreements about their income in retirement and so on, were much less conspicuous than amongst the peasantry of continental Europe.

Seventh, the prevalence in Austria and elsewhere, and the virtual absence in England of *Inwohner*, or inmates, and of sub-households generally. Though inmates, usually lodgers, existed in traditional times in our country, they were officially disapproved of; they were single individuals as a rule, not lodging families, and confined for the most part to towns. In Central Europe, as is made plain, such inmates and such households were institutions of considerable importance in the social structure and were used by the community to enable impoverished persons and families to subsist. In England Poor Relief operated very differently, and kept the casualties as independent households or even sometimes in institutions. Family and collectivity were differently related between the two systems.

The first of these seven contrasts is an entirely chronological one, the others could be called structural. It should perhaps be added that there were differences in purely demographic chronology between Austria and England of some structural importance, particularly in respect of expectation of life.

Mitterauer and Sieder lay great emphasis on increased expectation of life at birth as a dissolvent or as a source of distortion of the older familial order in their Europe. But, as we have seen, what is sometimes called the passing of traditional society had already taken place when expectation of life began its critical rise in our country. Therefore, it cannot have been affected in the way which is suggested for the Europe of this essay.

Complications of this kind should do nothing to deter the English speaking reader. And I fervently hope that these explanations from the English point of view will do something to encourage in him the enthusiasm which, I believe, the book he holds in his hand is likely to inspire.

November 1981

Introduction

The family represents a direct experience for everyone. It is impossible, then, to consider the family as a subject for professional research without being influenced by one's own impressions and ideas. And it is also impossible to write about the family without arousing in the reader memories of personal experiences and problems. One cannot deal with the family, whether as author or reader, without being in some way involved.

This personal involvement in the subject presents both an opportunity and a threat. On the one hand, greater interest is aroused; on the other hand, family problems are strongly emotive for every individual, and opinions about the family, marriage and the rearing of children are influenced by one's political and philosophical beliefs. It is the task of the historian to show how the seemingly 'natural' and enduring forms of family life came into being and how they change over time. This may well touch on particularly vulnerable areas of personal experience.

The authors of this book, however, have no wish to raise doubt and insecurity for their own sake; their hope is to make possible sounder judgements of present-day problems from knowledge of the function of familial connections in the past. Their object is to discover whether a study of historical origins and development can help people to make up their minds about such matters as role images of the sexes, sexual behaviour, the rearing of children, the care of the elderly, the position of the woman in the household and at her job. Does his specialized knowledge place the historian in a suitable position to call attention to the inevitable changes in the forms of family life, or perhaps even to consider alternative ways of living together? The authors are of the opinion that a modern social history of the family must ultimately succeed in doing this. In the present work they attempt to take a first step in this direction.

But the historian is not able to promote better understanding of present-day problems on his own. Social history has to call on the aid of other social sciences, and the construction of theories and models and the interpretation of modern data are heavily dependent on the social sciences. All attempts to relate the history of the family to present-day conditions are subject to the different ways in which theories of social development are constructed by historians and sociologists. The studies brought together in this volume reflect this difference in outlook. The presentation of types and tendencies, often in simplified form, necessarily overlook variations and deviations. They may appear too undifferentiated to the historian, while the sociologist may find the variety of historical family forms confusing. The high degree of abstraction is frequently fractured by the presentation of single examples. The authors are aware that they have not entirely succeeded in integrating the full range of social science literature into the subject under discussion. But by occasionally submitting a critical exposition of sociological theory, they hope to stimulate an interdisciplinary debate, a debate that is urgently needed, particularly with regard to the problems of the family.

Historians have not, up to now, paid enough attention to functional and structural changes in the family. The available literature either concentrates too much on regional characteristics, and is therefore difficult to use as source for a valid survey, or confines itself to changes in the numbers of births, marriages and deaths, and to such topics as the average size of households and families without taking into account socio-structural conditions and their effect on the quality of family life.

The essays presented here are based to a considerable extent on research carried out jointly by the two authors in the years 1975–77 as part of a research project financed by the Austrian *Fonds zur Förderung der wissenschaftlichen Forschung*. They aim to give not just a chronological description but also a sectional representation of the internal structure of the family over past centuries, thus illuminating the problems of the present. For since the object of our exercise is to analyse the past in order to assist in the interpretation of the present, we must follow those strands of past development that have led up to the contemporary problems of family life.

Our chief concern is the change from a society based primarily on a familial, domestic economy to an industrial society in which the family generally no longer forms the basis of the organization of labour. In the framework of this macro-historical analysis of family structure various developmental trends will appear. The most important is undoubtedly the change in the way authority is exerted in the family, which affects not only the relationship between spouses but also that between parents and children.

We begin with the family as a concept and with the various types of familial structures in Europe. Chapters on changes in family composition, family size and the family cycle lead on to a study of changes in the functions of the family. Patriarchal family structure is treated in such a way as to take account of its dependence on social and economic conditions. The second half of the book deals with relationships within the family: first with the place of young people within the family, then with the relationship between spouses, and finally with the position of the elderly.

The individual essays in this volume appeared originally as separate articles in the journal *Beiträge zur historischen Sozialkunde*, which is published by the Institute for Economic and Social History of the University of Vienna. Chapters 1–4 and chapter 8 are by Michael Mitterauer; chapters 5–7 are by Reinhard Sieder. The original essays have been brought up to date for the English edition of the book which appears four years after the German. For both editions they were revised for the purpose of producing a continuous text. The book takes the form of a general survey, without footnotes but with a select bibliography at the end of each chapter, and a detailed general bibliography at the end of the book. In this way we hope to reach a wider circle of readers than the historical and social scientific professions, and we shall measure our success by the extent to which we achieve this objective.

1

The Family as an Historical Social Form

Is the family a 'natural' community?

At first sight it may be surprising that the family should be considered a subject for historical research. According to general opinion, it is a static structure that would appear to be incapable of real change. It is conceived as a constant form of human life, remaining the same over time, a naturally established unit. The biological factors seem to be so evident that one feels that the family should be treated primarily in the framework of the natural sciences, perhaps as human biology. Even though social components may be noted, natural laws are often introduced into a discussion of the family. And seen in the light of natural laws, the family appears immutable, a structure that remains the same over time or one that should not be changed.

We are aware that this opinion is often held by people in public life. Whenever changing the family structure is raised as an issue, whether it be through the socio-political measures of governments or because of a change in social relationships, an attack on the natural order is immediately proclaimed. This concept of the family has also strongly influenced historical research. Until recently historians have paid scant attention to the subject of the family, at any rate in German-speaking countries. There is certainly no question of a continuous social historical research tradition. If the historian tackles the subject at all, he usually confines himself to what are considered purely biological data, such as number of children, age at marriage and so on. Socio-cultural aspects of the family are left out of account.

Against such a biological point of view the following may be said. It is true that the family is in great measure influenced by biological factors and is, because of this natural connection, a relatively stable entity. Nevertheless, the family has assumed so many forms in the course of history that it is impossible to consider it in any way a natural unit of human communal life, remaining the same over time. Obviously, the influence of biological factors in the development of family life cannot be ignored. But in essence the family is a social creation and, as such, a legitimate object of historical research, just as it has been for a long time a central preoccupation of sociology and ethnology. If academic interest in the family is to contribute to a better understanding of the present-day situation, then it is not the perennial natural conditions that should be our main concern, but the many ways in which these constants are combined in an ever-changing world.

The family as a model of social organization

Our interest in a social history of the family is not confined to what can be seen as the immediate precursors of the family of our own time. It leads us necessarily to an investigation of many social forms that we, at present, may not regard as familial, and should thus entail a consideration of further socio-historical connections.

The family is one of the most archaic forms of social community, and at all times men have used the family as a model for the formation of human societies. This is clearly shown by the way names derived from kin connections have been adapted to social forms in no way based on blood relationships – as, for instance, the use of 'father' and 'brother' in monastic groups. Indeed, in primitive cultures social unity is often conceived only within the framework of familial categories. The establishment of an artificial relationship becomes a certain means of forming associations. One might instance the important role played by adoption or by sworn blood brotherhood.

Association with the social concept of the family, as expressed in the adoption of familial terminology, is to be found in early times in the basic forms of social organization that were developed and modified in different ways. The brotherhood model occurs frequently in the original type of association, and persisted from the early medieval merchant and craft guilds to the labour unions of the nineteenth century. Although the structure of the family dependent on authority originally furnished the prototype of social forms organized on strictly hierarchical lines, it also produced societies of peers associated in equality. Where grown-up sons remained within the family and, after their father's death, continued to live together as his joint heirs, the family took on the appearance of a corporate fellowship. Thus corporations and unions were often rooted in the example of adult brothers within the family.

Much more hierarchical was the manorial community, where the authority of the *pater familias* remained more pronounced. This dependence was a product of the fact that members of the manorial community established in their own families patterns of authority that were similar to those they had experienced as servants of their lord. It is also evidenced by the term *familia*, which was applied to all the people who lived on a lord's estate.

The notion of a common derivation forms the basis of social association in ethnic units. Concepts such as *gens*, *natio* and so on indicate the origin of large groups of this type, though there is generally no genuine blood relationship. Common descent is, as a rule, a fiction, though one of great social significance. Comprehensive and complicated social structures are based on personal connections thought to have derived from family relationships. Starting with tribes, clans and races, the line of development proceeds to sovereign ethnic units of various types, and ends with the nations and states of our own day.

Repercussions of superordinated social structures on the family

Those simplified and schematically represented social forms that are derived from familial structures must be thought of as exceedingly diverse in space, time and type. Above all, it must be realized that changing family structures not only determine other social forms, but are in turn influenced by them. Examples of such repercussions may be seen in the three basic types of social structure, discussed below.

As fellowship associations of master craftsmen, the guilds, became [1] increasingly more exclusive from the late Middle Ages onwards, an apprentice could frequently achieve independence in his craft only by marrying the master's widow. As a result, a certain characteristic family constellation came into existence among lower-class artisans; the wife was often much older than her husband.

In order to prevent the fragmentation of peasant properties and to preserve the economic viability of the farm and the rendering of tribute, landlords usually favoured a closed inheritance system. As a result, those sons who did not inherit were forced to move away or to remain as unmarried servants on the farm. This was a state of affairs that affected the structure of the peasant family considerably, since age at marriage was higher or lower in accordance with inheritance customs that might favour the eldest or youngest son.

A complete change in the dominant force in society may also bring about changes in the structure of the family. Thus in Russia, in the period of the Tartar conquest, suppression by the overlords led to the suppression of the wife in the family. The connection between rising sovereign absolutism and the increase in the father's authority is also quite evident. The family may therefore always be seen as part of the diversity of social structures, the formation of which it has influenced, while these in turn have contributed to changes in the family.

Family and state

From a historical point of view, the common use of the image of the family as the 'germ-cell of the state' has only limited justification; it should certainly not go unchallenged as a general concept. The state is not the sum total of families in the same way that a beehive is constructed of cells. And the interaction between family and state is not to be seen as literally as the slogan 'If the family is healthy, then the state too is healthy' would have us believe (even if there were to be agreement about the meaning of 'healthy'). However, reciprocal influences do exist.

Certain familial characteristics of dominance and dependence do have their counterpart in public life and vice versa. Above all, functions observed originally in the context of household and family have been transferred, often indirectly, to superordinate social forms, in particular the state. Seen over a period of hundreds and thousands of years, such transfers of functions to higher social structures may be observed in practically all human spheres, in religious as well as legal matters, in business as well as in education. This process of the transposition of functions, which also occurs quite noticeably in the present time, constitutes one of the basic trends in the historical development of the family. In this way new social forms may come into existence on the lines of familial patterns – as, for instance, the transfer of parental rights to the teacher because of the adoption by the school of familial functions of socialization.

When one considers the interaction in the course of history between the family and the social structures of which families are part, then it may be established that in general the dynamic of development originates with the latter. Changes in family constitution respond to processes of social change more readily than they initiate and stimulate them. Family structure has a certain stability, frequently resulting in delays in adaptation and belated change. The historian's study of the phenomena associated with relatively slow development may be of special relevance to modern conditions. Such investigations may make it easier to judge to what extent, and in which directions, social changes may be necessary.

The connection between the social concept of the family and other forms of social organization is put forward here in an introductory fashion in order to clarify the significance of social historical preoccupation with the subject. The variety of social forms that have emerged from the family or have been created in its image while adapting its functions raises the question of what exactly the conditions are that allow us to speak of 'family' in an historical dimension.

Changes in the meaning of the word 'family'

In order to clarify the multiplicity of the concept of the family in the past and the present, we must deal with the historical as well as the modern meaning of the word. The history of the notion of the family reflects interesting tendencies in the development of this social form: an analysis of the meaning of the word is therefore valuable to a consideration of the changes inherent in the concept.

Let us begin with our present-day understanding of the word 'family'. There is no legal definition of the notion. In German legal tradition, civil law acknowledges only relationship, either as the duty of maintenance or as the right of inheritance. This relationship (in descending or ascending lineage) is usually inherent in our use of the word 'family', but in essence it is confined to people who are related to each other and live together in a household, nowadays nearly always both parents, or a single parent, together with unmarried or still dependent children. 'Family' signifying all the household has precise limits, as distinct from 'family' signifying all relatives, which includes an indefinite circle of blood relations and in-laws.

When we go back into history, we discover the interesting fact that in the late Middle Ages, and even in early modern times, the German language had no word for the group of parents and children that we understand as 'family' and that is characterized by sociologists as the nuclear or simple family. For lack of a suitable word, the complicated description 'with wife and child' was used. This should not allow us to conclude that social connections corresponding to those of our modern, simple family did not exist. Similar relationships did exist, of course, but they included a larger circle of persons, which, rather than just parents and children, is to be regarded as the definitive social group.

The present German word *Familie* came into general use only in the eighteenth century and is linked with the French word *famille*: this in turn is derived from the Latin *familia*. At that time it meant, in the first place, that small group, the nuclear family, that was already clearly in evidence in Western Europe but in Central Europe took longer to emerge as a distinct unit. For want of a proper term, the French *famille* was adopted but without any well-defined meaning, because *famille* and its Latin root had a connotation other than that of nuclear family.

The Latin word *familia* is very old and is derived, by way of the Oscan term *famel*, from a common Indo-Germanic root. The basic meaning of the word is 'house' – that is, the total number of people living in a house, including domestic servants and slaves. The position of children is, in principle, not distinct from that of slaves, though the term *liberi* indicates that by birth they are legally considered free. Likewise, *pater* and *mater* are notions that express not genealogical connection but dependence on authority. (Genealogical parenthood is expressed by *genitor* or *genetrix*. *Pater autem familias appelletur, qui in domo dominium habet . . . quamvis filium non habeat*, according to Ulpian.) The position of *pater familias* has, in fact, nothing to do with natural fatherhood. It derives, rather, from a specific position of authority. The *pater* was originally the master of the household, the *des-potes* (*domus-potis*), the person who had authority over wife, children, slaves and other persons belonging to the household, who collectively composed the *familia*.

In this sense the word *familia* was used throughout the Middle Ages and down to early modern times. It was applied to the various forms of large households (as, for instance, vassals, who were treated as the *familia* of the lord; the feudal *familia* who comprised the serfs; and the *familia regalis*, which joined the feudal lords in servitude to the king). The same applies to the use of the word in the Romance languages. The change of *familia* to *famille* and *Familie* took place later in Central than in Western Europe, although here again, it was not really before the seventeenth and eighteenth centuries. We can touch only briefly on the changes in structure behind the change in meaning. The following factors were influential.

1 The separation of the dwelling place and the place of work, which brought about a separation of the professional and the private sphere of life. This took place everywhere, though at different times in different social milieux, but it never occurred among the peasants. It has led to the characteristic present-day meaning of the word *Familie*, with its overtones of privacy and sentimentality.

2 The strengthening of the relationship between parents and children under the religious influence of both the Reformation and the Counter-Reformation, but particularly in the Age of Enlightenment.

3 The releasing of servants from the close community of the household. Because the conditions of their servitude (which, up to that time, had been extremely personal) became more business-like, the bonds joining them to the family were loosened and were increasingly replaced by service contracts, freely negotiated. Thus the split between related and non-related members of the family deepened.

4 The emergence of many households consisting only of members of the family, in the modern sense of the word: those of homeworkers and cottagers, rural artisans and early factory workers, clerks and so on. And so the household of the family became the dominant form.

From the 'whole house' to the family household

The need to designate by a new word the community consisting only of blood relations is connected with the special evolution of the German equivalent of *familia*, and this leads us to the meaning of the word *Haus* (house). Whereas in Latin *familia* no longer signified the house as a building but referred only to the group of people living within it, the German *hus* or *Haus* retained the old, inclusive meaning of both the building and the corresponding social group. This was the significance generally attached to the word *Haus* until the eighteenth century and was therefore, for the whole pre-industrial period, the standard word for the social form in question.

Traces of the old meaning of the word survive today, as in the old-fashioned expression that is still used in Austria: *Grüsse von Haus zu Haus* ('Greetings from house to house'). But the original connotation is retained in the official designation of the *Haushalt* (household), which is used to mean groups of people living together and is entirely divorced in meaning from the house containing them. Official statistics distinguish between households of solitaries, family households and institutional households, but they all have the same root: the *Haus*, in its former sense of social community. (Households of solitaries are represented by widows or widowers or members of the family who live independently; family households signify households reduced to the nuclear family; and institutional households are those built on the model of the family or derived from it – religious houses, for example.)

But it was just this separation of house from household, which took place for the most part in the very period when the smaller, private, nuclear family emerged, that made it impossible for the word *Haus* to be used any longer to denote a social form. All this seems to have occurred in Central Europe during the seventeenth and eighteenth centuries when, with growing urbanization, there was an increase in the numbers of those who, although they had their own families and therefore their own households, did not possess their own houses. Within the towns rented lodgings had been quite usual from earlier times. But in principle in old European society only those who owned their own houses were allowed to have families – that is, the nobility, the burghers, the peasants, but not the journeymen, the farmhands and so on.

We cannot consider here the many modifications and exceptions to this rule; they do not alter the principle of identity between house and household. As long as the house and the household (household in the modern sense) are roughly equivalent, it is possible to attach the same meaning to the building and to the social group. However, the word *Haus*, as used today, can no longer be applied to that social entity of the pre-industrial period, which again cannot be adequately described by the modern word *Familie*. Men- and maidservants, journeymen and apprentices are now no longer part of the family. The social historian Otto Brunner, following in the footsteps of the sociologist Wilhelm Heinrich Riehl, who was working in the second half of the nineteenth century, has suggested that the term the 'whole house' (*das ganze Haus*) be used for the older form of domestic unity. But this is not an entirely satisfactory solution either. If there is to be no misunderstanding, words that in their historical development have acquired many meanings should be avoided, and the social circumstances should be described by a phrase such as *Hausgemein- schaft* (domestic community) or 'domestic group', or some similar phrase.

The original connection between house and family is clearly discernible in specific forms of proper names, for the oldest family names are usually the names of houses. We see this particularly among members of the aristocracy, who called themselves after their castles and fortified manor houses; when the property changed hands, the noble family changed its name too. The same sort of thing also occurred among burghers and peasants. In many parts of the Austrian countryside, where there were scattered farms, the family name became permanent only in the nineteenth century. In peasant communities even today, the name of the farm is often of more importance than the family name, which may not be known at all. The fixing of family names in Central Europe was much more a concern of national government in the period of enlightened absolutism than it was of the country people. In England, of course, surnames had been fixed for the whole population three or four hundred years earlier.

The separation of house from family may also be perceived in the dropping of 'house' from proper names. The general dropping of 'house' names is part of this development. Following the French example, the numbering of houses on streets was adopted, and this represented quite a radical change for people at that time. Knowing where each citizen lived was of great importance to the state bureaucracy. The house, which had become a mere building, had also become entirely separate from the people living in it. Individual house names usually continued to be applied only to castles and to manor houses, single farmhouses, inns and the establishments of apothecaries. In the case of inns and apothecaries, it was the sign or name board that was crucial, for it was with this symbol that house-holds were identified, just as noble families were identified by their armorial bearings, which frequently referred to the names of their houses.

The lineage

The disappearance of the 'ganze Haus' (whole house) in the old European sense is illustrated by the substitution of house names by house numbers on the one hand, and by the definitive introduction of fixed surnames on the other. This development also indicates how-ever, that for a long time there had been an underlying, rival concep-tion of communal unity. Our present family names have been fixed in the agnatic male line. Whether one 'belonged' to a given family was determined, therefore, not by 'belonging' to a certain house, but entirely by genealogical descent in the paternal line. This other basic type of name-giving, the patronymic family name, was closely con-nected with this second conception of family from the very begin-ning. This leads us to consider another attribute of the social struc-ture, that which was based on ties of kinship – namely, the lineage.

The *Geschlecht* (lineage) was a group of people linked in real or imagined common descent. In German the word *Geschlecht* derives from Old High German *slahan-arten, nachschlagen*. The correspond-ing Latin word is *gens* or *stirps*, that is, *genealogia*. The Latin designa-tion *familia* or *domus* may be used to indicate genealogical relationship in the same way as the German *Haus*. It is of great significance that descent from a common ancestor might be either real or fictitious: this seems to have made no difference to the lineage as a social entity.

In more modern times the agnatic relationship does, of course, play a greater part in the perpetuation of the family name, although even today a legalized, artificial relationship, such as adoption, still occurs. (In England adoption is not an ancient institution that has survived until the present, but a twentieth-century innovation, which seems to argue for considerable differences in such matters across the face of Europe.) Lineage as a social form should be distin-guished from the household community. In ancient and medieval societies everyone belonged to a house but not necessarily to a lineage. In early Roman times only the patricians belonged to a *gens* at first; the formation of plebeian *gentes* occurred later. At first plebeians did not have their own *gentes* but belonged to the *gentes* of patricians. When a slave was freed, he adopted the *gens* name of his master. With the dissolution of the Gentile constitution, a simplification of the complicated system of Roman names also took place. The *gentes*, as communities of presumed common descent, were kept together by a common ancestor worship. Ancestor worship has generally played a decisive role in fostering lineage consciousness and persists to the present day in entirely secularized forms, particularly among the nobility. Through ancestor worship the lineage joins the living and the dead in one community. The dead play an important role in promoting the consciousness of belonging together through the lineage, which is distinct from the consciousness of a household community.

The awareness of lineage that arises from ancestor worship is confined, as in early Roman times, to small, dominant groups, most markedly princely houses. Sometimes such groups are referred to simply as *die Geschlechter* (for example, the *Geschlechter* of the patrician upper ranks in many cities) or the *Szlachta* (the assembly of the Polish aristocracy). This consciousness of belonging together because of a comon origin spread beyond the nobility and the patricians. But it could not take root in opposition to the house as a basis for the formation of a social group. These two competing principles may be seen at work most clearly among the aristocracy, whose members, for reasons of genealogical continuity, adopted the name of both the ancestral house and of the seat currently possessed, as, for instance, Hohenlohe-Waldenburg-Schillingsfürst and Waldburg-Zeil-Wurzach.

The sib

Another clear distinction must be made: that between family and sib. Historical literature, especially older legal history, distinguishes between a closed and an open sib system, which is supposed to have played a particular role in the early Germanic period particularly, but was also thought to have exercised a strong influence later. It was supposed that the closed sib were those descended through the male line (*Schwertmagen*) as opposed to those descended through the female line (*Spindelmagen*). This concept of the closed sib coincides entirely with that of the lineage and is therefore superfluous as a constructional aid. The open sib, on the other hand, would have comprised the totality of a person's blood relations. It is to be considered as having been led by a sib chieftain supported by a sib council, which would have carried out the sib law. The sib would have acted as the guardian of children under age and of widows.

To the world outside the sib would have appeared to be the association that carried on feuds and avenged bloodshed, that paid the blood price and gave aid to sworn brothers. Together, the members of the sib would have settled the land, and the eldest among them would have given his name to the settlement (German place names ending in '—ing'). When land was conquered, certain sibs would have settled there together and later formed the so-called *Markgenossenschaften* (Leagues of the Marches). Finally, the sib would also have constituted a division of the army. Apart from the sib, no one would have had any rights. Those without a sib would have been looked upon as unfree – 'more like a wolf than a man'.

This picture of the sib, which persists in German historical literature, is a pure invention of nineteenth-century academics. We need not go into the ideological background of this fabrication any further. Research may attribute those individual functions mentioned above either to the household community or to the lineage, or even to larger social forms above kin relationships. Kin relationships create bonds that go beyond the limits of house and lineage, such as those between people related on the mother's side. Thus connections between individuals are created, not enduring social groups. This is precisely the meaning of the Germanic word *sibb*: a very close, intimate relationship such as exists between blood relations. Because of such individual connections, contacts are established between groups of relations whose constituents constantly change, and which are formed only for a short time and for particular reasons (like witnesses to a charter in medieval times, for example, or contributors to a memorial volume).

Sibs, in the sense of cognate blood relationships, must certainly have existed. They must, nevertheless, have been ever-changing, fluid groupings that did not enjoy the permanence of house and, to some extent, lineage. They had no inner structure because their members played no clearly defined roles analogous to those of father, mother, child or servant in the household. The so-called *Sippenführer* (chieftain) is an academic invention. Consequently, there are neither standardized connections nor specific relationships between roles, only connections of association and friendship. Therefore the sib as a legal entity does not exist, and it can hardly be described as a social entity because of its ever-changing form. To avoid misunderstanding, it is best for European scholars to avoid the use of the word 'sib' in social history, and to employ, rather, the words 'house' or 'lineage' or at least 'kin'.

Sociological family types

That the concept of the sib has been used so readily by German writers, and so extensively, is worthy of consideration. It reveals that in the early stages of development we find a type of social grouping based on relationships to which our modern word 'family' cannot be properly applied because those living together are joined in a relationship that goes beyond that of parents and children. To introduce the word 'sib' here is tempting, but it does not accurately describe the nature of the group, since it is a matter not only of relationships but also of people living together in a household community comprising a larger circle of relations. Sociology describes this type (which has persisted to the present day in regions outside Europe, and on a reduced scale even within it)) as the 'extended family', in contrast to the 'nuclear family', and distinguishes as sub-classes the 'multi-generational family' and the 'joint family'.

The multi-generational family is one in which one or more married sons, with wife and children, live together with the father, who retains authority over them during his lifetime. The classical Roman patriarchal family of early times provides the best example. The second type, the joint family, is characterized by married sons staying together after the father's death, and sharing the inheritance, which remains undivided. This process may be repeated many times, so that cousins and nephews once removed may belong to this household community of relations. We may mention here the *frérèche* (*fraternitas* or community of brothers) found in many parts of France among the peasantry and the aristocracy during the Middle Ages and later, or the communal households that still exist in some Alpine districts. Both types are most clearly represented by the Yugoslavian *Zadruga*, which, with the increased life expectancy of modern times, is becoming more a multi-generational than a joint family.

This sociological nomenclature can also be used by historians, although with modifications and refinements. To characterize co-resident groups as families gives the impression that they consisted entirely of blood relations, which was certainly not the case; non-related persons, such as maid- and menservants, also belonged. 'Domestic group' may therefore be a better term, but it has the disadvantage of not indicating (without further explanation) relationships within the house other than those of parents and children. The sociological designation of extended family, on the other hand, is misleading because it assumes the present–day nuclear family to be the original form that has been extended in the course of its development, and this is not necessarily the case.

The concept of the nuclear family as the original, basic form also finds expression in the sociological differentiation between the 'complete' and the 'incomplete' family. But it is doubtful whether this family characteristic can also be applied to historical family types. If one characterizes a group as complete if it consists of both parents and one or more children and as incomplete if one parent or all children are lacking, then one assumes a continuing need for certain family roles. Even at the present time, this is in no way true of all phases of the family cycle. In historical times the completeness of certain groupings must be seen in the light of the respective family functions. In modern times the completeness of the nuclear family is judged by its primary function of rearing and educating the young, and this is justifiable during the phase of socialization. In former times a peasant or artisan family enterprise that was dependent on additional labour must surely be described as incomplete because its predominantly productive function could not be carried out adequately.

The house or domestic community as the basis of historical family typology

Sociological terms can help the historian to describe the various forms of familial living together in the past, but only up to a point; they cannot characterize in sufficient detail the many forms of historical family structure. This is mainly because sociology differentiates only with respect to the ties of kin that exist between persons living together. All the concepts used refer only to the persons within the house or household who are linked by blood relationship or through marriage. For a socio-historical analysis of family structure such a restriction is not acceptable. An historical reconstruction of family types that deals only with blood relations would not do justice to the existence of certain communities because, using an anachronistic criterion, it would exclude persons who consciously participated in a close-knit and active family life. One cannot at will isolate from the persons associated in the domestic group those who are joined together in a closer group and are presumed to represent the actual family. In attempting to construct types of family grouping, the historian must take into account all those who play a part in the house or household community in its entirety, whether they are related to each other or not. Numerous historical sources indicate that, in contemporary opinion, ties of kin played a secondary role in the structure of small groups, and that belonging to the family was characterized not by the degree of relationship but by the role played in the household. So, for instance, brothers and sisters were referred to as man- or maidservants, parents as *Altenteiler* (those who lived on the old man's part of the property) and relations as inmates. Accordingly, a historical family typology, as distinct from a sociological one, must be based in the first place on the various combinations of roles in the house. In this way one may identify a much greater variety of types for which it is impossible to find short, clear-cut descriptions. A detailed description of the multiplicity of different forms would have to indicate very complex configurations of familial roles.

It is important that the types of community that we come across in the historical sources can provide only limited insight into the dynamic development of the family; after a few years the constellation of persons might be quite different. In order to obtain a comprehensive picture of family structures, therefore, one would have to consider typical processes of change in the composition of groups. Of course, this applies to the sociological as well as to the historical family typology. For instance, a family of brothers who inherited an estate after the death of their father is quite different from the family that existed up to the death of their father, at least as regards the range of generations. The structural types put forward by family sociologists produce a much more static impression. One also has to take account of the fact that in the present and the recent past family structures have remained much more constant over long periods than they did in historic time. The social historian has to deal with groupings whose composition changes frequently. And a greater variety of roles also increases the possibility of changes in the grouping of roles.

Problems of delimitation

The greater differentiation between individual roles in family groups in the past corresponds to the differences in the degree of integration of those carrying out those roles in the family. A classification of families according to various combinations of roles gives rise to the problem of the delimitation of the family, which can be less easily solved for historical forms than for present-day ones.

At the core of the family, within the parent–child group, relationships were much more complex in earlier times than they are nowadays for sociologists. Particularly in country districts, because of higher mortality and economic necessity widows and widowers frequently remarried and as a result, step-parents and step-children were much in evidence. If a widow or widower had taken in the children of a dead partner's first marriage and then yet another marriage took place, then a grouping could arise in which there were children who were related by blood neither to the parents nor to some of their 'brothers' and 'sisters'. Such examples show clearly that the position of the son or daughter in the house did not necessarily depend on blood relationship, but it is evident that they were nevertheless part of the family.

The same applies to adopted or foster children. The numerous foster children found in Austria and Central Europe during the eighteenth and nineteenth centuries may well have been relations of the married couple at the head of the household where they resided. Some were perhaps illegitimate children of a sister or daughter, but this was by no means the rule. Here too the criterion of relationship does not necessarily apply for a person to be deemed to belong: the social connection is much more decisive. Because we regard socialization as an inherent function of the modern family, we ourselves have no difficulty in counting such children as members of the family either.

Difficulties arise in counting those types of familial roles which do not exist any more because of the loss of certain family functions. This is particularly the case with the various types of service. In pre-industrial society, in which the predominant form of labour organization was a family undertaking, the productive function was of decisive importance to the constitution of the family. The journeymen and apprentices, business and shop assistants, men- and maidservants who lived with the family therefore belonged to this group and have to be included in a family typology that is based on the constellation of roles. The same applies to the 'house personnel' proper, who cannot be considered as directly contributing to production (that is, the house servants, coachmen, valets, cooks, housemaids, children's nurses, and so on).

In Austrian towns the business and house personnel were generally not related by kinship to the master or mistress whom they served. But in peasant communities in Central Europe (in contrast to England, for example) domestic servants were very often related to their master or mistress. Brothers and sisters, nephews and nieces, distant relatives, and also former foster children frequently acted as men- and maidservants. It was not their kin relationships but the specific working roles that these people played in the family group that determined their membership of the family. Servants in both town and country were usually unmarried and without children. But this was not so in certain exceptional cases, and these raise delimitation problems. Should one consider the married manservant or the maid with an illegitimate child as heading their own family units? No simple answer can be given to this question. It depends on the degree of integration of a particular person in the household of the employer, which must have been considerable in the case of the domestic staff. In such cases one would probably have to speak of a family subsystem rather than of an independent family. Such more or less integrated subsystems are also to be found crystallized around other family roles.

A familial role that occurred almost exclusively among peasants in this region was that played by the *Altenteiler* (retired old people). The influence on family structure of the stipulated rights of the old could vary with local inheritance customs. These stipulated rights were arrangements for the housing and the care of the elderly.

It might be that these rights appertained solely to the old widowed peasant, or to the old widow of the farmer, or jointly to the surviving couple. If the eldest son or one of the older children took over the farm, brothers and sisters who were not yet of age continued to live with the parent or parents who were still alive. In this way, because of the provision made for the elderly, quite a conspicuous familial subsystem might be created, though it could hardly be considered an independent family. When such stipulated rights attached to a step-mother or to a step-father, they were clearly not connected with blood relationship. In many regions in Central Europe one frequently finds that farms were transferred to persons who were not in any way related by kinship to the previous holder. In such cases the retired peasants and those persons living with them should not be considered as belonging to the household in a different way from the blood relations. Indeed, the arrangements stipulated in the transfer agreement would be of greater importance to the degree of integration than kin connection.

An entirely separate household might be stipulated for the old or for those persons living with them, or possibly the partial or total integration into the household of the occupant of the farm. Next to the criterion of the household community, that of the sharing of the house would seem to have been of importance to the problem of delimitation. Living together under one roof would certainly bring about the greater integration into the household of the retired farmer or of his widow. But the extent of such integration would vary with the layout of the farm, which in turn would depend very much on the type of settlement. In scattered farmhouse settlements old people would often live in separate outhouses, but even then this would not create entirely separate households. Many other integrative factors have to be considered, especially continued co-operation in the running of the farm, which involved participation in the family producing unit. The greater the variety of family functions that permitted the partial or complete participation in familial community life, the harder it is to decide exactly who belonged to the family.

The problem becomes yet more challenging when we come to consider those who were described as inmates (*Inwohner*). Inmates generally comprised those living in the household in consideration of the payment of a rent or the rendering of a service, although sometimes there was no monetary compensation. They could be single or widowed persons, or married couples (or single parents) with children. In many districts the retired were also described as *Inwohner*, which indicates that there was sometimes no clear distinction between these two types of role within the household community. Often married brothers and sisters or relations of the residents counted as inmates. Men- and maidservants or other household servants who had been allowed to marry might also continue to live in the house in this position. But in most cases inmates were not related to the residents in this way. In country districts they had to share the work of the farm to a greater or lesser degree, so that one has to assume their partial participation in the family's labour organization.

The criterion of 'living under one roof' might be generally accepted, although inmates were also to be found in outhouses and in what might be called 'granny flats' in England today. They did not, on the whole, share in the activities of the household, but they certainly had to submit to the authority of the head of the house. In the towns there would not, as a rule, have been a strong personal relationship with the landlord of the house. Here lodging must have developed quite early on into an entirely businesslike association between landlord and tenant. Exceptions were married servants of the landlord and business assistants who lived with their small families in the house of their employer. One may assert that the integration of lodgers into the household community was greater in the country than in the town and that it was greater in earlier than in later times.

Multiplicity of types of historical family structure

The problem with *Inwohner* in the German-speaking areas of Europe is that a definition of the family, in the sense of the delimitation of the circle of persons belonging to it, is far more difficult for the past than for the present. This is due, above all, to the fundamental change brought about by the reduction in family functions. Those family functions that remain today relate to a fairly clearly defined group of persons. On the other hand, the greater number of functions performed by members of the family of the past resulted in a strongly differentiated interaction between them because of the various tasks allotted to them, and therefore in the more or less close integration of these individuals into the household community. With the reduction of family functions went a reduction in the types of familial role. The relative homogeneity of modern family forms contrasts with the multiplicity of roles in historical families.

There is as much variety in the family communities of the past as in the family structures of so-called primitive peoples put before us with such force by ethnologists and anthropologists. A backward glance at the variety of domestic group structures in the history of our own civilization can certainly achieve the same result. The strangeness of the ethnological material may well lead those who use it to regard the European family as a uniform and homogeneous family type, and thus to conceive of their own family structures as a static creation. The social historian of European family structures has, therefore, a very specific task: namely, to demonstrate radical change, as well as the considerable differentiations of family structure, both over time and between the regions of the European cultural area. The knowledge of fundamental change in the past enables us to envisage the possibility of fundamental change in the present.

Continual change in family structure

The variety of forms, as well as the changes in European family structure that inevitably followed upon changes in family functions, show clearly that the shape of our modern family cannot be attributed exclusively, or even primarily, to biological and natural causes. Transformation of the social system is much more likely to lie behind these far-reaching changes in the forms of family life. In the past these changes may have come about after some delay, and this may perhaps be the case in the present. To cling to outdated patterns of familial community life can lead to an unnecessary (if not a dangerous) restriction of opportunities for development, both for the individual and for the group. The constant adaptation to changed social conditions must therefore be a task to which social historical analysis should be able to make a considerable contribution. Putting existing structures into historical perspective can foster awareness of their changeability and give an impetus to alternative ways of thinking about them. Careful extrapolations from the study of past developmental trends may well indicate directions of development for the future. It is certain, moreover, that knowledge of the historical family gives us a better insight into the possibilities of varying membership of this primary group. Thus knowledge of the frequency with which non-related persons lived together with the family in the past may make it easier for us to adopt a different conception of future forms. The historical perspective will at any rate keep us from deprecating these notions as violations of the 'natural order' of things.

To appeal to the 'natural order' of the family and to claim that it must be retained at all costs may, from the point of view of social history, be seen as an attempt merely to retain a specific family structure that has developed over the centuries, with its corresponding patterns of behaviour and values. Certain factors, which appear constant over time, are seen in specific historical situations as essential for, or favourable to, society, but these factors may in due course be overtaken by social change. This applies especially to the model of patriarchal family structure, with its emphasis on the 'natural authority' of husband over wife and children. To describe certain relationships of authority and dependence adapted to the conditions of society in certain periods of the past as 'natural', and thus to declare them unchangeable, means legitimizing traditional structures of authority within the family and within the framework of the society with which the family is connected. If the historian can illuminate the original social conditions governing such relationships and show how they have lost their meaning in the course of historical development, then he may be able to create the conditions for the realization of greater equality and partnership.

SELECT BIBLIOGRAPHY

Berkner, Lutz Karl, 'The use and misuse of census data for the historical analysis of family structure', *Journal of Interdisciplinary History* 5 (1975), pp. 721ff.

Bosl, Karl, 'Die "familia" als Grundstruktur der mittelalterlichen Gesellschaft', *Zeitschrift für bayerische Landesgeschichte* 38 (1975), pp. 403ff.

Brunner, Otto, 'Das "ganze Haus" und die alteuropäische "Ökonomik" ', *Zeitschrift für Nationalökonomie* 13 (1950), pp. 114ff. (= Otto Brunner, *Neue Wege der Verfassungs- und Sozialgeschichte*, 2nd edn, Göttingen, 1968, pp. 103ff.).

Engelsing, Rolf, 'Das häusliche Personal in der Epoche der Industrialisierung', *Jahrbuch für Sozialwissenschaft* 20 (1969), pp. 84ff. (= Rolf Engelsing, *Zur Sozialgeschichte deutscher Mittel- und Unterschichten*, Göttingen, 1973, pp. 225ff.).

Genzmer, Felix, 'Die germanische Sippe als Rechtsgebilde', *Zeitschrift der Savigny- Stiftung für Rechtsgeschichte, Germanistische Abteilung* 67 (1950), pp. 34ff.

Gothein, Eberhard, 'Familie' in *Handwörterbuch der Staatswissenschaften*, 3rd edn, 4, Jena, 1909, pp. 21ff.

Grohne, Ernst, *Die Hausnamen und Hauszeichen, ihre Geschichte, Verbreitung und Einwirkung auf die Bildung der Familien- und Gassennamen*, Göttingen, 1912.

Haff, Karl, 'Der umstrittene Sippenbegriff und die Siedlungsprobleme', *Zeitschrift der Savigny-Zeitschrift für Rechtsgeschichte, Germanistische Abteilung* 70 (1953), pp. 320ff.

König, René, *Materialien zur Soziologie der Familie*, 2nd edn, Cologne, 1974 (1946).

Alte Probleme und neue Fragen in der Familiensoziologie, *Kölner Zeitschrift für Soziologie und Sozialpsychologie* 18 (1966), pp. 20ff. (= 'Old problems and new queries in family sociology' in Reuben Hill and René König (eds.), *Families in East and West*, The Hague, 1970, pp. 602ff.).

'Soziologie der Familie' in *Handbuch der empirischen Sozialforschung*, vol. 7, 2nd edn, Stuttgart, 1976 (1969), pp. 1ff.

Kohn, Georg, Gemeinderschaft und Hausgenossenschaft, *Zeitschrift für vergleichende Rechtswissenschaft* 13 (1898), pp. 1ff.

Kramer, Karl-Sigismund, 'Das Haus als geistiges Kraftfeld im Gefüge der alten Volkskultur', *Rheinland-westfälische Zeitschrift für Volkskunde* 11 (1964), pp. 30ff.

Kroeschell, Karl, 'Die Sippe im germanischen Recht', *Zeitschrift für Rechtsgeschichte, Germanistische Abteilung* 77 (1966), pp. 1ff.

Kroeschell, Karl, *Haus und Herrschaft im frühen deutschen Recht*, Göttingen, 1968.

Linde, Hans, 'Persönlichkeitsbildung in der Landfamilie' in *Soziale Welt* 10 (1959) (= Heidi Rosenbaum (ed.), *Seminar: Familie und Gesellschaftsstruktur*, Frankfurt, 1978, pp. 215ff.).

Lüschen, Günther, 'Familie und Verwandtschaft. Interaktion und die Funktion von Ritualen' in Günther Lüschen and Eugen Lupri (eds.), *Soziologie der Familie*, special issue 14 of the *Kölner Zeitschrift für Soziologie und Sozialpsychologie*, Opladen, 1971, pp. 270ff.

Mitterauer, Michael, 'Zur Familienstruktur in ländlichen Gebieten Österreichs im 17. Jahrhundert' in Heimold Helczmanovszki (ed.), *Beiträge zur Bevölkerungs- und Sozialgeschichte Österreichs*, Vienna, 1973, pp. 167ff.; extracts as 'Zur Problematik des Begriffs "Familie" im 17. Jahrhundert' in Heidi Rosenbaum (ed.), *Seminar: Familie und Gesellschaftsstruktur*, Frankfurt, 1978, pp. 73ff.

'Haus und Gemeinde in der mittelalterlichen Gesellschaft' in *Beiträge zur historischen Sozialkunde* 5 (1975), pp. 22ff.

'Vorindustrielle Familienformen. Zur Funktionsentlastung des "ganzen Hauses" im 17 und 18 Jahrhundert' in *Wiener Beiträge zur Geschichte der Neuzeit* 2 (1975), pp. 123ff. (= Michael Mitterauer, *Grundtypen alteuropäischer Sozialformen*, Stuttgart. 1979, pp. 35ff.).

'Auswirkungen von Urbanisierung und Frühindustrialisierung auf die Familienverfassung an Beispielen des österreichischen Raums' in Werner Conze (ed.), *Sozialgeschichte der Familie in der Neuzeit Europas*, Stuttgart, 1976, pp. 53ff.

Neidhardt, Friedhelm, 'Die Familie in Deutschland: Gesellschaftliche Stellung, Struktur und Funktionen' in *Deutsche Gesellschaft im Wandel 2*, 4th edn, Opladen, 1975.

Planck, Ulrich, 'Die Eigenart der Bauernfamilie und die bäuerliche Familienverfassung' (excerpts of Ulrich Planck, *Der bäuerliche Familienbetrieb zwischen Patriarchat und Partnerschaft*, Stuttgart, 1964) in Heidi Rosenbaum (ed.), *Seminar: Familie und Gesellschaftsstruktur*, Frankfurt, 1978, pp. 195ff.

Schlesinger, Walter, 'Randbemerkungen zu drei Aufsätzen über Sippe, Gefolgschaft und Treue' in *Alteuropa und die moderne Gesellschaft, Festschrift für Otto Brunner*, Göttingen, 1963, pp. 11ff.

Schmid, Karl, 'Zur Problematik von Familie, Sippe und Geschlecht, Haus und Dynastie beim mittelalterlichen Adel', *Zeitschrift für die Geschichte des Oberrheins* 66 (1957), pp. 1ff.

Schrader, Oskar, 'Familie' in *Reallexikon der indogermanischen Altertumskunde* 1, Berlin, 1917–23, pp. 284ff.

Schultz, Alwin, *Das häusliche Leben der europäischen Kulturvölker vom Mittelalter bis zur zweiten Hälfte des 18. Jahrhunderts*, Munich, 1903.

Schultze, Alfred, 'Zur Rechtsgeschichte der germanischen Brüdergemeinde', *Zeitschrift der Savigny-Stiftung für Rechtsgeschichte, Germanistische Abteilung* 56 (1936), pp. 264ff.

Schwab, Dieter, 'Familie' in *Handwörterbuch der deutschen Rechtsgeschichte* , Berlin, 1971, pp. 1067ff.

'Familie' in *Geschichtliche Grundbegriffe, Historisches Lexikon zur politisch-sozialen Sprache in Deutschland 2*, Stuttgart, 1975, pp. 253ff.

Schwägler, Georg, *Soziologie der Familie, Ursprung und Entwicklung*, 2nd edn, Tübingen, 1975 (1970).

Sprandel, Rolf, *Verfassung und Gesellschaft im Mittelalter*, Paderborn, 1975.

Stekl, Hannes, 'Hausrechtlich Abhängige – das Gesinde', *Beiträge zur historischen Sozialkunde* 5 (1975), pp. 34ff.

Thurnwald, Richard, *Wesen, Wandel und Gestaltung der Familie, Verwandtschaft und Bünden im Lichte der Völkerforschung (Die menschliche Gessellschaft 2)*, Berlin, 1932.

Weber, Max, 'Die Familien und Arbeitsgemeinschaften' (excerpts of *Zur Geschichte der Handelsgesellschaften im Mittelalter*, 1924) in Heidi Rosenbaum (ed.), *Seminar: Familie und Gesellschaftsstruktur*, Frankfurt, 1978, pp. 63ff.

Wenskus, Reinhard, *Stammesbildung und Verfassung*, 2nd edn, Cologne, 1977.

2

The Myth of the Large Pre-Industrial Family

Sociological models of development and their ideological background

Our present-day concept of the historical development of the family is not based primarily on historical research but has been subject to the influence of sociology. Historians have had very little to do with the subject hitherto, and have restricted their concern to certain aspects of it. It is only recently that historians have shown much interest in the historical development of the family. For sociologists, on the other hand, the family has been a central focus of research since the middle of the nineteenth century.

However they may vary, sociological theories about the development of the family have one thing in common: the acceptance of a general tendency for the family of many members to change to the family of fewer members. The process of industrialization is reckoned to have been the decisive factor in bringing about this change. Such a dichotomy between the large pre-industrial family and the small modern family dominates the relevant theories in sociological textbooks, and by no means only in German-speaking countries. And it is taken for granted that the large family size of former times was the consequence of numbers of relations, particularly grandparents, living in the household with the husband, wife and children.

The founder of empirical family sociology, the Frenchman

Frédéric Le Play (1806–82) was especially influential in furthering such notions about the development of the family. His concept of the 'stem family' (*famille souche*) as the dominant family form of older times found general acceptance. It was thought that three generations lived together in the stem family: the parents, who owned the house; their eldest son, who was to inherit the undivided property, together with his wife and children; and his younger and unmarried siblings. Le Play contrasts the stem family with the nuclear family consisting of parents and children only, termed by him the 'unstable' family. He describes it as a product of industrialization, a result of the changed social conditions brought about by the Industrial Revolution.

Le Play was not only an empirical social scientist; he was also a social reformer, as was his contemporary, Wilhelm Heinrich Riehl, who prepared the way for the emergence and development of family sociology in Germany. Both of these scholars became interested in past family forms because of their critical attitude towards the society of their own time. They asserted that the crises provoked by the radical social change that they witnessed could be attributed to industrialism and had to be overcome by reviving traditional family forms and their associated scale of values. By reinstating paternal authority, reviving family relationships and restoring declining morals, they hoped to stabilize society. Guidelines for social reorganization on the basis of the old order were derived from an analysis of the past. Their own political aims were legitimated by their view of history.

Although later social scientists may not always have been inspired by a desire to restore the old institutions, they were moved by similar dissatisfaction with the contemporary social situation and painted their picture of the family in the past accordingly. The egoism and individualism of the small modern family was contrasted with the feeling of responsibility towards relatives in need of help of former times, the coldly businesslike and impersonal social relationships of the present with the strong kin relationships that used to exist, the desire to develop one's own personality in the best way possible with the greater willingness to curb personal feelings for the mutual benefit of the family that formerly prevailed, modern individual freedom with the exercise of authority by the head of the patriarchal family, sexual licence with the willingness to abstain from sex by marrying late or, indeed, by remaining single. All these features of the family life of our age are widely held to contrast with the concept of the complex structure of the large family household of pre-industrial times, in which the married couple and their many children lived harmoniously with their old parents and with relations in need of support.

The current picture of older historical forms does not only bear the impress of social scientific theories and the critique of society associated with them. Even before the start of sociological research into the family, Romanticism and the Biedermeier culture in Central Europe fostered a widespread and enduring idealization of the family in past times. This found artistic expression in paintings of the family by Ludwig Richter or in the well-known ballad by Gustav Schwab: *Das Gewitter* ('The Storm'): *'Urahne, Grossmutter, Mutter und Kind in dumpfer Stube beisammen sind. . . .'* 'Great-grandmother, grandmother, mother and child sit together in the quiet room. . . .').

On the surface, such romantic idylls appear harmless; not so the motives behind the creation of this imaginary world. Le Play and Riehl made use of the appeal to authority in the structure of the historical large family to foster strongly anti-democratic tendencies. Less scientifically inclined contemporaries and followers employed these means in less subtle ways. It is not by chance that the demand to strengthen parental authority has been a constantly recurring item on the agenda of totalitarian and Fascist movements. The glorification of the large patriarchal family and the dependence of people related to it have been idealized as a beneficial historical model for the present. Certain potentially dangerous attitudes are often concealed behind such images of the family – hostility towards democracy, for example, and above all, hostility towards the emancipation of women. For woman occupied an inferior position in the paternalistic structure of the large family, which favoured the domination of the male. Le Play's concept of the family also displays anti-egalitarian features in placing the firstborn in a privileged position *vis-à-vis* the other sons.

Propagandists of the historical large family drew on agrarian society for material that seemed to corroborate their views. They therefore looked to the traditional peasant family for its renewal. In consequence, they had an aversion to all forms of urban and industrial living. And this resulted frequently, and by no means fortuitously, in the following antitheses: on the one hand, complaints about the decadence of the city, pessimism about the condition of the world and an essentially anti-modern attitude; on the other hand, the glorification of imaginary historical family forms strongly dependent on authority, the remains of which were supposed to exist in remote country areas.

Implicit in the contemporary picture of the family organization of earlier times were ideological concepts that could always be revived and brought back to life. The general tendency to regard the family as naturally ordained, so that it could retain its traditional structure or be restored to it, reinforced the dangers of such revivals. Knowledge of the size and structure of the family in the past is therefore of considerable importance to present-day society. Was the large family, as a community of several generations living together, really the dominant form in the pre-industrial period? Did it descend, unchanged, from as far back as the earliest development of society in Europe, and was it therefore an anthropological constant? Or is this to generalize about specific phenomena that should be seen in the light of the social conditions prevalent at the time? Are we creating a myth, an idealization of the past, to further the socio-political aims of the present?

Results of historical-statistical analysis

The transition from the large to the small family in the course of industrialization that is presumed by family sociologists is a phenomenon that can be disproved statistically. The most useful collated data are those available for England, the prototype of early industrialization. By carrying out a large number of tests, mainly on country communities, average sizes of households, going back to the sixteenth century, have been calculated. It is only in the context of the house or household that the family may be placed within the scope of a quantitatively defined social group. The network of family connections differs for each person concerned and cannot be statistically defined.

Average English household size calculated for pre-industrial times does indeed differ in certain respects from the present one, but the difference is not particularly striking. Whereas mean household size remained at approximately 4.75 persons throughout seventeenth, eighteenth and nineteenth centuries, the average today is 3.04 persons. It is hardly possible to speak of a large pre-industrial family in respect of these earlier periods. Even more important, it can be shown that the transition did not coincide with the Industrial

Revolution. On the contrary, in some industrialized localities a definite increase in family size may be observed during the course of the
nineteenth century. The marked reduction in average household size
in Britain did not take place until the beginning of the twentieth
century. It coincided with improved living conditions, an increase in
single-person households and a decline in the number of children
born. This development in England is by no means an isolated
phenomenon. In Vienna, for instance, the average household size was
4.68 in 1890, 4.4 in 1900 and 4.11 in 1910; it only dropped during the
following decades – to 2.9 in 1934, 2.38 in 1951 and 2.32 in 1961. A
direct connection between the industrialization process and a reduction in the number of persons living together in a household is not to
be seen in any of the Western industrialized nations.

Mean household sizes, such as we find nowadays in Western
Europe, were already present in the larger towns in the pre-industrial
period. In 1755 Antwerp had the same average (3.04 persons) as
England has at present. At the same time Brussels' average was
slightly higher, at 3.2 persons. The difference between town and
country may be observed as long ago as the late Middle Ages. In
Florence in 1427 3.8 persons lived together in one household; in the
surrounding districts, 5.1 persons. If one compares the average for
towns in pre-industrial Europe with our present, largely urbanized
society, far smaller differences may be noted. Test samples from
country districts give widely differing data for the seventeenth and
eighteenth centuries. The average values for most of the regions of
West and Central Europe fluctuate between 4.0 and 5.3, but can
be higher in many districts. Examples from Eastern and South-
Eastern Europe show particularly high average values.

A comparison of average household sizes is beset by uncertainty,
however. Those who work with local population data do not always
use the same criteria. And the question of which persons belonged to
a particular group cannot always be answered clearly. Apart from
parents and children, relations are generally included; there is usually
little doubt about the inclusion of domestic servants too. The situation of other non-related persons who lived in is more problematic,
especially when they were married and had children. Criteria of
function (that is, participation in production or consumption) must
decide the question of inclusion. The listings of the population do
not, on the whole, allow us to make such decisions. Comparisons of
average household size therefore always remain of somewhat dubi-

ous value. They can serve only as a tentative solution to the problem in which we are interested. Of far greater importance is the study of the inner structure of the groups who lived together as families.

Historical forms of the large family and their regional diffusion

Russia has provided us with the most impressive examples of the generational family. In a population listing from the Great Russian province of Rjasan of 1814, we find only 33.5 per cent of one- and two-generational families but 59 per cent of families with three generations and 7.5 per cent with four generations. The last was very exceptional in Central and Western Europe, where the proportion of three-generational families did not often reach that attained in Russia by the four-generational families. In some regions of Russia, domestic communities contained on average some 10 or 11 persons. Most of them were grouped around a core of two married couples or even more. Included were the descendants and the relations of the head of the family. It was probably the custom, prevalent in Russia, of periodically dividing up the common land that produced these highly complex families, for it was the number of married men per house that determined the share in the land each house was to have.

Very large family units with a complex structure have been discovered in the Baltic region of Eastern Europe. One example from Estonia in 1683 and another from Lithuania in 1797 show a proportion of 41 per cent and 64 per cent respectively of families grouped around two or more married couples. To this must be added a number of families (11 per cent in each case) that included relatives. In 26 or 43 per cent of these domestic groups, three generations lived together. Here too the lineal as well as the lateral extension of the family played an important role. The number of married servants who formed a family subsystem should be noted; many were relatives of the master or the mistress of the house.

The best-known and most intensely investigated example of the large family is the so-called *zadruga* in the Balkans. It occurs in Croatia, Bosnia, Serbia, Montenegro, Albania, Macedonia and Bulgaria and in historical times was the dominant type of family in large areas. Of particular interest is the unusual way in which this form of the large family was capable of extension. In the nineteenth century *zadrugas* comprising more than 80 people were observed. This was not the rule, of course, but domestic groups of 20 to 30 members were not uncommon at that time.

According to a census of 1863, in a group of listed villages 70–90 per cent of the population lived in families of more than six persons. Data about the *zadruga* have been recovered from as far back as the fourteenth century. In a list of 1330 were found, in typically large families, between 7 and 11 adult men and, correspondingly, between 16 and 25 family members. The adult married males around whom the large families were ranged belonged mainly to a patrilinear lineage. The role the male line played in the construction of the family is characteristic of the *zadruga* structure and is certainly connected with the marked ancestor veneration found among south Slavonic peoples.

Large families were also prevalent in many parts of Hungary. This may be illustrated for the late eighteenth and early nineteenth century by the examples of two villages with 31 and 32 per cent of three-generational families, as well as 39 and 36 per cent of complex families with at least two nuclei each. It is true that in the Hungarian region examples of the complete opposite may also be found. Two population lists from the mid-sixteenth century show respectively only two and 3 per cent of three-generational families. Other material from later times also indicates very varied family sizes.

The Italian material so far researched also indicates little uniformity. Rural communities with only 9 or 11 per cent of complex households may be contrasted with three places in Tuscany with very high rates (39, 44 and 45 per cent) of such family forms. These data are from the eighteenth century. According to the *Catasto* for Tuscany of 1427, the highest proportion of complex family forms in country districts amounted to only 20 per cent.

For France the prevailing family forms are relatively well documented. More and more evidence supports the fact that complex families comprising distant relations predominated in some country districts of south and central France. And it was not only a question of three-generational families; fairly frequently several brothers lived together in the *frérèches* mentioned above. High proportions of complex families occurred in the districts of the Limousin, where in many communities more than 40 per cent of the families were non-nuclear. The manorial system must have influenced the existence of complex family forms in south and central France. The prevalence of undivided inheritance may also be an explanatory factor.

North of the Loire, conditions were quite different. Here the nuclear family undoubtedly predominated. Two population lists of the eighteenth century show 76 and 81 per cent of simple family households (households without living-in relatives). Complex family forms amounted to only 3 and 2 per cent. Members of three generations lived together in 8 and 5 per cent of the families.

Northern France obviously belongs to that wider zone of Western and Central Europe where, even in country districts in the remote pre-industrial period, multi-generational families played a relatively minor role. England is the best researched country in this respect. In the 65 communities for which reliable population listings from the end of the sixteenth to the early nineteenth century have been investigated, the proportion of multiple family households was not more than 5 per cent and that of extended families not more than 12 per cent. This sample gave an average of 5.7 per cent of three-generational families.

For the Netherlands extensive research produced practically identical outcomes. Belgian examples also accord with this picture. Few analyses have yet been carried out for Germany, but so far they have not shown fundamentally different results. The situation in Austria confirms that the area in which multi-generational families were relatively poorly represented probably took in the whole of Central Europe in pre-industrial times.

The sources that have been investigated in Vienna are just as voluminous as the English material. They stretch from the end of the Middle Ages to the twentieth century. The proportion of families in which members of three generations lived together is, according to these sources. fairly small. The highest percentages were found in districts with a wealthy peasantry. The conclusion that residence with elderly parents or relatives varied with class agrees with results of research carried out in other regions. In the countryside three-generational families were almost entirely lacking among the lower classes, and it is fairly clear from the Austrian material that the proportion of complex and extended families was lower where the settlement was near a town. In towns themselves it was minimal. This difference between town and country has been confirmed by parallel research in other regions. In spite of the relatively small number of complex and extended families, the Austrian sources nevertheless indicate quite a high average number of persons per house or household. This may be explained mainly by the relatively high proportion of servants.

In so far as present research allows us to compare European families, it may be said that multi-generational families and others with living-in relations were relatively rare during pre-industrial times in large regions of Western and Central Europe. This stands out clearly when the data for these regions are contrasted with those for Southern and Eastern Europe. The problem is how to determine to what extent percentages from individual lists warrant conclusions about the prevalence of certain family structures. Placing a person in a certain family position is like a momentary photographic exposure. Family structures are only fully discernible in the course of the family cycle. The fact that a certain family structure is the dominant one in a region does not mean that the whole population lives in such family constellations. Furthermore, the conclusion that the cohabitation of members of three generations depends on the phase of the family cycle is correct. For instance, in families of young farmers, shortly after the transfer of the farm, one or both parents would be more likely to be present than in families of farmers between the ages of 50 and 60. But this does not justify our drawing the conclusion that the stem family structure applies to the whole population when only a small proportion of multi-generational families appears in one listing. Local population listings show, in more or less representative cross-section, how many and how frequently phases of family cycles in which members of more than one generation lived together occurred in the population. In societies in which the house remained in the family by inheritance, it was natural for a young couple to live together with at least one parent for part of their lives. Such constellations cannot be taken as indicative of stem family structure when they occur in very small proportions in the same way as when they occur in very large ones. In many parts of Central and Western Europe peasant families rarely passed through the phase of generational co-residence, and when they did, it was only for relatively short periods of time. They did not always live together, and even seem to have avoided doing so. That is the decisive structural characteristic that must be explained.

The stem family and retirement rights

In the light of the consecutive phases of the family cycle, yet another distinction must be made with regard to the co-habitation of members of three generations. We speak of stem family forms in the narrow sense when in a multi-generational family authority resides in the first generation. Members of the second and third generation must then submit to the dominion of the patriarchal master of the house. This happens in the lineally extended forms of the *zadruga*, and also in many regions of France.

Another form of the three-generational family appears to be characterized by the peasant's stipulated retirement rights, which have already been mentioned. The arrangement of stipulated retirement rights is spread all over Central and Western Europe – from Ireland to the Sudeten, from Norway to the Alps. Where the old farmer or his wife is already living in retirement, the family authority resides in the middle generation. This family structure is therefore quite different from the original stem family, a point often neglected in discussions about historical forms of the large family. In this type of family constellation it is frequently only the surviving mother who represents the first generation, whereas in the stem family the father of the house stands at the head of the generational line.

It appears particularly significant for relationships within the family that in the stem family the adult married son and the daughter-in-law have to submit to the authority of the father as head of the house. Such conditions of dependence do not as a rule exist in the three-generational family forms prevalent in Central and Western Europe. But cohabitation with aged parents can produce strains. The old farmer living in retirement is not to be thought of as enjoying life as represented in idealized pictures of the old being cared for in the peasant household.

The essential difference between the two fundamental types of multi-generational family, therefore, consists in the possibility of the master of the house yielding his position, during his lifetime, to his successor. This solution was of particular importance to the farming population. The arrangement of retirement rights originally had economic roots, since it seems to have been intended to guarantee the management of affairs by a master of the house who was in full possession of his physical faculties. That was obviously in the interests of the landlord, who needed to ensure orderly domestic management in order to safeguard the regular payment of his dues. The development of certain retirement arrangements obtaining in a particular district depended on many factors: on local inheritance customs (retirement occurred more frequently with indivisible than with divisible inheritance); on the size of the property (owners of large farms could hand over earlier and more easily than was possible with medium-sized and small farms); on the local farming system; on agrarian market conditions; and so on. This created a variety of types of retirement rights, which had an effect on the number of multi-generational families.

The institution of retirement rights goes back to the Middle Ages in Central and Western Europe. Industrialization in no way reduced its importance. The cliché of the large pre-industrial family may at best be understood to mean that the size of the agrarian population was reduced partly as a consequence of industrialization, and that the characteristic family forms vanished accordingly. But it has been established that the proportion of three-generational families increased, particularly in the period of industrialization. The cause of this phenomenon was certainly not a change in inheritance custom but rather increased life expectancy or good agrarian market conditions. This not only brought about a rise in the number of families in retirement in country districts, but also led to an increase in the proportion of three-generational families in many towns and industrial areas.

Demographic factors

Given the demographic preconditions – life expectancy in particular – one must ask how far conditions in the pre-industrial period allowed members of a three-generational family to spend a large part of their lives together. The decisive factors were, on the one hand, average life expectancy; on the other, the age gap between the person handing over the household and the person receiving it, which was determined by average age at marriage, birth intervals, the survival of children and specific inheritance customs.

In Central Europe average life expectancy at birth has risen by 30 years in the last 100 years – for men from 30 to 65 years, for women from 35 to 68 years. But we cannot really use these figures, as the low life expectancy of earlier times was the product of high infant and child mortality. The possibility of members of more than one generation living together was influenced more directly by the average age at death of married couples. For instance, in France in the sixteenth and seventeenth centuries it lay between 55 and 60 years. During the same period the average age at marriage in northern France was between 25 and 30 years, a little higher for men than for women. If one hypothesizes that after one year of marriage a child was brought into the world, and that the child was a son, who lived and remained as heir in his father's house and after a year of marriage himself became a father, then even in such a case the statistical possibility of grandfather, father and child living together in one household existed only for a relatively short time.

Such a calculation does not, however, take account of the fact that additional factors may have increased significantly the actual gap between the generations. There was, in the first place, the high mortality of children and young people. In France at that time only half of those born reached their twentieth year. It was generally the second or third child who survived. Among country people, as among the middle and lower classes in the towns, birth intervals would be about two years. (We will deal below with the question of shorter birth intervals among the upper classes.) Because of higher male infant mortality, the chance that the first surviving child would be a boy was less than 50 per cent. These factors would cumulatively affect the possible existence of a three-generational family. In many country districts not the eldest but the youngest son inherited. Where such inheritance customs prevailed, the difference in age between father and youngest son has to be calculated, and this was greater in earlier times than nowadays. The difference in age between the first- and the lastborn could be over 20 years. In farming circles the children were often the result of more than one marriage: remarriage after the death of the wife was an economic necessity. Despite the impossibility of divorce, second and third marriages played a much greater role in old European society than at the present time. The traditional wicked step-mother in our fairy tales has its origin in these marital relationships. There was always a considerable difference in age between the husband and the second or third wife, and she would, as a rule, survive him. Relatives of the first generation who shared in the life of the three-generational household were frequently widows of a second or third marriage and were blood relatives of neither the master of the house nor his family.

The European marriage pattern

This discussion about the possibility of multi-generational families is based on demographic data influenced both by biological conditions and by social conventions. Age at marriage is the crucial social variable here, and there is widespread misinformation about the average age at which the first marriage was contracted in old European society. All too often notions are based on marriage customs prevailing in princely houses rather than among the mass of the people, where very different factors were decisive. Political alliances were secured by promises of marriage when the two participants were still children, and these were quite often followed by an early wedding. There were generally no financial difficulties. The continued existence of a dynasty might also necessitate an early marriage. These motives were only of importance among the ruling houses, and quite different marriage conditions might well prevail even among the higher ranks of the nobility. Literary evidence often presents us with an entirely misleading picture. When in Shakespeare's *Romeo and Juliet* Lady Capulet admonishes her 14-year-old daughter:

> Well, think of marriage now; younger than you,
> Here in Verona, ladies of esteem
> Are made already mothers: by my count,
> I was your mother much upon these years
> That your are now a maid. . . .

We have in no way a typical example of marriage patterns in the pre-industrial world.

Farmers, artisans, tradespeople and even the nobility, for the most part, married no earlier then than do people in our modern, industrial society. On the contrary, a considerably later age at marriage was quite usual, at any rate in those regions of Central and Western Europe where multi-generational families seldom occurred. A sample of six selected English parishes from the years between the end of the sixteenth and the end of the eighteenth century shows that in the age group 20–24 years only 16 per cent of the men and 18 per cent of the women were married, compared with 45 and 50 per cent of those in the age group 25–29 years. (Mean age at first marriage in fifteen English parishes over these centuries never fell below 26 for women; for men it varied between 27 and 28.) A series of Austrian examples from the seventeenth and eighteenth centuries shows that nowhere more than 13 per cent, and generally less than 10 per cent, of the men between 20 and 24 years of age were married; for women in the same group there was one instance of a proportion of 30 per cent, but on the whole it was under 20 per cent.

The analysis of the registers of country parishes in northern France for the pre-industrial period shows an average age of 25 years at marriage for women and a somewhat higher age for men. In southern France, a region of complex family forms, the comparable ages were lower. However, a contrast with South-Eastern and Eastern Europe should be noted. In Belgrade in 1733–34, 33 per cent of the men and 92 per cent of the women were married in the age group 20–24. On one domain of the Great Russian province of Rjasan, where multi-generational families were common, age at marriage was particularly low. Most of the men were already married by 16 and women by 15.

These figures show a fundamental difference in marriage conditions, persisting until recent times, between countries of Western and Central Europe on the one hand and those of Eastern and South-Eastern Europe on the other. The Western and Central European marriage pattern, more simply called the European marriage pattern, is unique; the Eastern and South-Eastern European pattern, on the other hand, corresponds much more with conditions outside Europe. A two-generational family prevails in countries that follow the European marriage pattern, but a tendency towards large family units, including more than one married couple, exists in Eastern and South-Eastern Europe.

Extended families and the problem of subsistence

Differences in age at marriage are to be explained not by varying physiological development – the earlier or later start of puberty – but entirely by social conditions. There were marked regional differences, it is true, in the age at which puberty began, but this does not seem to have affected marriage age. There was, however, a clear connection between the average marriage age and the generational composition of families. The impression is that in large regions of Western and Central Europe families of three generations were avoided, or at least restricted to a relatively short phase, by keeping marriage age high. The establishment of retirement rights did, of course, encourage multi-generational families, but such forms of co-residence were by no means actively sought. For the farming household, retirement rights always represented a great burden, at any rate for the owners of small and middle-sized properties, and were avoided when possible. The inevitable result was a relatively high marriage age. Frequently the heir had to postpone marriage until after the death of the old farmer. The causal connection between the low proportion of three-generational families and high marriage age is to be seen thus: on economic grounds, the co-residence of more than two generations was undesirable or impossible, and consequently the time of marriage was delayed.

If it is true that large families, both three-generational and complex, were largely absent from a zone that stretched right across Central and Western Europe because the estates could afford little encumbrance, we may be allowed to speculate about the origin of this situation. The ability to feed the individual family must have been limited in these regions, mainly because of the agricultural conditions brought about by the formidable colonization movement of the High Middle Ages. Cereal crops became prominent, and scattered farms and hamlets were replaced by village clusters. The cultivation of the land was intensified because of the spread of the 'three-field system' (except, of course, in the mountain regions). It went mostly hand in hand with new kinds of land division into strips, the so-called *Gewannfluren*, with strict allocation of certain parcels of land to individual farmsteads in the village. This development was accompanied by the planned development of the village, and these denser settlements resulted in an increase in the population.

All these things seem to have influenced the size of the peasant household, for the land belonging to the farm could now provide food only for a limited number of people. The group that made its living off one property could not increase at will. Families of the size of the *zadruga* were quite impractical, given the strictly limited nourishment that this intensive land cultivation could provide. It should be noted that the extensive changes in the agrarian structure brought about by the colonizing movements of the High Middle Ages were confined precisely to those regions in which the European marriage pattern and corresponding family forms developed. The country districts of Eastern and South-Eastern Europe were not affected by these settlement movements; consequently, there was not such a decisive change in living conditions, and older, less intensive forms of the domestic economy remained.

Town and country

So far we have dealt mainly with the conditions governing the emergence of multi-generational and complex families in a peasant society. They were certainly of great importance to a population that was, on the whole, dependent on a land economy. It is true that in agrarian societies there were also non-farming people, among whom the elderly had no retirement rights and family structures were quite different. Neither the available houseroom nor the material resources would, as a rule, allow for the co-residence of members of more than two generations. Additional means of earning a livelihood from trade or industry occasionally permitted earlier marriage and larger families. But these were exceptional circumstances. In general, large families were not characteristic of the lower classes in the country-side.

Among the inhabitants of the towns in pre-industrial times extended family forms were really to be found only among a small section of nobles, patricians and rich merchants. And here too it was mainly domestic servants who contributed to the larger size of the households. Among those who plied a craft or traded, multi-generational and complex families rarely occurred, for by contrast with peasant families, retirement rights did not obtain among arti-sans. Additions to the nuclear family comprised journeymen, apprentices and servants, but not relatives living in. Among the lower classes in the town, such family forms were also absent, but co-residence with other non-related persons played a greater role.

It cannot be maintained, therefore, that the dominant family form of pre-industrial times was the large family community in which several generations lived together. Even if restricted to the peasantry, the concept does not apply to large regions of Western and Central Europe. The analysis of early population censuses shows that the large households that were listed comprised different family constel-lations and by no means only those of relatives living together. The one-sided academic preoccupation with the question of the nuclear as opposed to the stem family has ignored this diversity of forms. Dur-ing the period of industrialization forms of familial living together did indeed undergo genuine changes, but these were not occasioned solely by industrial development.

Effects of industrialization

In the pre-industrial period practically the only production unit was the family itself. That applied equally to agriculture and to crafts; mining and building were in general the only economic enterprises that were organized on a large scale. Family units without productive functions had existed since pre-industrial times, however – the families of day labourers in town and country. But with the creation of large industries, families without productive functions became a mass phenomenon. Increasing bureaucratization had the same effect. Once the rule, the productive family unit now became the exception.

This development exercised a decisive influence over the composition of family units. The bonds created by the division of roles in the work that people did together were loosened. Above all, there was no longer any need to marry when the household was transferred or to remarry after the death of a partner. Especially in the farmhouse, but to a great extent in the artisan's household too, the central position of master and mistress of the house had always had to be filled. Widows and widowers were seldom found as family heads; households of widows were found mainly in the towns. Worthy of notice in this context is the difference between the proprietor of the house and the inhabitants living with him as tenants or in some such relationship of dependence, of whom there were many, particularly in the towns. Whoever held the position of master or mistress of the house had generally had to be married in the pre-industrial period, hence the remarkable proportion of second and third marriages. The married couple as nucleus, a two-person focus, was usual in families who owned a house at this time. There were few single-person households, so common today, and the phenomena of the 'empty nest' and the incomplete family were rare. Such forms occurred mainly among lodgers. It is not the nuclear family that is the result of industrialization and its accompanying modernization, but the increasing emergence of the incomplete family, in which there is no compulsion always to fill the two central roles. The deliverance of a large number of families from the function of production must be seen as the background to this development.

For the sake of the domestic economy, above all in agrarian societies but sometimes also among townspeople, it was necessary that at least one child should remain in the house as heir. When such conditions of production prevailed, the parent-child group would appear to have been the predominant family constellation. But when individuals earned a living outside the home, all the children would leave the parental home, particularly when there was an opportunity for neo-local settlement. With increased life expectancy, the phase during which parents lived without their children lengthened. The increase in the number of such 'empty nest' families is a characteristic of the development of the family in recent times and is connected, among other things, with the process of industrialization.

Another aspect of the loss of productive functions is the decrease in, or disappearance of, servants. As long as the family as a community had to meet a prescribed work schedule, a constant labour force was necessary, supplied on the one hand by the children of the house and, on the other, by men- and maidservants.

Servants and size of household

The proportion of domestic servants in individual households and in the population as a whole in pre-industrial times was quite considerable – on average between 7 and 15 per cent. Towards the end of the nineteenth and at the beginning of the twentieth century this proportion decreased markedly. The reduction in the number of domestic servants accounts in large measure for the small average size of households in recent times.

For the servant the opportunity to marry came only at the end of his term of service. Research into modern sources from Central and Western Europe has shown that married men- and maidservants who lived with their children in the family of their employer were rare. Length of service was therefore associated with the average marriage age. Again, the figures that have been calculated in this connection seem to show real structural differences between Central and Western Europe on the one hand and Eastern Europe on the other. The lower marriage age in the countries of the latter region corresponds to a smaller number of servants, particularly of women servants. The characteristic European marriage pattern apparently accords with a longer phase of service. But in traditional European society service was also apprenticeship. The effects of the specific European marriage pattern on the length of service and apprenticeship may therefore be seen as part of the overall social and cultural development of Western and Central Europe.

Large families because of large numbers of children?

Inaccurate estimates of the size of the pre-industrial family have also been made because of persistent misapprehension about the number of children born to a marriage. An entirely false impression has been created by well-known pictures of the family life of personalities of the ruling houses, as, for example, the eighteenth-century Austrian empress, Maria Theresa, in the midst of her many children. Again, we are deceived about numbers of children by the succession of births in genealogical tables, including those of burghers and peasants. Conditions in the upper classes made familiar by pictures and literature are not representative, for statistical research has led to the astonishing finding that among these classes birth intervals were considerably shorter than among the peasant and artisan classes. This phenomenon is explained by the fact that in the seventeenth and eighteenth centuries mothers in the upper classes did not suckle their own children but employed wet nurses. This was responsible for their having babies more frequently than those who breast-fed their babies. It is uncertain whether the average birth interval of two years among the broad masses of the population is only to be explained by reduced fecundity or also by abstinence during the period of lactation. Given the long birth intervals and the relatively high age at marriage, a peasant wife would have brought hardly more than eight children into the world by the end of her fertile period, if indeed she lived so long. When one takes account of the high mortality among infants and children, one should perhaps reckon that four or five offspring survived. If a first wife died young, there would be the children of a second or third marriage to add to the family group. But the number of children registered did not correspond to the actual number in the house, for sons were sometimes sent away from home at 10 or 12 years of age, occasionally earlier; daughters were usually sent into service somewhat later.

At the time when younger children were born, therefore, the older ones were frequently no longer at home. In this respect, differences may be observed between peasants and artisans. Whereas on the farm the labour force was filled in the first place by the farmer's own children, so that a large number of children lived with their parents, this was not the case with those carrying on businesses in the towns, where one should assume that a smaller number of children were born, even in pre-industrial times. Increasing urbanization and a decrease in the proportion of peasants in the total population must also have led to a smaller average number of children and a decrease in the size of the family, though not to the extent often imagined.

The idea that every family had large numbers of children in earlier

times is based on the same sort of generalization as that which has led
to the conclusion that the old were cared for in the context of multi-
generational families. With increased life expectancy and favourable
market conditions in the nineteenth century, the number of retirements among Austrian peasants suddenly increased in some districts,
and the proportion of the elderly who were cared for in this way
increased correspondingly. With the decrease in child mortality, and
as procreation remained constant, the number of surviving children
increased markedly. At the same time, compulsory education and
reduced opportunities for going into service led to children staying in
the parental home for longer. It was, however, only during a passing
phase that a relatively large number of children lived with their
parents; this was certainly not characteristic of the whole pre-
industrial period. To invoke this allegedly natural constant of a
healthy family life in an attempt to discredit the smaller families
that people have in the contemporary world has the same ideological
implications as those we discussed in relation to the notion that the
elderly were cared for within the large family that was supposedly
the norm in pre-industrial times.

Trends in structural changes

A review of historical development shows that certain changes have
taken place in the size of the family and the household, though by no
means considerable ones. The background to these changes was,
apart from industrialization, such modernizing trends as urbanization
and bureaucratization; these, it may be noted, were already evident
before the Industrial Revolution. The change cannot be defined
entirely as a reduction in family size but rather as an alteration of the
composition of the household brought about by changes in its functions. There was no general historical trend from the large to the small
family. Moreover, the popular sociological concept of an evolution
from the multi-generational family type in the past towards the isolated
nuclear family of the present does not fit reality. The larger domestic
groups of earlier times were conditioned by other structural
characteristics, such as families living with servants and other
non-related co-residents. And it must be emphasized that the complete
nuclear family is in no way the only family constellation of modern
times. One only has to consider the various forms of the incomplete

family, households of single persons, 'empty nest' families or unmarried couples living together.

The range of possible ways of living together has increased in recent times. The withdrawal of various family functions has made the relationships that they implied irrelevant to the composition of the family today. Particularly important is the fact that the family has lost its function as a production unit. The constraints implicit in the need to fill the roles attributed to members of historical families has had a persistent influence on social attitudes. Hostility towards the unmarried, for example, or those who remained childless is to be seen in this light. In a world in which the roles of master and mistress of the house were necessarily associated with marriage, while single and widowed persons generally lived in conditions of dependence, the prestige of married couples is understandable. To apply such an attitude to present-day conditions, and to judge the single working woman by these standards, is entirely anachronistic. The value placed on fertility in a predominantly agrarian society has, on the whole, a functional basis. To pass judgement on voluntary or involuntary childlessness in our day ignores the fundamental changes in family functions that have taken place over the years. The higher value placed on sons and the veneration of the lineage that have persisted into the present are likewise relics of the past. To take over and hand on such traditional standards of value is quite unjustifiable, in our view at least. It leads to the confirmation of inequalities that should really be eradicated, and it prevents members of society from taking full advantage of the opportunity to devise a personal lifestyle and of ways of living together that have been made possible by historical developments.

SELECT BIBLIOGRAPHY

Anderson, Michael, *Family structure in nineteenth century Lancashire*, Cambridge, 1972.

Andorka, Rudolf, 'Peasant family structure in the eighteenth and nineteenth centuries', *Ethnographica* 86 (1975), pp. 341ff.

Arensberg, Conrad M. and Kimball, Solon T., *Family and Community in Ireland*, 2nd edn, Cambridge, Mass., 1968.

Bahrdt, Hans Paul, 'Wandlungen der Familie' in Hans Paul Bahrdt, *Wege zur Soziologie*, Munich, 1966 (= Dieter Claessens and Petra Milhoffer (eds.), *Familiensoziologie*, Frankfurt, 1973, pp. 110ff.).

Berkner, Lutz Karl, 'The stem-family and the developmental cycle of the peasant household: an eighteenth century Austrian example, *American Historical Review* 77 (1972), pp. 398ff.

'The use and misuse of census data for the historical analysis of family structure', *Journal of Interdisciplinary History* 5 (1975), pp. 721ff.

Braun, Rudolf, *Industrialisierung und Volksleben*, Erlenbach/Zürich, 1960.

Brooke, Michael Z., *Le Play: engineer and social scientist*, London, 1970.

Deenen, Bernd van, *Die ländliche Familie under dem Einfluss von Industrienähe und Industrieferne* (*Sozialpolitische Schriften* 13), Berlin, 1961.

Durkheim, Émile, 'La famille conjugale', *Revue Philosophique* 20 (1921), pp. 2ff.

Engelsing, Rolf, 'Das häusliche Personal in der Epoche der Industrialisierung', *Jahrbuch für Sozialwissenschaft* 20 (1969), pp. 84ff. (= Rolf Engelsing, *Zur Sozialgeschichte deutscher Mittel- und Unterschichten*, Göttingen, 1973, pp. 225ff.

Goode, William J., *World revolution and family patterns*, Glencoe, Ill., 1963.

Goubert, Pierre, 'Family and province: a contribution to the knowledge of family structures in early modern France', *Journal of Family History* 2 (1977), pp. 179ff.

Hajnal, John, 'European marriage patterns in perspective' in D. V. Glass and D. E. C. Eversley (eds.), *Population in History*, Chicago, 1965, pp. 101ff.

Halpern, Joel M., 'Town and countryside in Serbia in the nineteenth century' in Peter Laslett and Richard Wall (eds.), *Household and family in past time*, Cambridge, 1972, pp. 401ff.

Hammel, Eugene A., 'The Zadruga as process' in Peter Laslett and Richard Wall (eds.), *Household and family in past time*, Cambridge, 1972, pp. 335ff.

Kaufmann, Albert, *Demographische Struktur und Haushalts- und Familienformen der Wiener Bevölkerung* (dissertation, University of Vienna), Vienna, 1967.

Klapisch, Christiane, 'Household and family in Tuscany in 1427' in Peter Laslett and Richard Wall (eds.), *Household and family in past time*, Cambridge, 1972, 267ff.

König, René, 'Alte Probleme und neue Fragen in der Familiensoziologie' in *Kölner Zeitschrift für Soziologie und Sozialpsychologie* 18 (1966), pp. 1ff. (= 'Old problems and new queries in family sociology' in Reuben Hill and René König (eds.), *Families in East and West*, The Hague, 1978, pp. 602ff.)

Laslett, Peter, 'Size and structure of the household in England over three centuries, *Population Studies* 23 (1969), pp. 199ff.

The world we have lost, 2nd edn, London, 1971 (1965).

Introduction to Peter Laslett and Richard Wall (eds.), *Household and family in past time*, Cambridge, 1972, pp. 1ff.

'Mean household size in England since the sixteenth century' in Peter

Laslett and Richard Wall (eds.), *Household and family in past time*, Cambridge, 1972, pp. 125ff.

'The comparative history of household and family', *Journal of Social History* 4 (1970–71), pp. 75ff.

'Characteristics of the Western family considered over time', *Journal of Family History* 2 (1977), pp. 89ff. (= Peter Laslett, *Family life and illicit love in earlier generations*, Cambridge, 1977, pp. 12ff.

Laslett, Peter and Clarke, Marilyn, 'Houseful and household in an eighteenth-century Balkan city' in Peter Laslett and Richard Wall (eds.), *Household and family in past time*, Cambridge, 1972, pp. 267ff.

Le Play, Frédéric, *Les ouvriers européens. Etudes sur les travaux, la vie domestique et la condition morale des populations ouvrières de l'Europe*, 6 vols., Paris, 1855–78.

Mackenroth, Gerhard, *Bevölkerungslehre, Theorie, Soziologie und Statistik der Bevölkerung*, Berlin, 1953.

Mitterauer, Michael, 'Zur Familienstruktur in ländlichen Gebieten Österreichs im 17. Jahrhundert' in Heimold Helczmanovszki (ed.), *Beiträge zur Bevölkerungs- und Sozialgeschichte Österreichs*, Vienna, 1973, pp. 167ff.

'Vorindustrielle Familienformen, Zur Funktionsentlastung des "Ganzen Hauses" im 17. und 18. Jahrhundert' in *Wiener Beiträge zur Geschichte der Neuzeit* 2 (1975), pp. 123ff. (= Michael Mitterauer, *Grundtypen alteuropäischer Sozialformen*, Stuttgart, 1979, pp. 35ff.

'Auswirkungen von Urbanisierung und Fruhindustrialisierung auf die Familienverfassung an Beispielen des österreichischen Raums' in Werner Conze (ed.), *Sozialgeschichte der Familie in der Neuzeit Europas*, Stuttgart, 1976, pp. 53ff.

'Zur familienbetrieblichen Struktur im zünftischen Handwerk' in *Wirtschafts- und sozialhistorische Beiträge (Festschrift für Alfred Hoffmann)*, Wien, 1979, pp. 190ff. (= Michael Mitterauer, *Grundtypen alteuropäischer Sozialformen*, Stuttgart, 1979, pp. 98ff.

'Faktoren des Wandels historischer Familienformen' in Helge Pross (ed.), *Familie wohin?*, Reinbek, 1979, pp. 83ff.

Plakans, Andrejs, 'Peasant farmsteads and households in the Baltic littoral, 1797', *Comparative Studies in Society and History* 17 (1975), pp. 2ff.

'Seigneurial authority and peasant family life', *Journal of Interdisciplinary History* 6 (1975), pp. 620ff.

Planck, Ulrich, 'Die Eigenart der Bauernfamilie und die bäuerliche Familienverfassung' (excerpts from Ulrich Planck, *Der bäuerliche Familienbetieb zwischen Patriarchat und Partnerschaft*, Stuttgart, 1964) in Heidi Rosenbaum (ed.), *Seminar: Familie und Gesellschaftsstruktur*, Frankfurt, 1978, pp. 195ff.

Riehl, Wilhelm Heinrich, *Die Familie (Die Naturgeschichte des Volkes als Grundlage einer deutschen Social-Politik*, vol. 3), Stuttgart, 1855.

Schwägler, Georg, 'Anfänge einer Familiensoziologie bei Wilhelm Heinrich Riehl und Frédéric Le Play' (excerpts from Georg Schwägler, *Soziologie der Familie*, Tübingen, 1971) in Dieter Claessens and Petra Milhoffer (eds.), *Familiensoziologie*, Frankfurt, 1973, pp. 15ff.

Ussel, Jos van, 'Die Kleinfamilie' (excerpts from Jos van Ussel, *Sexualunterdrückung, Geschichte der Sexualfeindschaft*, Reinbek, 1970) in Dieter Claessens and Petra Milhoffer (eds.), *Familiensoziologie*, Frankfurt, 1973, pp. 95ff.

Walter, Emil J., 'Kritik einiger familien-soziologischer Begriffe im Lichte der politischen Arithmetik des 18. Jahrhunderts' in *Schweizerische Zeitschrift für Volkswirtschaft und Statistik* 97 (1961), pp. 64ff.

Woude, A. M. van der, 'Variations in the size and structure of the household in the United Provinces of the Netherlands in the seventeenth and eighteenth centuries' in Peter Laslett and Richard Wall (eds.), *Household and family in past time*, Cambridge, 1972, pp. 125ff.

3

The Emergence of the Modern Family Cycle

The family as a developing community

Generally speaking, we would not associate the phrase 'family history' with the social history of the family; we think of it as the history of an individual family, not as the development of the family as a basic form of human community life. For us the phrase rings of ancestors, relations and lineage rather than of the common past of those who are presently united in one household. This last notion is at best taken into consideration as the final chapter of an historical presentation of the succession of generations.

As we have remarked, apart from biographers, it is sociologists rather than historians who have occupied themselves with the development of the family household over time. And the preoccupations of sociologists are different from those of historians. Whereas family history (in the sense familiar to genealogists) occupies itself mainly with tracing the descent of individual families, the sociology of the family deals with typical developmental phases of present-day families, and these form the subject of research into the family cycle.

This type of research has lately acquired considerable importance for the sociology of the family and must therefore also influence the social historian when he is dealing with the social history of the family. It must be a valid proposition for him too that the family as a social group is not static but dynamic. Research into the position of the individual in the family, as well as the size and structure of the family, is too restricted on its own.

Local population listings, which are the basis of such research, offer a momentary glimpse of conditions, but if they are placed within the framework of overall development, they gain in explanatory value. An individual's family life, his place within the group, his connections and interactions with other members of the group, are determined not by familial formations that remain the same but by groupings of persons living together that perpetually change over time to a greater or lesser extent. Dealing with historical family structures and their development must therefore include research into the history of the family cycle. Work on typical phases in the development of family groups represents a distinctive historical approach, but it is an approach markedly different from that of the traditional family history of the genealogists. A social history of the family that concerns itself with developmental cycles is, in general, concerned with certain types of cycle, not with individual family fortunes. The rich source material collected by genealogists, when arranged systematically, can be of great assistance to the reconstruction of the types of cycle that are relevant to social history.

Sociological models of life-course phases

Sociological concepts of the family cycle cannot be adopted without modification by social history. However, it is precisely these changes, when compared by the historian with the sociological schemata of progressive phases, that illuminate important aspects of social change. The realization that there is no such thing as a basic model of familial development that remains the same over time and in different areas raises the question of the causes of regional differences and structural change over time. Research into the history of the family cycle may lead one to appreciate that models of family sociology, and their interpretation, cannot be seen as absolute.

There is no consensus in sociological literature about the critical points that mark the individual phases of the family cycle. Phases that occur in practically all models of the cycle are as follows:

1 young married couples without children;
2 married couples with children of pre-school age;
3 married couples with children of pre-adolescent age;
4 married couples with adolescent children;
5 parents living alone in the home after the departure of the children;

6   a single surviving parent living alone or in the household of one
of the children.

These phases may be further subdivided. Phase 2, for instance, can
be separated into the periods before and after a child's attendance at
nursery school, with an agreed age limit of three years. Phase 5 may
be divided into the time when the breadwinner is still working and
the period after he retires. Such phase models may be supplemented
with more exact data for the ages at which the critical events in the
life of the individual usually take place.

A schematic representation of the family cycle in the United States,
for instance, is based on an average age at marriage of about 23 years
for the man, and about 20 years for the woman. An average number of three to four children, who are born up to the twenty-eighth
year of the woman's life, and a phase of living with the children of 20
to 25 years may be assumed, so that, with a male life expectancy of 70
years, this phase is followed by an 'empty nest' phase of another 20 to
25 years. The somewhat higher female life expectancy would lead
one to assume that a wife might live alone as a widow for another six
years.

Critical points in the family cycle, seen in historical perspective

Some of the critical points in the phases of the modern family cycle
may be transferred, without much difficulty, to historical times.
This applies to marriage, the birth of the first child and the deaths of
both marriage partners. We have at our disposal, with respect to
several centuries in the past, accurate information from church
records about the average age at marriage, the average length of
marriage up to the birth of the first child and the average life expectancy of adult men and women. The ages that mark the limits of
these phases in the family cycle can therefore be determined.

Considerable difficulty is encountered, however, if we attempt to
apply modern standard divisions to the family cycle of the past. We
cannot equate the events that demarcate the part of socialization that
takes place today outside the home – at school, for example – with
particular phases in periods when children were brought up entirely
or primarily in the household of their parents or employer. Before
general education became compulsory, only children in certain sections of the population attended school, and it was only in these

sections that the period of education represented an identifiable phase in the family cycle. Even when education was made compulsory, it was at first not generally enforced, and the length of schooling varied considerably in different regions and over time. It was much later that nursery schools became important in the developmental phases of the family community. Because attendance at nursery school has never been compulsory, this particular subdivision of phase 2 is of questionable significance even today. All the phases of model cycles that are based on attendance at public educational institutions imply that the family has been relieved, more or less, of this part of its socializing function.

There are also problems when one tries to use categories such as adolescence and pre-adolescence as divisions of the family cycle in the past. Although the process of physical maturation is in itself a biological constant, the age of puberty varies considerably over even relatively short periods of time. Phases of adolescence can in no way be determined by purely biological criteria. The duration of adolescence, and the problem of when to assume its beginning and above all its end, depend very much on socio-cultural factors. Here again the markedly differing length of education or apprenticeship plays a decisive role, a role that has varied over time and space and according to the age at which an individual has started work.

Just as the age at which people have started to work has been subject to considerable change in the course of history, so has the age of retirement. Retirement, as we understand the word today – that is, as a particular phase of the lifecycle – generally applies only to wage earners, and then only after the introduction of old-age pensions at a compulsory retirement age. This transition applies therefore, even nowadays, only to the wage-earning section of the population (by far the majority in modern industrial nations). Its historical development presupposes a process of bureaucratization and industrialization. Such a phase is not to be found in a pre-industrial society dominated by family enterprise. The institution of peasant retirement, which was prevalent in many parts of Central and Western Europe but by no means among all country people, is not to be compared with the retirement of modern wage earners.

Research into the sociological family cycle is based on a specific procreative pattern that has emerged fairly recently. It assumes, in the first place, that the number of children is small, that births follow each other at relatively short intervals and that they generally occur in the first years of marriage. For only then do we find a close association of siblings, who go simultaneously through the socialization phase and who depart from the family at more or less the same time, thus making possible a prolonged 'empty nest' phase.

We do not question the validity of these assumptions for the contemporary world. They are invalid, however, in the context of the development of the family in history. Even if it is a proven demographic fact that family limitation did take place in parts of Europe (in England, for example) after the seventeenth century, it was by no means practised in all sections of the community and could hardly have created close-knit sibling groups.

Among peasants in most parts of Europe, parental attitudes towards children as a labour force would usually prevent any restriction on the numbers of the succeeding generation. Other sections of the population were also very fertile. Taking into consideration the high infant mortality during the first months after birth, the distance in age between the surviving children was generally greater than nowadays. Women's reduced fertility during the nursing period, which often lasted a long time, had the same effect. The frequency with which the widowed remarried, particularly among the peasants, resulted in a succession of siblings from several marriages, often widely separated in age. In such conditions the children could not pass through a synchronized socialization phase; it is therefore impossible to construct a clearly defined family–cycle model for most historical family forms, taking as a model the socialization process as we know it today.

Does the family cycle accord with historical fact?

In the modern family cycle, the entry of children into the parental home, as well as their departure from it, take place in the course of a more restricted period of time than was the case with the families of the past. The number of children and the length of birth interval do, of course, affect this concentration. It is undoubtedly true that today the age at which children take up a job and become self-supporting depends in the first place on the length of their training. This differs in different classes of the community, but less among members of a family within one particular class. Training usually takes place while children live in the parental household. With the conclusion of training and the taking of a job comes the possibility of marriage and the setting up of one's own household. This too is historically a relatively new situation. It presumes, in the first place, a wage-earning economy, with the possibility of neo-locality, that has been brought about, for large sections of the population, by the increase in urbanization.

In societies in which family enterprises were the foundation of industrial structure, quite different conditions obtained. Those children who were not to succeed to their father's farm or shop, and could not be employed as fellow workers, left the parental household at quite an early age. Their education took the form of service in the house of a stranger; the length of their service did not depend on a specific programme of further education or apprenticeship, but on obtaining a position that would enable them to marry, establish their own households and maintain families. But the son or daughter who was to succeed to the family enterprise did not leave the household, at least in Central European areas. This applied especially to farming at those times and in those regions where *de jure* or *de facto* inheritance held sway. In merchant houses and artisan businesses that were tied to house ownership, this had the same effect on the family, but enterprises not tied to house ownership were less likely to be influenced. The situation in noble households was similar, although these were not 'family enterprises' in the strict sense of the phrase.

Where a child remained in his family of origin up to the time he took over the parental house, the family cycle had no 'empty nest' phase, of course. The question then arises of whether under these conditions one can speak of a family cycle at all, as it is understood by sociologists of the contemporary family. Sociological models of the family cycle stipulate a precise limit to its duration: either the establishment of a new household or the death of the surviving marriage partner after the departure of all the children. But when a young couple joined the parental household in the past, they did not, as a rule, start a separate household unit of production and reproduction. On the contrary, the existing household persisted. This was true particularly in those peasant families that were governed by retirement rights. The death of the surviving partner, in fact, did not mean the end of the existence of the household in question. It is, therefore, quite appropriate to speak of the perennial peasant family, and this leads one to question whether the family-cycle models of contemporary sociology can be used at all for analysing family forms of the past. In all historical family forms in which the household is continuous, perennial (based, that is, on the inherited possession of a house), one finds analogous conditions.

However important the dynamic view of the family cycle may be to the researcher's understanding of such family structures, the validity of the concept of the family cycle would appear to be problematic if it is applied too mechanically. If one wishes to avoid misunderstandings, it is wise to use more general terms, such as 'stadia' or 'stages of development'.

The continuing development of a household characterized by the perennial peasant family was by no means brought about only by successive transfers of property from father to son or father to son-in-law. In many farming communities, and in trading and crafts as well, continuity was effected not by the handing over of the household to a member of the next generation but by the remarriage of the widow. The precondition for such a succession was community of property between the marriage partners.

In the towns such forms of married property rights can be traced back as far as the high Middle Ages. In the case of the peasant household, the transfer of property to a second husband had several advantages. The farm was saved from the burden of providing support in retirement for the widow and her children who were minors; furthermore, the number of persons in the household remained constant, which was an advantage both for the subsistence of the family and for the continuity of labour organization. If the widow of a peasant household head remarried, there was a change of only one person in the family group. It is certainly not possible to treat such a break as the beginning of a new family cycle. We have the same problem with the identification of developmental forms in present-day families. It is true that remarriage among widows and widowers has decreased substantially in the last hundred years, but the increase in second marriages after divorce poses, in principle, similar problems of formalization.

Characteristic stages in the development of historical family types

The perennial character of households based on a family enterprise, therefore, casts some doubt on the concept of the family cycle in the historical context, and the modern division into phases corresponding to stages of socialization does not seem applicable to the past. We can, nevertheless, recognize characteristic periods of development in these family structures.

They are marked less by age-specific problems of education than by the requirements of labour organization. In the household structure of familial economic units, it was the productive function that was of importance to the life of the group, not the socializing function, as is the case nowadays. The need to secure the means of subsistence by a communal domestic economy influenced familial interaction in different ways. It even influenced the composition of the household community. The possibility of labour being supplied by parents, adolescent children and perhaps relations too governed the intake into the household of additional workers. These were primarily the servants, but married or single inmates could also be called upon to maintain the labour force of the family enterprise. Changes in the personal composition of the household often took place to meet these economic requirements. In the lifetimes of the two central figures of the group, the master and mistress of the house, age-specific stages characterized certain types of constellation of roles within the household community. These stages do not have the same clear-cut limits as those defined by their socialization function in the context of family cycles; nor do such stages correspond to regularly recurring constellations. Still, specific conditions at various stages of the development of the domestic community undeniably favoured certain constellations, which frequently occur in the sources.

The phase following the transfer of the farm to the young farmer, which generally coincided with his marriage, was frequently characterized by relations who lived in. When the transfer of the farm had been occasioned by the death of the father, the mother or mother-in-law went on living in the house. An elderly widowed farmer seldom managed on his own. Work on the farm made it necessary that both central positions should be properly filled, so the death of the wife generally meant that the widowed farmer handed over the farm to his successor. He then continued to live in the household of the young farmer. When the transfer took place during the lifetime of both old people, there was a double retirement to be faced. Such family formations varied in accordance with the regional inheritance and transfer customs in Central and Western Europe, and these also affected the presence of siblings in the household.

Where primogeniture held sway, minors among the siblings

accompanied the parent or parents into retirement on Austrian farms. Even where ultimogeniture prevailed, the young farmer might have to reckon with the presence of at least some of his siblings: older brothers and sisters often stayed for a few years as servants on the farm. The presence of siblings as servants in the period after the young farmer had taken over was characteristic of this period of the development of the family household and was governed not only by the obligation to care for near relations but also by labour requirements. At this stage the head's own children were not yet available to help with farm work. Periods of pregnancy and of nursing between births prevented the young wife from participating fully in the running of the household. In this phase of development related or non-related workers were therefore particularly necessary.

As soon as any of the children of the farmer had reached the age at which they could work in the house or on the land, the need for additional labour was reduced, so servants were frequently no longer engaged. If the farmer married in his late twenties, this generally did not happen before his fortieth year. Since the parents would then no longer be alive, a nuclear family may well have formed at this stage. If the old people had had rooms reserved for them on the farm, when these were no longer occupied they might be used for housing inmates. At this stage, then, the typical household might consist of parents, children and inmates. In the third phase of the lifecycle of the farmer and his wife, we again have to reckon with an increased need for servants. Some of the adult children would have already left the farm; the ability of the ageing couple to work would have diminished; and the assistance of servants was correspondingly more important. Where the institution of retirement had a legal basis and was an economic possibility, the retirement phase followed immediately. It coincided with the initial phase of the new young farmer who had taken over, married and had himself become the hub of the developmental cycle of the household.

Throughout rural areas of Central and Western Europe retirement rights were the most obvious reason for the existence of the three-generational peasant family where such are found to have existed. The stem family form, which came into existence because the successor to the farm married before succeeding to his inheritance, occurred less frequently. The stem family arrangement also solved the problem of the need for additional workers as the old couple's capacity for work diminished. Servants did not have to be taken on where this arrangement was adopted. An additional reason for the creation of the three-generational family was associated not so much with its *productive* as with its *protective* function. In many Austrian regions the illegitimate children of daughters were frequently to be found in the households of old farmers; the daughter either lived in the parental home or was in service elsewhere. This occurred in Austria particularly in the nineteenth century, and the phenomenon may have been connected with a markedly later age at marriage, which seems to have given rise to an increase in illegitimate births among the agrarian population.

Variations in phases of development

Many other circumstances determined whether constellational types that were linked with specific phases initiated primarily by labour requirements actually occurred in the peasant household. In the first place, there was the question of what crop was grown. Vine growers, for example, needed additional workers at different seasons of the year and preferred to make use of short-term additional wage earners rather than full-time servants living with the family. In the second place, local inheritance customs played their part. Where the inheritance could be divided, we often find small properties on which servants were unnecessary and which could not support the retired farmer. Third, there were economic considerations. When their economic situation was bad, many farmers could not afford servants, although they may have needed them. The same was true in years of pestilence. Epidemics could result in such a loss of men that the necessary assistance was not available.

Marked divergences from the ideal development of family constellations could therefore arise from differences in economic structure and conditions. In addition, long-term trends that promoted change brought about alterations in the succession of phases in the structure of the household. The increase in life expectancy since the eighteenth century has been of particular importance. Connected with this, but related to other factors as well, was the rise in the age at marriage of the country population. Both these trends led to changes in the decisive points in the lifecycles of peasant domestic groups. Another long-term trend was the decline of the influence of the landlord. His economic interest had less effect on the moment at which the farm was handed over and on the type of transfer arrangement. Increasingly, these were left to the family itself to organize. In the same way, a decrease in remarriage among widowed farmers' wives and an increase in direct father-to-son successions played a decisive role in the developmental stages of the domestic group. The transfer of the farm from father to son was a precondition for the regular succession of phases in the development of the peasant family.

In other historic forms of the domestic economy, particular requirements of labour organization were reflected in the developmental phases of the household: different economic conditions gave rise to varying household formations. In the urban artisan family, for example, the retirement principle played no part, for among the crafts the labour force needed for production was provided primarily not by the artisan's own children but by journeymen or apprentices living with the family as domestic servants. This was a developmental phase in which children, or at any rate sons, were frequently absent. As a consequence of late marriage and a great difference in age between spouses, many marriages among artisans remained childless. In their need to fill the central roles within the family, however, artisans resembled farmers: in their family cycles too, there was generally no 'incomplete' phase during which a single or widowed person stood at the head of the household.

Stability and change in composition

Labour requirements quite frequently caused changes in the membership of all domestic groups that functioned as family enterprises. By contrast, in families without these productive functions the circle of persons who lived together remained relatively constant over long periods of time; these households found it unnecessary to take in additional workers and therefore saw fewer changes in membership than did families with productive functions. And they were also affected less by the economic necessity to remarry, which was a factor that disrupted the continuity of many family groupings. It may be said that in general the development from a society based primarily on a domestic economy to one dominated by a wage-earning labour force changed household structure to a considerable extent because people lived in the same family groups for a much longer time.

This decisive change in the continuity of the membership of the family circle has not been the result of industrialization alone. The creation of large-scale business has undoubtedly altered the whole structure of industry and labour, but wage earning, we must remember, was already in evidence in the pre-industrial period, particularly in the towns. Increasing urbanization, just as much as industrialization, has contributed to its spread. In terms of the organization of labour in society, the emergence of relatively stable domestic groups has been associated with the formation of the three large social orders: labourers, clerks and officials. Sociological research into the family cycle is directed at specific relationships in these sections of the population as a whole, which now prevail in all European industrial nations. The reduction of the family community to a parent–child group is taken for granted. This would have been impossible if the family had not been relieved of its productive functions.

In the past the chances of the same members of a family living together for a long time varied considerably, even if the family had no productive functions. Families of day labourers in a city would, of course, be quite different from the families of the higher officials of the prince or the city. However, all families without productive functions were fundamentally the same in one crucial respect – the household group did not change in accordance with the periodic labour requirements of the family enterprise, which is why we may find the same succession of phases in the developmental cycles of groups as diverse as these.

Other factors were also of importance to the increasing homogeneity of the membership of the family circle. Increasing life expectancy was one; decreasing child mortality was another. Then there were changes in procreative patterns; compulsory education, along with a longer period of training; and better housing conditions, even for the lower classes. All these developments have affected considerably the stability of family composition. Whereas in peasant households in the seventeenth and eighteenth centuries hardly a year passed without at least one person coming or going, the developmental cycle of a present-day family shows an unchanging membership over years, even decades.

Effects on family life

The radical change in the length of time during which people have had to live together is clear and can be measured. There can be no doubt that it must have affected personal relationships within the family. But we have little documentation on the way such circumstances influenced family life in former times, and we are reduced to a great extent to speculation. Statements by individuals about the quality of family life are rare and cannot be taken as representative evidence. Any attempt to apply socio-psychological knowledge of the present to the family formations of the past seems methodologically questionable. At best one might be allowed to draw negative conclusions about which demonstrable effects of phase changes in today's families cannot be applied to historical family forms because of differences in composition and in phases of development. Yet judgements of this kind have a certain value, for they show quite clearly that many phenomena that are assumed to be constant by family sociology, socio-psychology and psychoanalysis have historically only a relative application.

One may safely assume that the increasing stability of family composition has promoted those changes that have given rise to the growing intimacy, emotionalism and sentimentalism of family life. It is generally thought that the eighteenth century saw the beginning of this change, which gave us many of those standards of value and behaviour that we associate, as a matter of course, with our present-day notion of the family.

This 'privatization' of the 'whole house' is frequently attributed to a change in ideas fostered by certain writers susceptible to the contemporary intellectual climate. Phrases such as 'the discovery of the child' are typical of this point of view. It is more likely that the increasing closeness of the family group is to be explained by the gradual separation of the place of work from the home, which seems to have been the case for an ever-increasing proportion of the population. This separation, however, does have the same root as the growing permanence of family groupings, namely, the abolition of the domestic group as the basis of production. The fact that a smaller unit of parents and children now live together over a longer period of time must deepen emotional relationships. Increased life expectancy has led to longer marriages. Emotion plays a much greater role in family formation because the choice of a marriage partner is no longer influenced by economic considerations.

The reduction in child mortality, together with higher life expectancy, must explain why even a small child is the focus of much affection today. Such strong ties between parents and children would not have existed when 20 per cent or more of all children born did not survive their first year of life. Then there is the change in the procreative pattern, which also has its roots in the different industrial structure that has been a result of the reduction in the number of family-based enterprises. A decrease in the number of children has given rise to smaller families living together for longer periods of time, which must undoubtedly have led to a deepening of personal relationships.

The departure of a member of the family in the past and in the present

Greater permanence in the composition of the family group, together with the emotional deepening of family relationships partly caused by this, have had the result that the departure of any one family member causes great grief. The contrast with family relationships in the past is very stark in this context.

Changes in membership took place so frequently in a peasant household of the eighteenth or nineteenth century that there could be no comparable sense of loss throughout the group. If a young wife died after a few years of marriage – and this happened quite often because of the great danger at and after childbirth – a second marriage was contracted after only a short period of mourning. A new housewife was needed to help in the management of the farm. Parents had to assume that several of their children would die young. Reactions of people of the eighteenth and early nineteenth centuries to the death of a child seem extremely hard-hearted to us, but they become understandable when the high mortality rate is taken into consideration. Soon after one child had died, the next might come into the world, and so on until the end of the woman's period of fertility.

Among peasants, however, little importance was attached to actual parentage. Foster children might be taken in, orphans of relations or neighbours; young relations often came into the household as men- or maidservants and were then treated as children of the family. On the other hand, people often sent their children into service at an early age and without a great sense of loss. Very young servants, many of whom were relations, usually stayed a fairly long time; older servants changed their position quite frequently, as did inmates with their dependants. In these circumstances, it was impossible to forge the strong emotional bonds that might have been fostered by a longer stay in the household.

In the context of the modern family cycle, the departure of a member of the family must be seen in a quite different light. The early death of a marriage partner or of a child is now an exceptional occurrence and leaves a pronounced gap in the household. Remarriage by a widowed partner may lead to psychological disturbance among the children, which would probably not have happened in historic times, in view of the frequency of second marriages. The same applies, of course, to the departure of one of the parents when a marriage ends in divorce. Today the separation of parents must have much more serious consequences for the children than the early loss of father or mother in former times.

The death of a marriage partner in old age has also taken on a quite different significance. Because of the lower age at marriage and higher life expectancy, the average marriage lasts much longer now. After living together for a very long time one partner finds the other's death much harder to bear; in most cases, it entails total isolation for the surviving partner. This certainly did not always happen to the family groupings of the past. Also in our day grown-up children leave the parental household and make their homes elsewhere, so that eventually all the children leave their parents' home. This did not happen when at least one child, the heir, continued to live in his father's house.

Lower age at marriage and higher life expectancy also help to ensure that children nowadays seldom live with their parents until the end of their lives. The 'empty nest' phase has become more frequent and longer-lasting in the contemporary world. The knowledge that they will have to face a long period of being alone together may inspire a keen fear of separation in the parents, especially in the mother, who is confined to the household sphere and emotionally more deeply involved. This anxiety is intensified by the fact that the departure of the children is not spread over a long time, as formerly, but is concentrated into a relatively brief period. The shorter birth intervals between surviving children, together with the clearly defined opportunities for independence and marriage at an early age, form the background to this development. In the charged emotional atmosphere of the modern nuclear family, the time of the children's departure constitutes a particularly painful and critical phase of the family cycle.

Increased intimacy as the possible root of psychological disturbance

With the greater permanence of the family group of individuals living together, family life has certainly gained in feelings of affection. For the individual member of the family, this may mean a greater opportunity to satisfy emotional needs. But at the same time it has made the family more susceptible to crises. Contemporary psychiatry has ascribed many psychological disturbances to the family circumstances of patients and to emotions prevalent within the family that are the product of the intensification of the emotional atmosphere. From the socio-historical point of view, these may be seen as relatively recent developments – developments that include over-organization by the mother, and among the children emotional fixations and dependence on parents, as well as the problems that arise as a result of difficulty with, or even the failure of, essential attempts to break free from parental dependence. In families that were ruled by less intense personal relationships, with a less closed and less intimate atmosphere and a more fluid structure, such social disturbance and tendencies to psychological illness would be unlikely, as Richter maintains in his classic work *Patient Familie* (*The family as patient*).

More intensive familial interaction, brought about by the greater conformity and continuity of family structure, causes the modern family to be not only more intense in its feelings but also more individualistic. People who are together for a long time are inclined to turn in upon themselves and live in separate, closely knit groups. Common experiences and memories link individuals very closely and leave a permanent imprint. Specific habits, attitudes and reactions arise from long-lasting co-residence. Certain ways of relating to each other are ritualized within the family. This individualism may even lead to the creation of a special family language.

In a family whose composition changed frequently such individualism would be impossible. The developmental cycle of the family of the past would preclude such special relationships and individual lifestyles. Domestic groups were probably much more similar to each other, but there would be marked differences between local settlements, village communities, parishes and so on. Nowadays the individualism of family life constrasts sharply with the more unified standards of public life.

Problems of isolation

In one sense, increasing intimacy and individualism seem to have led to the isolation of the modern family. The contrast between private and public life has become more marked. The greater permanence of the small family group may be set against the greater mobility of society as a whole. The static situation within the family, as it affects relationships between its members, may cause tension when individual members have to cope with the dynamics of public life. Thus one can speak of 'structural opposition of family and modern society' (Schelsky). These tensions affect different members of the family in different ways. It is much harder for the woman running the house than for the man to make outside contacts and to build personal relationships that are often so different from relationships within the family. If she is divorced or widowed, the woman's situation is still more difficult, and the risk of loneliness is particularly pronounced. Children growing up in the closed family circle have to face the problem of a more or less rapid adaptation to different patterns of behaviour when they leave it.

The crises that may arise from such intense relationships would certainly be mitigated if familial ties could be extended to a wider circle. If the small, isolated family were to foster its contacts with the outside world, it would take the edge off the problems of opposing familial and social relationships. It would, of course, not be possible to emulate the frequent changes in membership of families of the past. Indeed, the deeper personal relationships of the modern family constitute an advance of positive social value. But seen as an alternative form, the historical family may suggest, perhaps, that it is not necessary to confine family life to the parent–children group, and that integration into the social world immediately surrounding the family may reduce susceptibility to crisis.

Towards the polarization of generations?

If we contrast the succession of phases in the modern family cycle and the phases of historical domestic groups, we observe a number of remarkable differences. An analysis of family composition in respect of the age of individual persons deserves particular attention. Speaking generally, we may say this: the transition has been from a consid-

erable variation in ages, with phase-specific changes in the age relationship between group members, to stable generation clusters in the
parent–child group. Such a statement may be too general because it
ignores regional differences and, above all, differences between classes. It is true that age constellations similar to those of modern family
cycles occurred in former times, especially in those families that were
reduced to the circle of parents and children as a result of economic
constraints. But in households based on family enterprises, particularly among the peasants, all ages were represented.

The first reason for this was the great difference in age between
marriage partners found in Austria and Central Europe. This age gap
was sometimes decades in the case of second or third marriages. It
was not always the husband who was much older; it could also be the
wife. There might also be great differences in age between siblings as
a result of gaps between surviving children. These were all the more
pronounced when one or more children remained in the household
or when children were the products of successive marriages. Servants
usually occupied an age position between parents and children; only
young owners of farms had servants older than themselves. Finally,
there was the retirement arrangement, which required a developmental stage in which members of three generations lived together.

These conditions may be contrasted with those of the modern
family cycle, whose course is structured quite differently. It is characterized by smaller differences in age between marriage partners, by a
smaller group of siblings nearer to each other in age, and by the lack
of additional family members. As long as parents and children live
together, there is no alteration in this constellation of ages. It is not
easy to estimate how the different age patterns of the families of
former times influenced relationships between family members and
the development of the individual, but by studying a few examples
we may be able to get a better idea of such differences.

Equality in age and partnership

Whereas near equality in the ages of spouses favours a partnership
relationship, in the past the difference in age arising from frequent
remarriage may have contributed to greater dependence, at any rate
in those marriages in which the man was considerably older than the
woman. There is some evidence to suggest that the wife was then

treated almost as a child by the husband. It is not by chance that wherever there were deeply implanted patriarchal structures, the husband was much older than the wife. This patriarchal situation prevailed in large regions of South-East Europe, where the reverse position, that of the wife who' was older than the husband, occurred only rarely. A similar situation could also occur among the nobles and the urban upper classes.

However, among peasants and artisans whose farms or work-shops could be transferred by a widow, marriages between older women and younger men also took place. To what extent this resulted in relationships of dependence the sources do not permit us to say, but we may assume that the woman occupied a relatively strong position when the second husband's management of the farm was only an interim measure. The difference in age between mar-riage partners did not merely modify authority relationships; it must surely have influenced sexuality within marriage.

As regards the relationship between family and child, modern research into the family cycle assumes that the most important factor for the family now is the age of the child. Thus the family passes through the pre-school phase, the school phase, and so on. In earlier times a father or mother in a household based on a family enterprise had to deal with quite different situations. Their role was determined by many and diverse relationships with children of very different ages and with young servants who occupied a similar position. The parents were therefore confronted, at one and the same time, by a variety of tasks, demands and expectations. It seems likely that with this pattern in relationships between the children, the roles of father and mother would be multifarious but would remain much the same over time. Variations corresponding to successive phases that are postulated for the present time would seem to have been improbable in the past.

The socializing function of servants and siblings

The socialization of children is quite different at present from what it was in the past because then there was a greater variety of ages in the family. Whereas in the modern family, whose generations are polar-ized, the parents represent the exclusive or at any rate the primary means of socialization, one must assume that in historical families servants and older siblings also exercised a strong influence. The educational function of domestic servants was most obvious when they acted as nursemaids, governesses and tutors, especially in upper-class households. But even if they did not carry out such special tasks, servants must have influenced growing children. Where there was a great difference in the ages of siblings, the older ones would almost certainly have set an example for the younger ones. Apart from the parents, there would have been several persons in the household who exercised influence over the children in their early years. This is not the case with the modern family cycle. This difference between past and present should also be taken into account when considering the psychological development of the child in its early and later life. We might well wonder about the probability of the development of an Oedipus complex in such circumstances. Many assumptions of psychoanalysis can apply only to the small child in the restricted parent–child group that remains constant over time.

Effects of placement in the sibling rank order

It must be assumed that historical changes in the family cycle have brought about different relationships between siblings. In present-day families, siblings spend their childhood and youth together, in the same grouping. Individuals continue to occupy the same position in the sibling ranks, which is of great importance for their later development. Psychological theories have attempted to classify the effect of such sibling positions into certain main types and to delineate various character profiles. There is, for example, the eldest sister among sisters or the youngest sister among brothers, each with her specific personality. The theories even go so far as to pursue the effects of such placements into the next generation. In this way they analyse the consequences for the relationships between the children of a father who is the youngest brother among sisters and a mother who is the eldest sister among brothers and so on (Toman). Such speculation is surely only realistic if the whole sibling group is known to have undergone the relevant experiences as a closely knit community. This means that they are separated by only a few years and that there has been no change in individual position in the rank order of siblings over a period of time.

It is unlikely that a child's character was formed by his or her position in the sibling group of the family of the past because of greater differences in age, less stability in the composition of the family and frequent changes of position. No more than one in ten families in today's Federal Republic of Germany experiences the loss of a child, whereas until the late nineteenth century high child mortality practically always removed a brother or a sister. On top of this, siblings left to get married or to go into service or apprenticeship, although they might return home for short periods. In the past, therefore, the position of the individual child in relation to his brothers and sisters changed frequently during his childhood and youth and could not, therefore, have had much influence on the child's personality. Where we can trace the influence of the child's position in relation to his siblings at all, it is generally attributable to some later development.

More important for the child were the decisions taken by his parents about his future. The scion of a noble family might be destined to take orders, as can be gathered from the records of those who were named after a cleric among their relations. Primogeniture in these classes influenced the child's life from the cradle. A similar influence must have been exercised among the peasantry by their specific inheritance customs. It might be worthwhile to investigate whether such historic traditions, still evident in present-day veneration of the male descendant (*Stammhalterdenken*), would affect the empirical findings in connection with the influence his position in the sibling group has had on the individual child in the modern world.

Polarization of the generations and 'secondary patriarchalism'

It cannot be proved beyond doubt to what extent the general development from a uniform distribution of ages to a polarization of generations in the family has favoured the emergence of generational conflict. Such polarization must be associated with people's ages; yet conflicts arise not from differences in age but from relationships of authority and dependence. The hierarchy of age is not always identical with the distribution of social power within the family. However, the succession of phases in respect to authority in households based on family enterprises was distinctly different from that in modern families. While the household functioned as a unit of production, there was a need for clearly defined and uninterrupted authority. From the time he took over the farm until his death or retirement, the farmer was both household head and business manager, and he wielded unrestricted power, as did his wife in the narrower sphere of work allotted to her. Similar conditions obtained in family enterprises of other kinds.

The situation changed with the loss of the family's productive function. Its now dominant socializing function does not require the same kind of parental authority. On the contrary, with the subjects of socialization increasingly making their own decisions, the authority of the socializing agents ought to be reduced. That no account has been taken of these changed conditions until the present time, and not always even now, is due to the tenacity with which certain patterns of family behaviour, though no longer functional, are kept alive.

Thus we find what may be called 'secondary patriarchalism' in the families of wage earners who strive to maintain the authority inherited from the time of the family economic enterprise. But this state of affairs is already past its peak. Empirical research shows that since the beginning of this century adolescent children have been involved more and more in family decisions. The gradual reduction of parental authority that reflects the socializing function of the modern family poses real problems that may be difficult to resolve and may lead to conflict.

SELECT BIBLIOGRAPHY

Berkner, Lutz Karl, 'The stem-family and the developmental cycle of a peasant household: an eighteenth-century Austrian example', *American Historical Review* 77 (1972), pp. 398ff.

Cuisenier, Jean (ed.), *The family life cycle in European societies*, The Hague, 1977.

Glick, Paul C., 'The Family Cycle', *American Sociological Review* 12 (1957), pp. 164ff.

Haller, Max, 'Lebenszyklus und Familientheorie', *Kölner Zeitschrift für Soziologie und Sozialpsychologie* 26 (1974), pp. 148ff.

Hareven, Tamara K., 'The family as process: the historical study of the family cycle', *Journal of Social History* 7 (1974), pp. 322ff.
    'The family cycle in historical perspective: a proposal for a developmental approach' in Jean Cuisenier (ed.), *The family life cycle in European societies*, The Hague, 1977, pp. 339ff.

Hill, Reuben and Rodgers, Roy H., 'The developmental approach' in Harold T. Christensen (ed.), *Handbook of marriage and the family*, Chicago, 1964.

König, René, 'Soziologie der Familie' in *Handbuch der empirischen Sozialforschung*, vol. 7, 2nd edn, Stuttgart, 1976, pp. 1ff.

Laslett, Peter, 'Le cycle familial et le processus de socialisation: characteristiques du schéma occidental dans le temps' in Jean Cuisenier (ed.), *The family life cycle in European societies*, The Hague, 1977, pp. 317ff.

Meistermann-Seeger, Edeltrud, *Gestörte Familien*, Munich, 1976.

Mitterauer, Michael, 'Familiengrösse – Familientypen – Familienzyklus' in *Geschichte und Gesellschaft* 1 (1975), pp. 226ff.

Mitterauer, Michael and Sieder, Reinhard, 'The developmental process of domestic groups, *Journal of Family History* 4 (1979), pp. 257ff.

Richter, Horst Eberhard, *Patient Familie. Entstehung, Struktur und Therapie von Konflikten in Ehe und Familie*, Reinbek, 1972.

Rosenmayr, Leopold, 'Schwerpunkte der Soziologie des Alters' in *Handbuch der empirischen Sozialforschung* 7, 2nd edn, Stuttgart, 1976, pp. 218ff.

Rosenmayr, Leopold and Rosenmayr, Hilde, *Der alte Mensch in der Gesellschaft*, Reinbek, 1978.

Rowe, George P., 'The developmental conceptual framework to the study of the family' in Ivan Nye and Felix M. Berardo (eds.), *Conceptual framework in family analysis*, New York, 1966, pp. 198ff.

Schelsky, Helmut, *Wandlungen der deutschen Familie in der Gegenwart*, 5th edn, 1967 (1953).

Shorter, Edward, 'Der Wandel der Mutter–Kind Beziehungen zu Beginn der Moderne', *Geschichte und Gesellschaft* 1 (1975), pp. 256ff.

Sieder, Reinhard, 'Strukturprobleme ländlicher Familien im 19. Jahrhundert', *Zeitschrift für bayerische Landesgeschichte* 41 (1978), pp. 173ff.

Toman, Walter, *Familienkonstellationen. Ihr Einfluss auf den Menschen und seine Handlungen*, 2nd edn, Munich, 1974 (1964).

4

Has the Family Lost its Functions?

The present position of the family and its future prospects are often painted in very dark colours in our day. The family is considered to be in a condition of crisis and incipient dissolution: it sometimes is prophesied that it will disappear as a social form. Symptoms of disintegration and disorganization have been recorded, and the family is said to be ailing, increasing pathological problems for individuals. Prognostication and political aims coincide when radicals predict the death of the family.

Social scientists have provided a basis for pronouncements about the decreasing significance of the family as a form of social organization; they speak of a clearly recognizable tendency towards a loss of functions by the family, towards a reduction to its rudimentary functions. They do, indeed, acknowledge the durability and elasticity of this social form, attributes that have made it possible for the family to resume functions it had given up and to assume new ones that it fulfils in a satisfactory manner. Because research into the subject has been confined to a limited period, sociologists are unable to conclude whether this loss of function is a long-term trend or merely a temporary movement. With regard to long-term developments, they have to rely on the findings of historians.

Traditionally, historians have been little concerned to diagnose the present or foretell the future. The attention they have paid to major developments in the history of the family has been so restricted that it cannot be said that they are on an equal footing when it comes to a discussion with social scientists. However, although little is known as yet about historical changes in the social functions of the family, it is possible to arrive at certain definite conclusions.

The processes discovered by family sociologists are certainly part of a long-term trend in development and the historian can perceive the overall tendency far more clearly than the sociologist. As far as we can look back into the past, the family has always surrendered some of its social tasks to superordinate social structures. This has happened to a far greater extent than is suggested for the present day by sociologists, for the number of functions of the modern family is only a meagre remnant of the wealth of functions it fulfilled in former times. We may even be permitted to wonder whether, from an historical point of view, the age-long process of reducing family tasks and allotting them to larger social forms can be characterized as a loss of functions. It might be better to speak of the family having been *relieved* of some of its functions, and this is more than terminological hair-splitting. Different words stand for different values, as will be shown.

A few introductory remarks are necessary before embarking on a consideration of the theory that the family has been relieved of some of its functions. We must begin by pointing out that there can be meaningful discussion of the question of trends of development only if the investigation remains within the framework of one clearly defined context. We shall, therefore, deal only with European – and more especially Central European – developments. Furthermore, it would appear that within any one society, changes in family functions have not occurred at the same time among all social classes. Although parallel developments have taken place, there have been differences in the phases of development, which may have led to the simultaneous appearance of family forms relieved of their functions to various degrees.

Generally speaking, then, in the towns, with their highly complex and differentiated forms of living together, change came before it did in country districts. When one compares family life on a remote mountain farm with that of the household of an employee in a great city, one is immediately aware of the enormous differences in their functions. For the peasant family, the transfer of functions to larger social forms usually took place much more slowly, so that old-fashioned forms were often retained. In the past it was markedly more common to find the old and the new existing side by side. In a period when the family had a greater variety of functions, the simultaneous presence of family forms relieved of their functions to various degrees was more noticeable than it is in modern times, when conditions are more homogeneous in this respect. We must, therefore, distinguish temporal differences, such as those between the family of the late Middle Ages and the family of the eighteenth century, and must also allow for a regional dimension. The most important criterion of family type, however, has always been social status: the overriding reality is the division between nobility, craftsmen and peasants.

It must be pointed out that any classification of family functions (for instance, with respect to socialization or production) must be undertaken on an entirely systematic and analytical basis. Functions in an historical context should always be seen as an indivisible whole. There are no sharply defined boundaries between them; they are interconnected and condition and influence each other. It is impossible, therefore, to isolate the seemingly 'purely biological' function of procreation from the seemingly 'purely social' function of child rearing, because there is unity of psychological impression in the phase of early childhood. It is impossible too to separate bringing up children from protecting them, or the securing of food from the organization of labour. Changes in one kind of function involve changes in another, as, for example, when the procreative pattern is adapted to new forms of production.

Religious functions of the family

The religious functions of the family were the first to lapse. It is true that even today the family fosters religious belief, but nowhere, at any rate in the main European communities, was it the dominant form of worship in the past. The characteristic family cult was ancestor worship as a house cult. Where ancestors were venerated at their graves near the house or in front of pictorial representations of them within the house itself one may assume that the family was a community of worship.

But not every form of ancestor worship was a cult confined to a particular house. Relatives from many associated households might join in ancestor worship. Again, not every house cult was an ancestor cult. The Roman *penates* were gods of the larder and had nothing to do with sanctified ancestors. Ancestor worship in the house was seldom the exclusive cult form of a society. There were also the cult of the community, the cult of the tribe, the cult of the nation. With the predominance of one or other of these cults, the family's function faded to a greater or lesser degree.

In early European society the ancestor cult of the house would appear to have been quite general. Many sources provide evidence of the belief that the spirits of the dead did not leave their earthly dwellings, that the dead could cause calamities and confer blessings, that they required sacrifices and veneration and avenged neglect. Evidence that fits with this imaginary world has been supplied mainly by archaeologists. It instances the nearness of farms to burial places, gifts found in graves and, above all, the importance of ancestors in pictures. These pictures were intended both to secure protection from ancestors and to put an end to their restless wandering by identifying them with their pictorial representation.

There is linguistic evidence as well. The German word *Erbe* (heir), we are told, is derived from *erfa*, which means to make a sacrifice to an ancestor. There was also the widespread practice of naming a child after its ancestor, which was originally connected with a belief in reincarnation.

It is mostly relics and remnants of tradition that enable us to draw conclusions about the dominance of the household worship of ancestors in early European society. In that society, as opposed to various non-European cultures, such cult forms must have waned quite early. Christianization marked their final disappearance. Where Christianity came up against the remains of an ancestor cult, as in the Scandinavian countries, there was sharp conflict, which ended in the relegation of these cults to the status of superstition. Inevitably, a compromise had to be reached with the tradition of the household as a cult community. The medieval house church or chapel was the product of such a compromise. It was, above all, the families of princes and nobles that clung to the archaic forms of the house cult. The court bishop, the castle and house chaplain were the last representatives of the old household priests.

The ancestor cult was also maintained by the rulers and the aristocracy in Christianized forms. We can see this, for example, in the veneration of princely and noble ancestors as saints: St Wenzel and St Ludmilla in Bohemia, St Stephen in Hungary, St Olaf in Norway, St Edward in England, the *pius marchio* Leopold in Austria. As a late and

particularly grand example of ancestral worship we may mention the
Eisernen Mander (Iron Men) of the sepulchre of Emperor Maximilian
I in the Hofkirche in Innsbruck. The princely and noble ancestral
galleries in later castles perpetuate this worship in secular form. This
tenacious clinging to the ancestor cult by princely and noble families
is to be associated with the legitimization of sovereignty by means of
the sanctity of the lineage.   Apart from the relics of such customs
among the upper classes, local populations may undoubtedly be seen
as cult communities among the Christian people of the European
regions. Everywhere in Christendom religious social life was based
primarily on the parish. The placing of burial grounds around the
church would seem to indicate that the original family-cult forms
had been integrated into the parish community, which then proceeded as a corporation, as it were, to take over other functions from
individual households – for instance, in business or the care of the
needy. This group, therefore, provided one of the oldest and most
significant foundations for the development of communal life, especially in country districts.

However, the parish community as a type of local or regional cult
association was preceded by earlier community organizations
stretching back into pre-Christian times. It was in connection with
matters of worship that communal and corporal forms of organisation generally took shape in very early times. The surrendering of its
function of worship by the household or the family was of crucial
importance to the development of larger, superordinate social forms.

Judicial functions

Another archaic family function, often closely connected with the
ancestor cult, was the duty of blood revenge. It was usually the same
group of persons on whom this duty devolved: the adult males of the
house, in particular the nearest agnatic relatives. When this group
became aware of an offence perpetrated against the family, they were
duty bound to direct their revenge against the whole of the clan to
which the offender belonged. This form of collective self-help was
found only where primitive justice prevailed. In remote country districts in which central authority had but little power, these conditions
could still be found until quite recently, as, for example, in Albania,
Montenegro or Corsica. But in general they disappeared at quite an

early date. In the early Middle Ages Germanic tribal law provided for the settlement of disputes by deeds of atonement, the so-called *Wergeld* (blood money). The abandonment of acts of revenge lies at the heart of the developing public system of jurisdiction.

The decrease in the dispensing of justice by members of the family was accompanied by the growth of a legal system in the framework of ordered social forms. This development took place not only because the family surrendered its duty to avenge its members, but also because the judicial powers of the head of the family were increasingly restricted to the house. In earlier times he had carried out this duty in full measure and, according to general opinion, legitimately. He was even able to pronounce the death penalty, certainly on slaves and, most important, on children, by expelling them from the house, and on his wife as well if adultery or any such grave offence had been committed. In regions in which public law did not generally prevail, a wife could be disposed of until recent times.

Protective functions

The atavistic phenomenon of blood revenge may, in a very broad sense, be counted among the protective functions of the family: if something cherished by all and worthy of protection had been violated, the crime had to be avenged. To give protection is, in general, a central family function, which becomes more important the further back we go in history. On the one hand, the natural world presented a greater threat to the individual; on the other hand, the community provided far less social security. Therefore the primary family group had to meet a much greater need for protection. In considering the secular process that relieved the family (the domestic group as a whole, that is to say) of many of its protective functions, one has to take account not only of the smaller number of persons in need of protection, but also of the decrease in the occasions on which protection had to be provided.

One function of which the house was relieved quite early was the protection it gave to a guest. A stranger enjoyed protection only in so far as he was taken in as somebody's guest. At the same time, he had to submit to the authority of his protector, as is indicated by the Slavonic word for master, *gospodi* (host). With the development of transport, the protection of strangers was transferred to higher levels of authority. The merchant, for example, was under the protection of the king. Hostelries for the accommodation of travellers were given special guarantees of peace.

The withdrawal of domestic servants from the family's protection is of much greater importance than that of guests. This was caused, on the one hand, by the fact that contractual labour increasingly took the place of personal service and, on the other hand, by the transformation of the family enterprise into organized, large-scale business.

In a predominantly agrarian society with few and poorly developed communal settlements, families had to contend with greater dangers than do those living in present-day urban societies. Great physical strength and the ability to use weapons were needed for the defence of life and property and protection against wild animals. Protective functions were therefore mainly in the hands of adult men, above all in those of the master of the house. This is one of the reasons why a patriarchal order prevailed.

Certain protective measures typical of the countryside were superfluous in the fortified towns, and others could more easily be organized by the community, so that individual households were inclined to give up these functions. Defence against an enemy or police protection were formerly arranged on a co-operative basis. Requirements of protection clearly differed between town and country. In urban areas it was impossible to be self-sufficient in providing the family's food, and with increasing differentiation in labour conditions, security of livelihood was often threatened. As the wage-earning economy replaced the subsistence economy, the incapacity to earn one's livelihood became a problem of survival, and the classic risks of old age, illness and invalidity assumed increasing importance.

Co-operative organizations, therefore, had to take over the guaranteeing of security from the urban family. Guilds and associations of artisans relieved the family of its protective functions, as indeed did the confraternities that increased considerably in the late medieval cities. At the same time, a greater number of hospitals took over family functions; these were, in the first place, institutions where casualties were cared for – casualties of all kinds and not simply the indigent and the ill. The hospital for the sick, in our present-day meaning of the word, was a later development.

Particular difficulties arose in connection with the care of the old and the ill with the emergence of independent wage earners and their spread throughout the population. Personal service within the house had been in the nature of an agreement, whereby it had been the master's duty to care for his servants when they were unable to work. But this duty lapsed when the domestic servant turned into the independent wage earner, who could then no longer count on the assistance of his employer in this way. Wage earning meant above all that the labourer was paid as an individual, regardless of his domestic situation. If the support of members of the family was precarious anyway, the care of widows and orphans might become impossible because of illness or old age.

Wage earning by the industrial masses has brought with it a need for protection that could not possibly be met by the family. It was not until the late nineteenth and early twentieth centuries that the state dealt with this situation by providing social security, on which the wage-earning section of the population, and increasingly the self-employed too, depend. Central functions of help and care that, until recently, were assumed mainly by the family have now been taken over by the state.

Economic functions

The period of the Industrial Revolution – which occurred, it must be remembered, much more recently in Central than in Western Europe – was the period during which the family ceased to provide the basic form of labour organization, and this was of decisive importance in phasing out its economic functions. It is true that earlier in human history the family had already given up some of its productive activities. In principle, every division of labour between household communities means a reduction of the productive functions of the respective households. Economic differentiation brought about by the development of transport and communications can therefore be seen as an important part of the great process of freeing the family from its productive functions.

The peasant household community, as an ideal type, represents the basic structure increasingly changed by the growing division of labour. The farmstead has always appeared to be non-specialized in its production; it has always been an all-embracing family enterprise that retains out-dated features in its social organization. Economic differentiation, which had met with success in town centres, was pursued further with increasing urbanization. Household communities in the towns were therefore foremost in relieving each other of their productive functions.

There was no clear difference betwen types of family enterprise. The peasant was not occupied exclusively with farming, nor the artisan with his craft. In pre-industrial times members of the peasant household worked at spinning and weaving and other crafts, both for their own use and for the benefit of their lord. Conversely, townsfolk were not occupied solely with industry and commerce. Our picture of the economic structure of the medieval urban area should not be restricted to the great commercial cities. A more usual type was the so-called *Ackerbürgerstadt*. City dwellers often possessed within the city walls allotments that they cultivated, where they might also keep cattle, while outside the walls there were fields and vineyards. There was no hard and fast distinction between country and town households.

Nevertheless, in its economic aspect the farmstead was primarily a unit of subsistence; the artisan's household was a commercial unit. Providing for the needs of its inhabitants was the main consideration of the first, although this did not mean a closed economy; in the second, the market was of prime importance. With increasing market production, securing one's livelihood became more precarious. This necessitated the security provided by co-operative associations like the medieval guild system. As people increasingly joined superordinate co-operative societies, the functions of the household and the family declined.

Although greater economic differentiation altered the system of family production and specialization produced many different family types, yet the family as a unit of production remained virtually unchanged. It was the progress of industrialization that relieved the family of its productive functions. Family enterprises increasingly gave way to large-scale industry, with organized labour in factories, which gradually took over the tasks previously carried out by the family.

During the period of industrialization, when the family enterprise disappeared, the masses became independent wage earners. However, wage earning outside the family enterprise did not make its first appearance at this time. Many centuries before there had been families in different sections of society that were free from productive functions. Mining, for instance, was organized quite early on a large-scale industrial basis, as were the building and transport industries. Day labourers on the land, in forestry and especially in viniculture, were very common.

The most important effect on the family of the change to wage earning was nevertheless the separation of place of work and dwelling, as has been pointed out above. This separation, characteristic of the present-day family, was caused not only by changes in production but also by the growth of the bureaucracy, which played an equally important role. In Central Europe this began with the centralization of the royal administration during the period of absolutism (seventeenth–nineteenth centuries) and has proliferated at all levels of government since. During the nineteenth century both civil servants and clerks multiplied. The family's loss of functions was brought about by those working in offices just as much as by those in factories. Since the early nineteenth century, wage and salary earning has taken place outside the family in nearly all sections of society. These decisive changes greatly reduced the economic functions of the family. Housework, in the modern sense of the word, remained the only productive domestic activity, carried out by domestic servants when they were available and, latterly, entirely by the housewife. During the nineteenth and early twentieth centuries much more was involved in housework than is appreciated nowadays. During this period, functions continued to be shed by the family, mainly because food and clothes formerly produced within the household became available on the market. New kinds of service were offered that relieved the family of the need to provide them itself. Except in times of crisis, there was no need to be self-sufficient, to grow and preserve one's own fruit and vegetables. The reduction in productive functions emphasizes the character of the household as a unit of consumption.

Socializing functions

In modern times the socialization of children is taken to be the central function of the family. It is, in fact, a legacy of earlier, more extensive family duties and has been extended and differentiated in recent years. General and, more recently, compulsory education has resulted in a reduction in the family's socializing functions.

In early European society the rearing and training of offspring took place mainly within the household. This statement needs qualification, however. In the pre-industrial period education was by no means confined to the parental house, for children frequently left home at an early age to receive their training elsewhere. Knowledge and skills were transmitted mainly by the older to the younger generation as they worked together in the family enterprise: children and young people learned by precept and experience. If a child could not acquire a particular skill in his own home, he had to seek training elsewhere.

Even the son who was destined to carry on his father's work usually entered another household to complete his training. Service was a form of education undertaken by all young boys, by the sons of noblemen as pages, by journeymen and apprentices in crafts and commerce, by the farm servant on the farm and by the clerical scholar in the monastic community. The youngster entering a new household held a position similar to that of a child: he had to render service and obedience, but he also had the right to expect maintenance and protection.

Training outside the parental home lies at the root of all forms of school. The medieval *schola* attached to monasteries served, in the first place, to educate those who were to enter these establishments. This type of education had its own special characteristics. Within the larger religious community the *schola* at first formed a separate group under the leadership of someone whose task was exclusively educational, the so-called *scholasticus*. It is also important to note that in schools general subjects were taught as well as those required for special callings. Eventually, the *schola* also catered for children who were not destined for a religious career. It therefore constituted an educational institution apart from the household and marked the beginning of the surrender of certain socializing tasks by the family.

In medieval and early modern times education outside the home varied for different sections of the community in accordance with the social structure of the times: grammar schools were established for the offspring of well-to-do burghers; there were schools that taught the three Rs to children of artisans; there were special schools for young nobles. Public education, in our sense of the word, did not exist. It is significant that the introduction of compulsory education took place in the period of absolutism, when integration of the whole state was attempted. In Central Europe it did not come about until the early seventeenth century in the Lutheran territories, and it spread from there to the Catholic lands. In Austria, for instance, it did not occur before Maria Theresa's reign (1740–80). It was accomplished gradually, with marked differences between various sections of the community. There was much opposition to it in country districts. Children of factory workers were included at a late date.

And there was a great difference between the schooling of boys and that of girls: the tradition that only boys should be educated was perpetuated by the public school system. The introduction of general compulsory education did not, therefore, result in the family giving up all its educative functions, nor did the family surrender these functions at the same time in different regions and among different classes.

There was never more than a partial surrender by the family of its socializing functions to community or state educational institutions. Unless he went to a boarding school, the child was away from home for only part of the day. Also the school did not take over his education until the child had reached his sixth or seventh year, which for a very long time has been the traditional time for the termination of that part of the child's education for which the mother is mainly responsible. If the child attended a kindergarten or nursery school, this date was advanced. (These institutions were founded in Germany at the middle of the nineteenth century and have increased in importance ever since.)

The reproductive function

There is little to separate the early phase of primary socialization from that of reproduction, which among human beings is prompted by a symbiosis of biological and socio-cultural factors. We have now come to the hard core, as it were, of family functions. Notwithstanding the central importance of reproduction to the family, we may discern certain changes in the course of history, which, in a sense, may be taken as a partial shedding of functions by the family. Whereas in pre-industrial times the period of marital fertility was, on the whole, fully exploited, there was a steady decline in the birth rate during the nineteenth and twentieth centuries.

Several contributing factors may be mentioned. One was the rapid decline in child mortality because of advances in medicine and hygiene, which practically doubled the child's chances of survival. At the same time, as more and more people became wage earners, children became an additional expense to the family instead of providing labour for the family enterprise – farm, craft, shop or service. Expenditure and the period of maintenance for children increased considerably. The ambition to improve one's living condition, and thereby one's social standing, also made for a reduction in the number of births. All this has been enormously facilitated by new methods of birth control. Procreative patterns changed drastically. The rearing of children is now confined to a relatively short phase in the family life cycle by comparison with pre-industrial times. Considering the total duration of marriages, parents have been increasingly relieved of the task of primary socialization.

Cultural functions

In spite of these losses of function, which have affected its very core, the family has not surrendered all of its functions. Those that have been relinquished in the course of time were all calculated to ensure the survival of members of the group, to secure their existence and to counter the threats of nature. But even as these tasks were abandoned, new activities developed that were not directly concerned with survival but rather enhanced the quality of life. In contrast with the functions we discussed earlier, we might simply call them cultural activities. In this connection, as well as in connection with the other functions we have discussed, it is surely preferable to talk of the family being relieved of its functions rather than losing them. It must be remembered, however, that these secondary, cultural functions are not restricted to the family as a social unit.

It is greater leisure that has enabled the family to assume these new functions. Leisure time, in the modern sense of the word, is quite a recent phenomenon, closely connected with those losses of function that we have been discussing. Leisure time has increased as the work imposed by society has decreased. It developed with the reduction of such work within the family and with its separation from the family. The multiplication of the family's cultural functions is in many ways connected with those functions of the family that are vanishing. Often it is merely a question of endowing the remaining functions with new and more elaborate shapes, as may be seen from customs that perpetuate those cults that have become obsolete.

Games may be mentioned as an example. Many children's games still contain elements that are recognizable as preparation for work to be undertaken within the family. The ambition to add comfort and luxury to a home that was formerly designed merely to secure survival is another example of this process of development. Similarly, the custom of a family's sitting and eating together at table has been much elaborated. Gardening as a leisure activity has developed from the growing of fruit and vegetables. Keeping animals as pets has its origins in raising livestock. The enjoyment of leisure is an increasing preoccupation, and the family is becoming more and more a unit of consumption. (Such changes do, of course, take place at different times in different classes of society.)

Will the family become functionless?

We realize, as we look back into the past, that family functions have tended to change in accordance with a recognizable trend. This raises the question of whether, in the light of our historical knowledge, we should allow ourselves to forecast future developments. The question touches on fundamental problems of historical research and its practical possibilities. We cannot deal with this abstract problem here but must content ourselves with a consideration of the concrete theme of family development.

The historian is able to note, especially when his view ranges over a long period, that there has been an essentially uni-directional trend in changes in the social structure of the family. Admittedly, there have always been situations in which the family has had to resume tasks that it had given up long before. During and after periods of war, for example, many households have aimed to become self-sufficient by producing their own food. Thus the family has resurrected some of its productive functions from time to time. The repression of religion, and thereby of religious community life, has often caused the family to appear to be the only forum for religious belief. We could cite other examples of the family's resumption of tasks it had abandoned, but on the whole these are exceptions. They serve to illustrate the extraordinary elasticity of the family in dealing with danger and crisis but in no way contradict the general trend of development.

The secular process by which the family has surrendered its functions to superordinate social forms is, in principle, irreversible. To revert from modern civil justice to archaic blood revenge would be impracticable; to give up public education and bring up children entirely within the household would hardly be feasible; it is most improbable that family enterprise could replace the now dominant forms of large-scale business and labour organization. Though it is a negative assessment, the historian is at least able to say that certain past family forms will have to be excluded from his prognosis for the future. A return to the plethora of functions exercised by the European family of pre-industrial times would seem to be impossible.

The fact that certain long-term processes in the surrender of family functions are not reversible must not, of course, be seen as the automatic result of social development; it is much more the case that new ways of thinking on the part of the individual and society as a whole would reject such a return as primitive. It would not be sensible to give up the progress achieved in the mastering of the natural world and in the organization of human community life. The institutions that took over from the family were maintained and improved in the past because they offered certain advantages; the question of who benefited from these advantages is scarcely our concern. The trends we have described were therefore initiated by rational thinking and deliberate action. They arose from the necessity to deal with critical situations; they were not dictated by some prior law of social development, as people tend to believe. The role played by purposeful change must therefore be considered in every attempt to forecast the future shape of the family.

We have seen that the surrender of functions by the family in the past went hand in hand with the adoption of functions by existing or newly created social institutions. Schools, businesses, communities, above all the state, with its multiplicity of social facilities, may be cited here. Urbanization, industrialization, bureaucratization assisted in, or forced, the surrender of family functions. The development of the family structure, therefore, must always be seen in the context of such overall social changes. The future shape of the family will depend on whether this framework alters or remains the same. We may reckon on a further loss of functions by the family if present developmental trends continue and larger social forms are created and endowed with greater power. The decrease in those family functions that have the character of necessary tasks and duties may be accompanied by an increase in activities that will improve the quality of family life. This may be seen as a shift of emphasis from institutionalized to voluntary activities. The character of the family as a social group will undoubtedly change, but it should not be assumed this will entail its decline or dissolution.

These considerations lead us to attempt an evaluation of the changes that have taken place in the social structure of the family, and here history may be better qualified to make a contribution than to forecast the future. The proposition that the family has been relieved of its institutional functions must be viewed favourably because there is an undeniable historical connection between this development and emancipation – and by this we mean emancipation not only within the family but also within and between different social groups. The first results in a lessening of patriarchalism in the family, the latter in a lessening of the importance of status in society.

Emancipation resulting from loss of functions

When the father was head of the house and also its priest, he occupied a sacred, patriarchal position that ensured the enduring dependence on him of members of his household. Such dependence rested finally on religious grounds and was therefore unshakeable. This gave rise to a rigid patriarchalism. The religious power of the head of the family led to the formation of large households and even to the subjection of married sons. It also resulted in a preference for sons rather than daughters, as evidenced by inheritance rights. The abandonment of the ancestor cult created conditions conducive to the weakening of patriarchalism and social order characterized by male predominance.

In society at large the ideology of ancestor worship led to the veneration of the lineage. Consequently, there was little chance of improving one's social standing. Mobility was also spatially limited, mainly because sons were tied to the paternal house as the centre of their cult. The rise of new social forms seems to have been inhibited by the religion of ancestor worship. By contrast with East Asia, for instance, the wealth of new social forms developed in European countries may have been due, among other things, to the relatively early disappearance of the ancestor cult. Communal and corporal social forms, above all, were important emancipating factors.

As the family was relieved of the need to provide immediate armed protection, it became less important for its members to bear arms. The offering of protection always demands authority. Because the father had less need to bear arms, there was less need for him to exercise authority within the family. The custom of blood revenge linked the ability to bear arms with the right to mete out justice, which was therefore primarily a male affair. The administration of justice is the basis of political power in the community and in all larger forms of community life. Only with the limitation of the protective and legal functions of the master of the house did legal and political emancipation of those dependent on him become possible. And this, in turn, led to the recognition of the personal rights of women, of adult children, and, above all, of the various types of servant.

Similar changes took place in the political system too. With the decrease in the protective functions of the family, it became possible to extend political rights to persons other than male property owners. Under the earlier system, the privileged position of a noble house owner derived from his military and protective obligations in what can also be seen as a great household, his domain.

The surrender of the family's productive functions led to a decisive weakening of patriarchalism. The father lost his position as leader of the labour organization and, with it, the strongest institutional support for his authority over the members of the household. With the disappearance of the family enterprise, there was a change from personal service to contractual labour. This process of emancipation gave work outside the household to persons who had hitherto been dependents. Members of the family (and this included the children and the wife) now had a chance to earn their own living and thus became economically independent of the head of the household. The increase of wage labour reduced the importance of the parental inheritance and thus was also a factor in emancipation.

As long as the family was the dominant form of labour organization, fixed roles were allotted to its members by the division of labour. With the lapse of productive functions, greater freedom was allowed to both husband and wife, as well as to sons and daughters. In the family enterprise, as we have remarked, key roles always had to be filled. A widow or widower had to marry again; a son who took over the family enterprise was obliged to marry, although up to then he had not been allowed to. His choice of a marriage partner suited to his particular occupation might be limited. But after the family had given up its productive functions, there were greater opportunities to choose an appropriate partner. This was also true among members of the higher social classes after they had freed themselves from their preoccupation with considerations of lineage.

The separation of the place of work from the home gave greater freedom to members of the family to organize their own lives. The availability of more space led to the development of the individual. Neo-locality replaced patrilocality in the case of newlyweds who had a new opportunity to decorate and furnish their home in accordance with their own private desires.

Socialization within the family was crucial to the stability of pre-industrial society. In essence, the son was brought up in his father's profession or in the profession of the master of the house to whom his father had entrusted him. In such a system there could be only specialized education, because preparation for a profession meant participation in the work of the household. By contrast, the advance in public schooling has meant greater social mobility, greater opportunities for bettering oneself. Education has ceased to be practical and specialized. It has opened up greater professional possibilities and has delayed the final decision about what calling a child is to follow – an important step towards the right to determine his own destiny. The school has opened up new vistas for the child and, by fostering his development, has helped him to realize his own personality. The teacher is now next to the parents in importance in a child's education. The peer group as a factor of socialization has also to be reckoned with. Common education in state schools has brought children of different classes together and has made for a levelling of social distinctions. The lowering of the age at which socialization outside the family begins has brought with it greater equality of opportunity.

Finally, the reduction of the phase of childbearing and the restriction of primary socialization has had certain emancipatory effects. The endless sequence of pregnancy and lactation meant that the mother of pre-industrial times was very much tied to the home. With smaller family size and the reduction in family duties, her role as wife and mother is no longer fixed and ties have been loosened, thus enabling her, at least at certain times, to pursue her own career.

From domination to partnership

The whole process of the reduction of functions may be seen as the development of the family structure from a rigidly hierarchical institution to a partnership of individuals. Members of the family have gained greater independence and the right to live their own lives. This applies, above all, to the relationship between marriage partners, but also to that between parents and children.

As we look back in social history, the causal connection between the change in familial functions and personal emancipation helps us to understand why the pronounced patriarchalism that formerly characterized European family life does so no longer. This patriarchalism did not result from the suppression and exploitation of the wife by the husband and of the children by the father for its own sake; it arose from the need to secure the family's existence by concentrating tasks and duties in the family, which in turn required a strongly hierarchical organization. The mastering of nature, better ways to ensure human survival, the emergence of social forms that helped to relieve the family of its institutional functions – all these made the emancipation of its members possible.

But even when a further decrease in family functions brings further emancipation, as is to be expected, there is one relationship to which this can never fully apply: the relationship between parents and children. As a social form that gives protection, the family must always have a head; as a socializing agent, it must always be able to exercise authority.

It would be an unwarranted simplification to say that relieving the family of its functions has always resulted in emancipation. On the contrary, there are historical examples to show that such processes can lead to new relationships of dependence and to crises within society. Indeed, the disappearance of the family enterprise at the time of the Industrial Revolution had a number of adverse consequences. The wife employed outside the house today may well have a sense of personal fulfilment, but surely those women who were forced by poverty to work in the early industrial period could in no way have felt emancipated. Even if one were to regard it as an advance that, by contrast with apprentices, wage earners were able to marry, the wage-earning family found itself in a catastrophic economic situation and was even more dependent than before. If one thinks that the condition of the free wage earner was emancipated by comparison with the dependent position of the artisan working in his master's household, one must not forget his relative lack of protection when in need. We also have to take into account the fact that the transition from one situation to the other was accompanied by hardship. When journeymen were allowed to marry, for example, they continued to receive the customary wage that they had been paid as single journeymen. Again, the transfer of the family's productive functions to the large industrial business did not involve the transfer of the family's protective functions. The crises that have followed in the wake of the disappearance of family functions have been caused, for the most part, by the failure or the lack of readiness to adapt on the part of society as a whole.

Difficulties of adaptation arise when the standards of value, the patterns of behaviour and the views of former times are retained when conditions have changed. Under conditions of advanced industrialization, we can find ourselves saddled with a procreative pattern that was justified in the peasant household but is no longer wholly appropriate. Ideas about the upbringing of boys and girls still hold sway that have their roots in the long-lost division of labour between husband and wife within the family. Claims to inheritance and property that were legitimate in a social world that has long since disappeared still retain their value. Such a cultural lag is often to be noted in the history of the family because of its inherent conservatism. The historian interested in emancipation is therefore presented with special opportunities to investigate the social context in which traditional ideas, values and patterns of behaviour have originated. If he can indicate the conditions in the past from which they have sprung, he may well have a contribution to make to changes of consciousness that are long overdue.

SELECT BIBLIOGRAPHY

Ariès, Philippe, *L'enfant et la vie familiale sous l'ancien régime*, Paris, 1960.
Bahrdt, Hans Paul, 'Wandlungen der Familie' in Hans Paul Bahrdt, *Wege zur Soziologie*, Munich, 1966 (= Dieter Claessens and Petra Milhoffer (eds.), *Familiensoziologie*, Frankfurt, 1973, pp. 110ff.).
Claessens, Dieter, *Familie und Wertsystem*, Berlin, 1962.
Claessens, Dieter and Menne, Ferdinand, 'Zur Dynamik der bürgerlichen Familie und ihrer möglichen Alternativen' in Dieter Claessens and Petra Milhoffer (eds.), *Familiensoziologie*, Frankfurt, 1973, pp. 313ff.
Egner, Erich, *Entwicklungsphasen der Hauswirtschaft*, Göttingen, 1964 (excerpts as 'Epochen im Wandel des Familienhaushalts' in Heidi Rosenbaum (ed.), *Seminar: Familie und Gesellschaftsstruktur*, Frankfurt, 1978, pp. 92ff.).
Freudenthal, Margarete, *Gestaltwandel der städtischen bürgerlichen und proletarischen Hauswirtschaft unter besonderer Berücksichtigung des Typenwandels von Frau und Familie, vornehmlich in Südwest-Deutschland 1766—1933*, vol. 1, Würzburg, 1934 (excerpts as 'Strukturelle Merkmale des proletarischen Familienlebens' and 'Bürgerlicher Haushalt und bürgerliche Familie vom Ende des 18. bis zum Ende des 19. Jahr-

hunderts' in Heidi Rosenbaum (ed.), *Seminar: Familie und Gesellschafts-struktur*, Frankfurt, 1978, pp. 342ff. and 375ff.).

Haensch, Dieter, 'Zerschlagt die Kleinfamilie?' in Dieter Claessens and Petra Milhoffer (eds.), *Familiensoziologie*, Frankfurt, 1973, pp. 363ff.

Horkheimer, Max, 'Die Erziehungsleistung der bürgerlichen Familie' (excerpts from 'Allgemeiner Teil', in *Studien über Autorität und Familie*, Paris, 1936) in Heidi Rosenbaum (ed.), *Seminar: Familie und Gesellschaftsstruktur*, Frankfurt, 1978, pp. 425ff.

Linde, Hans, 'Persönlichkeitsbildung in der Landfamilie', *Soziale Welt* 10 (1959), pp. 297ff. (= Heidi Rosenbaum (ed.), *Seminar: Familie und Gesellschaftsstruktur*, Frankfurt, 1978, pp. 215ff.).

Lupri, Eugen, 'Industrialisierung und Strukturwandlungen der Familie' in *Sociologia Ruralis* 5 (1965), pp. 57ff.

Mayntz, Renate, *Die moderne Familie*, Stuttgart, 1955.

Mitterauer, Michael, 'Vorindustrielle Familienformen. Zur Funktionsent-lastung des "ganzen Hauses" im 17. und 18. Jahrhundert' in *Wiener Beiträge zur Geschichte der Neuzeit* 2 (1975), pp. 123ff. (= Michael Mit-terauer, *Grundtypen alteuropäischer Sozialformen*, Stuttgart, 1979, pp. 35ff.).

Ogburn, William F. and Nimkoff, Meyer F., *Technology and the changing family*, Cambridge, Mass., 1955.

Pfeil, Elisabeth, 'Die Grossstadtfamilie' in Günther Lüschen and Eugen Lupri (eds.), *Soziologie der Familie* (special issue 14 of the *Kölner Zeitschrift für Soziologie und Sozialpsychologie*), Opladen, 1971 (= Dieter Claessens and Petra Milhoffer (eds.), *Familiensoziologie*, Frankfurt, 1973, pp. 145ff.)

Planck, Ulrich, 'Die Landfamilie in der Bundesrepublik Deutschland' in Günther Lüschen and Eugen Lupri (eds.), *Soziologie der Familie* (special issue 14 of the *Kölner Zeitschrift für Soziologie und Sozialpsychologie*), Opladen, 1971 (= Dieter Claessens and Petra Milhoffer (eds.), *Familien-soziologie*, Frankfurt, 1973, pp. 169ff.

Rosenmayr, Leopold, *Arbeit und Familie in der ländlichen Region*, Vienna, 1964.

'Ist die moderne Familie eine "Problemfamilie"?' in H. Asperger and F. Haider (eds.), *Das Werden sozialer Einstellungen in Familie, Schule und anderen Sozialformen*, Vienna, 1974.

Schelsky, Helmut, 'Die Gestalt der Landfamilie im gegenwärtigen Wandel der Geselschaft' in *Die Landfamilie. Schriftenreihe für ländliche Sozial-fragen* 9, 1953, pp. 44ff.

Wandlungen der deutschen Familie in der Gegenwart, 5th edn, Stuttgart, 1967 (1953).

Schneider, Lothar, 'Charakteristika des Haushalts des Fabriksarbeiters' (excerpts from *Der Arbeiterhaushalt im 18. und 19. Jahrhundert. Dargestellt am Beispiel des Heim- und Fabriksarbeiters*, Berlin, 1967) in

Heidi Rosenbaum (ed.), *Seminar: Familie und Gesellschaftsstruktur*, Frankfurt, 1978, pp. 334ff.

Schrader, Oskar, 'Ahnenkult' in *Reallexikon der indogermanischen Altertumskunde*, vol. 1, Berlin, 1917–23, pp. 18ff.

'Blutrache' in *Reallexikon der indogermanischen Altertumskunde*, vol. 1, Berlin, 1917–23, pp. 152ff.

Schultz, Alwin, *Ds häusliche Leben der europäische Kulturvölker vom Mittelalter bis zur zweiten Hälfte des 18. Jahrhunderts*, Munich, 1903.

Ussel, Jos van, 'Die Kleinfamilie' (excerpts from *Sexualunterdrückung, Geschichte der Sexualfeindschaft*, Reinbek, 1970) in Dieter Claessens and Petra Milhoffer (eds.), *Familiensoziologie*, Frankfurt, 1973, pp. 95ff.

Weber, Max, *Wirtschaft und Gesellschaft*, 2nd edn, Tübingen, 1956 (1921).

Wittfogel, Karl A. 'Wirtschaftsgeschichtliche Grundlagen der Entwicklung der Familienautorität' in Erich Fromm *et al., Studien über Autorität und Familie*, Paris, 1936, pp. 473ff.

Wurzbacher, Gerhard, *Leitbilder gegenwärtigen deutschen Familienlebens*, 3rd edn, Stuttgart, 1958.

Die Familie als Sozialisationsfaktor, Stuttgart, 1968.

5

The Young in the Family

The young in simple and complex societies

Every society is concerned to bring up its offspring in accordance with its cultural and social ideals. The more thoroughly a society is steeped in tradition, the less it needs to reflect upon its style of socialization and to develop specific educational institutions. In familial societies, the family itself – the family of origin and that of the employer – is able to initiate growing children into society. But in all societies with a more complex structure, the young form social groups in which they learn a great deal that the family is not able to teach them. In this sense, the existence of youth as a social phenomenon is closely connected with the transmission of cultural inheritance. Youthful patterns of behaviour and thinking, as well as the extent to which these can be controlled by society, influence sociocultural continuity or discontinuity. The central issues, therefore, are how a society brings up its young people and thus influences its future, and what connections exist between socialization and historical change or indeed historical continuity.

In complex societies, education and professional training are generally the task and purpose of specific institutions – for example, the school. In simple societies, the socialization of the young is an automatic by-product of daily life, and we may expect the family to play a greater part in it. Our interest, therefore, is directed at discovering under what conditions of increasing differentiation in society the family loses its significance for the young, and under what conditions the young are increasingly socialized in separate social groups.

In simple societies of country folk and peasants (this was also true of town dwellers in earlier times) what the young have to learn is, in essence, confined to those occupations, patterns of behaviour and ways of thinking that govern their daily lives. When he participates in the life of the family and community, the growing child acquires thoughts and habits typical of the culture and society in which he lives. And this occurs because as a child and as a young person, his time, his movements, his consciousness and his emotions are confined to the relatively small group of persons who live on the farmstead and in its immediate surroundings.

By contrast, the high degree of differentiation in a modern society has resulted in the individual's being a member of various social groups, institutions and so on other than the family. The domestic group and its neighbourhood no longer form a relatively autonomous society in which all types of behaviour patterns and ideas are to be found. Even the so-called 'private sphere' of people is interwoven with structures of the economy and administration, with politics and with commerce. The primary group of the family no longer determines the socialization of the young to the same extent as before. It provides only one socializing instrument among many and is itself modified by encroaching social institutions that are assuming many of the functions that it previously fulfilled.

The transition of society from the domestic organization of pre-industrial to industrial conditions of living and working has brought about a growing alienation of the adolescent from the family or the domestic group and his increasing integration into peer groups. The growing privacy of the family – that is, the restriction of its tasks to the fields of reproduction and socialization – has caused a transfer of the formerly familial tasks of general education and job training to extra-familial, societal institutions (school, place of work, club). The fact that adolescents are now influenced more and more by social systems that have become increasingly structurally homogeneous as regards age, rather than by heterogeneous primary groups, has created a specific youth culture, juvenile manners and values and the socio-cultural phenomenon of youth at large. It seems useful, therefore, to make a clear distinction between the modern societal concept of youth and one that was based on young people who were organized differently according to their local and occupational background, as in traditional European society.

The present discussion, however, will deal with only one of the different areas of interaction of the young, that is, the family or the domestic group. We shall concern ourselves neither with the historical development of class-specific youth groups nor with the emergence of youth as a socio-cultural phenomenon. Rather, we will look at the social context of the family and examine the period in an individual's life between physical maturity and social maturity or marriageability.

The family is the primary group that is of importance to the social development of the adolescent by way of familial socialization, and it is structurally opposed to the more comprehensive societal fields of juvenile interaction. In addition to this, the family, as it changes socially and economically, must be understood as a social correlative, as it were, of more comprehensive social spheres of young people that are increasingly homogeneous in their age composition. We shall examine all this below.

In an attempt to fix the beginning of the phase of youth in an individual's life, one is tempted to take puberty as a point of reference. But it has to be borne in mind that this event has not marked a critical social point of equal importance at all times and in all societies, and that its effect has differed according to historical, cultural and class-specific conditions.

According to Siegfried Bernfeld, there is a physiological, a psychological and a social dimension to puberty. Even the biological onset of puberty is subject to variations in time, class and culture. For the last hundred years there has been an acceleration of puberty in Europe. While in the 1850s the average age of the menarche was still about 16 years, for instance, it is between 12 and 13 at present. The age of physical maturation varies according to the degree of urbanization, social rank and ethnic and various other factors. We know from English and German research that the difference in the age of the menarche between girls from poor and girls from rich families amounted to two years around the middle of the nineteenth century. Today the average difference is between two and three months (Tanner). The date of puberty still varies according to social class and geographical region. It is an almost undisputed fact that class-specific habits of nutrition are responsible for the date of maturity and the acceleration of puberty over the last century.

Subject to variation of class and culture to an even greater extent than the process of *physical* maturity is *social* maturation, the phase at the end of which the young person is considered socially and economically able to assume an independent position, whatever this may be under prevalent social conditions. As a rule, it has meant the possibility of marrying and having a family, at least in Western and Central European societies. For this social phase of maturation Bernfeld has coined the term 'extended puberty', (*gestreckte Pubertät*), denoting the prolongation of a phase of social dependence caused by socio-cultural and economic factors in spite of actual physical maturity.

Two things in this socio-cultural definition of a phase of youth point to the family: on the one hand, the connection between the status of social maturity and the state of marriage or the possibility of founding a family; on the other hand, the fact, characteristic of pre-industrial societies, above all, that the phase of social maturation was experienced in conditions of familial or domestic dependence.

Both these elements weighed more heavily on the situation of the adolescent in the domestically constituted traditional European society than they do on those in industrial societies. On the one hand, industrial societies have developed non-familial social forms (boarding houses for apprentices, boarding school, flat sharing); on the other hand, they have split up the process of social maturation, in its former comprehensive sense, into partial processes of maturation, which do not necessarily coincide with each other. Marriage is an example. People are now increasingly in a position to marry even when they still have to undergo professional training.

Our general proposition would be that the social shape of the phase between physical maturity and the assumption of adult status in modern Western and Central Europe depends, above all, on the degree to which the young person in this phase of his life is integrated in the production of goods and rendering of services, or the degree to which he is subject to a specific process of socialization outside the sphere of production – at school, for example – in order to qualify him for his future occupation.

The duration of this phase, which is characterized by lack of autonomy and domestic or familial dependence, does not necessarily correspond with the period in which the individual undergoes training, as it is not determined by the time needed to acquire knowledge and skills. It was the socially and economically powerful (masters, farmers), guided by their corporate interests, who decided the duration of this phase of youth in domestically organized societies. Examples of this are the rules laid down for service on the farm and for the number of years of itineracy required from journeymen in order to control access to full positions in farming and the crafts. In the long run, increasingly formalized and institutionalized kinds of training, stretching over uniform periods, have replaced periods of training and apprenticeship determined by individual and special circumstances.

In the course of the following historical outline of the living and working conditions of young people in the family household, a certain narrowing of our focus will have to take place. The reason for this is that whereas we are able to examine both the living and working conditions of the young person in the traditional European family, our concentration on the family will make us lose track of the conditions governing his job qualification and his conditions of work because of the family's loss of productive function as a consequence of industrialization.

Nevertheless, for the young in industrial societies too the family is one of the most important fields of interaction, and the dependence or 'semi-dependence' of the young (Gillis) on their parents and on the family is one of the main factors responsible for their specific social status.

We will be concerned below with individual young persons within the family and with the social significance of the family in the shaping of the socialization process in the light of the historical development of Central Europe since the Middle Ages.

A strictly chronological exposition would seem neither feasible nor fruitful. If, therefore, we pose the question of which structural and functional conditions govern the place of the young within the family, then a long-term historical comparison reveals two main possibilities. In all traditional societies or spheres of society, on the one hand, the family organized as an economic unit is a place where the young are trained for work; in industrial societies, on the other hand, the family generally represents a place where the young only live and recuperate in order to regain energy that is to be exploited outside the home.

In pre-industrial times, when the family was still a productive unit, it provided a place of instruction and of service for the young. This is exemplified by families of peasants, artisans and shopkeepers. Such a situation is still found in modern times, though to a lesser degree, in those families that run small businesses. In all these family types, the sphere of reproduction (what we now call the 'private sphere') and

economic activities are, in fact, identical. When we consider the peasant family of pre-industrial times, we find that family, household and
economic enterprise were one and the same. Accordingly, the presence of the young was determined by the requirements of the family
enterprise.

The young in the peasant family

It may be said that in traditional rural societies the young were
regarded mainly as a labour force for use in the peasant family enterprise and were therefore employed to meet the demands of that
enterprise. This meant that –as in all simple, 'closed' societies – there
was no need to develop separate institutions and techniques of socialization. A deliberate system of 'education' was neither possible nor
necessary in the remote farmstead or village, for the manners,
attitudes and skills to be acquired by the young were transmitted
within the framework of the domestic group or village; the young
learned 'empirically'.

Because the psycho-social development of the young clearly
depended on interaction with members of the family and on the part
they had to play within the farmer's 'whole house', there was little
chance for them to develop their own interests or to foster individual talents and ambitions. If we take into account the very small
number of 'careers' available in country districts in pre-industrial
times, it will be appreciated that the possibility of satisfying the
desire to follow a certain calling was very slim, as there were few
options from which to choose.

When we look more closely at the young from the social classes
inferior to that of the farmer (that is, the families of cottagers,
inmates and day labourers), then their social position may be
described as underprivileged, as were the cultural and economic
resources of their families of origin. Children of cottagers and
inmates acted as herdsmen on meadows and commons, as cowherds
and dairymaids, and as servants. Their parents sent them away from
home as early as possible, for to look after them was economically
demanding. In contrast with the farmer's family, their labour was
rarely employed in the parental home.

Children born out of wedlock and children who were sent by their parents to live with other families often formed, together with orphans, a large proportion of the group called *Zuchtkinder* (children in care). The household lists from pre-industrial times, which are the sources for these statements, do not mention adolescent children in care. This is because foster children of this age entered into service, as did some of the farmers' children, and were given the status of servants.

A large number of peasant children also left the parental farm at an early age to hire themselves out as servants. But if they were needed as labourers by their parents, they tended to remain at home for a long time. Where inheritance customs marked out the eldest son as the heir, his privileged position allowed him to marry as soon as he was able to take over the farm. He had probably assumed his future role from an early age, and his siblings had to accept their less privileged positions. The eldest son, who was destined to succeed, therefore became accustomed to associating with those in the group of siblings who were socially less significant because they were younger and were not yet able to work, or not to the same extent. It may be taken for granted that this was of great importance in shaping the character of the future manager of the household economy of the farm and, more particularly, in fostering in him a sense of patriarchal responsibility and authority, which were also copied from his father.

In other districts the inheritance went to the best-qualified son – that is, the son whom the old farmer (and, incidentally, the lord of the manor) considered the fittest to take over the farm. We may take it that the resulting competition among siblings would not have allowed for the development of emotional ties as we know them today, particularly as in many cases the less privileged siblings would have had to leave the parental farm to hire themselves out as servants or day labourers. This also applied where it was not decided at an early stage who should be the successor (as, for instance, where the youngest son had the right to inherit) and where there were no binding inheritance rights at all.

Differences in prestige and function among the children of cottagers and day labourers must have been very small. In their cases there was generally no inheritable property so there was no need to train a future successor to be aware of his privileges and his responsibilities.

Psychological aspects of socialization on the farm

In country and farming families social relationships were determined by the economic and labour requirements of the family enterprise. Emotional and affective relationships, which nowadays would seem to constitute the typical 'family' character of a small group, were consequently much less common than they are today. Even the relationship between mother and infant was usually less intense than it is now. Until the middle of the nineteenth century there was, among large sections of the population, little tenderness and loving intimacy. Lack of attention and care, as well as poor feeding and unhygienic conditions, led to the death of many children in infancy, which probably discouraged mothers from lavishing much love on new-born babies. There was little appreciation of the need to cherish an infant, to give it the security of a warm nest and, as it grew up, to help it to develop its own personality. The further socialization of the young was also hampered by this lack of feeling. In pre-industrial times mother fixations and other neuroses fostered by what might be termed 'emotional overload' and so often found in the small modern family can hardly have existed in the country. Even today they are not evident in remote country districts.

The relationship between parents and those youngsters who were destined to inherit differed from their relationship with those who were not. Because a son frequently had to wait a long time to take over the farm, the relationship between the head of the family and his future heir was often marked by the farmer's considerable psychological, social and economic influence over his son, and there may have been latent conflict between them. This is also evident from the retirement agreements that provided for the old age of the farmer. The provisions were often very detailed, which suggests that relations between the generations were rather strained.

Their natural parents were of less consequence to the sons who were not destined to inherit, since they often left the parental home at an early age to hire themselves out as servants on other farms. This was also true for those daughters who did not remain in their parents' house but spent their youth as maidservants on other farmsteads or in patrician houses in towns. Girls were rarely able to join outside groups in pre-industrial times, for their work and social activities were confined largely to the domestic group. The division of labour between husband and wife in agrarian societies bound the woman to the house and its immediate surroundings, and in effect allowed only the man to participate in social and political activities in the 'public sphere'. Because her life was filled with the duties of looking after the children, the kitchen and the livestock, the woman was judged incompetent to deal with public affairs and to join social and political associations. Thus there were no societies for the female young to join, as there were for the young men of the village. Indeed, village girls stood under the protection of these male fellowships. In many respects, as in those of morals and sex and the question of choice of partner and marriage, the male young exercised the right to control the girls. Within the family, therefore, there was a distinct and fixed division of roles for the young, based on sex. The girls remained restricted to the confines of the house and from an early age assumed the roles of housewife and mother, busying themselves with the concerns of the house and the family and, in the main, leaving to the men those outside contacts that might enhance social status.

When one considers that servants changed their jobs frequently, often annually, it becomes clear that for the majority of young persons in country districts there was no such thing as long-term dependence on one and the same father figure, but very long dependence on a constantly changing series of masters; at a later period this dependence might well last for the rest of their lives. Psychoanalytical explanatory models, such as that put forward in the Freudian doctrine of the Oedipus conflict, can therefore be applied only in a modified form to these family relationships. Among the lower classes in both town and country, parents had little influence over the development of those children who left home at an early age. On the other hand, for those children who remained at home and sometimes for young servants, the master and the mistress were personalities of overriding importance throughout a long period of their lives.

The early entry of the young into their active working life led them to adapt quickly to a form of behaviour that met the purposes and requirements of the family enterprise. The young shared a world identical with that of the adults, and their values were accepted as a matter of course. They clung to traditional ways of thinking and feeling, and these were confirmed by their undifferentiated environment. They were presented with no competing standards of values or modes of thinking such as might have been promoted by different socializing institutions like the school.

THE YOUNG IN THE FAMILY

Recent trends in peasant families

Twentieth-century industrial penetration into what was formerly a country and farming lifestyle in peasant areas in Austria and elsewhere has broken down some of the social and mental attitudes antagonistic to emancipation. Technical innovations in production and general social changes that have reduced the importance of practical training have increasingly deprived peasant patriarchalism of its economic justification. The rural exodus and non-agricultural employment in the country have assisted the young to enjoy an improvement in their lot. The specific socializing conditions of the peasant family have become inadequate to supply the knowledge and skills required for rationalizing and improving farming methods. Primary and vocational schooling have undermined those traditional values and social practices that tended to stand in the way of adaptation to changed conditions.

Personal planning has begun to play its part in the choice of a calling and in the selection of a partner, as well as in procreative behaviour and in the education of children, which up to recent times had been dictated by tradition and by the interest of the group. The socialization of the rising generation, which in traditional peasant society had been directed mainly towards the family, has become increasingly directed towards the children. The growing concern with the child's talents, the greater attention paid to personal independence rather than, as formerly, to the wellbeing of the group, as well as the acknowledgment of the need for intimacy in the young, highlight their slowly changing position in the peasant family.

Nevertheless, entrenched mental attitudes favourable to authority and the interests of the group, and therefore inimical to emancipation, cannot be ignored. Some of the young among our peasantry are still forced, by the economy of the farm, to restrict their choice of marriage partner and of occupation. A heavier load is sometimes placed on the young because there are now fewer people to cope with the work of the farm. Only members of the farming family itself are left to do it. A young man may experience difficulty in finding a spouse who is prepared to undertake the onerous tasks of a farmer's wife. These are only some of the problems that the young farmers of today may have to face because of the specific character of the peasant family as an economic unit.

The young in the craftsman's family

In the craftsman's family the young occupied a position similar, in some respects, to that which they occupied in the farming family, for the household of the master craftsman was where the training of apprentices and, to some extent, journeymen took place. There were, however, considerable differences. Sons and daughters of the master craftsman were not taken into their father's enterprise as frequently as were those of the farmer. Girls were not involved directly in most enterprises, although they were, of course, expected to help in the household. (There is some evidence to suggest that in England girls were sometimes involved in such enterprises, however.)

Contrary to common opinion, few craft enterprises were handed down from the master to one of his sons. The low capital investment required to found an enterprise and the mobility of artisans' sons that was enforced by the guilds favoured the settlement of the sons of the masters in different places some distance away. Artisan enterprises were handed down from father to son only among those crafts for which technical equipment (like a scythe smith's tools) was needed or which were associated with certain topographical conditions (like milling). In Austria it was not until the nineteenth century that there was an identifiable trend towards the patrilineal inheritance of craft enterprises. Frequently they were transferred by way of a daughter to a son-in-law, or by way of the master's widow to her second husband.

Teenage sons were not often found in the artisan's household, for if they did follow their father's calling, they usually served their apprenticeship in the house of another master craftsman. (In peasant families the heir at least spent the whole of his youth with his parents.) In Central Europe it was common for vocational training to take place in another master's establishment. The master craftsman played the part of father to his apprentices and journeymen, just as the farmer did to his farmhands. But because the period of training for young apprentices was a long one, their relationship with their masters was probably closer and more intimate than that of most farm servants, who frequently changed their jobs. We can take it that the youngsters who entered the craftsman's family as apprentices at a very early age were more fully integrated into the family than the journeymen and subject to a greater extent to the authority of the master.

Professional qualifications and social control

The craft guilds of the Middle Ages regulated conditions of work, both as to quality and as to time, in order to guarantee the economic independence and security of their members. But in doing so, at any rate in the late Middle Ages, they crippled individual initiative and rejected innovation as unfair competition. This conservative attitude remained entrenched because the guilds had their own judiciary, their own administration and their own social life. It is clear that the conservative lifestyle of corporations engendered a specific attitude towards the young, with a corresponding system of socialization that aimed to preserve an established, unchanging social and economic system.

Among the peasant population the most important instrument of social stratification was control over the means of production by way of the inheritance and transfer of land and other property. For craftsmen ownership of the means of production as such was of less consequence. The tools required for a craft or trade were infinitely easier to acquire than land. Many artisans did not own a house but rented lodgings and shops. What was important, however, was the craft apprenticeship. The binding regulations that governed professional qualifications (non-existent among the peasantry) acted as a lever by which the guilds wielded their power, their most important instrument of social control.

After the restraints imposed on admission to apprenticeship by the criterion of 'honest birth', it was the fact that training was provided exclusively for male youths that was of crucial significance in Central Europe. Girls and women were excluded from learning and practising most of the independent trades. Young men passed through the various stages of their training and were able to gather considerable professional and social experience on their journeys, but girls or women, in most cases, never left the house of their parents or husbands. A girl's education was confined to religion, housekeeping, perhaps a little reading and writing. Most of what she learned she was taught by her mother. From her she also learned, at an early age, to adopt an attitude of subordination and dependence that would befit her future role as wife and mother in the patriarchal family.

Contemporary guild documents provide a clear picture of how the training of male apprentices was organized. The festive initiation into the guilds was usually preceded by the signing of a contract between the parents of the trainee, or the person who stood surety for him, and his future master. This agreement provided for the necessary clothing, for the period of training and for the apprenticeship premium which had to be paid, together with the period of probation, which could vary from two weeks to several months. From the moment that the trainee was admitted into the guild, he belonged to his master's household and had to submit unconditionally to its discipline. The master stood *in loco parentis* to the young pupil, who was not allowed to go out without his master's permission, to leave the house at night, to 'gamble, drink, or behave in an unseemly fashion'. A ruling dating from the eighteenth century stipulates that work and business could only be carried out as honourably as they must be if, from the beginning, the young apprentice was 'taught to fear God and to obey his master as he would his own father'.

The master had not only to teach the trainee the rules and skills of his craft but also to bring him up to become an 'honourable member of the craftsman's guild'. It was therefore laid down in the orders of the guild that 'the master should be of good conduct and with his wife should maintain a happy and healthy household.'(It was often necessary to urge masters to treat their apprentices with more leniency.) It was, on the other hand, the master's duty

to protect the young pupils from the journeymen who might well abuse him; punch-ups, fisticuffs and horseplay are only too frequent. . . . Master, remember your duties! The apprentice has been given into your care by the guild to look after him, body and soul, as the rules provide. You will have to render account for this apprentice, and you must look after him as you would look after your own child! (From a trade charter of the eighteenth century).

The age of entry into apprenticeship was laid down as not younger than 10 years and not older than 18 years. The period of training was usually three years but could be shorter (about a year for glaziers and two years for beer brewers, for example).

The integration of apprentices and journeymen into the families of their masters should not allow us to gloss over the fact that these were labour conditions involving absolute dependence and exploitation, and not familial relationships in the modern sense. Identity of family, occupation, life and work inevitably blended childhood into working youth. It is interesting to note that at the beginning of the period of apprenticeship, as at the beginning of the period of service on the farm, a different figure of authority took the place of the natural parents but familial organization and the role of the young in the family group remained practically unchanged. In this way a certain continuity of social structure was ensured for the young. Traditional European society passed on norms, attitudes, manners and skills in a familial or domestic framework. The same is true, by analogy, for the socialization of the young in the noble and bourgeois upper class, with which we shall not deal here.

A growing division of labour in society made it impossible for the individual family or domestic group to carry out the required tasks of socialization on its own. The relations of production and their growing dynamism and complexity made it imperative to transfer certain educational processes from the domestic to the spreading 'public sphere' and to create specialized institutions for the education and the training of the young. The development of education from what had originally been a clerical office, but had become secularized and run by the state, led to a marked division between manual and intellectual work. As a consequence, the institutions for the education of adolescents were developed separately in the two fields.

General, all-round education designed for the recruitment of an elite henceforth took place in the new *Gymnasien* (grammar schools). The professional training of young workers, however, continued to take place in the artisan's shop, although it began to be accompanied by evening classes and *Berufsschulen* (continuation schools) in the nineteenth century. General education organized by the state and job training in crafts, commerce and industry organized by private business have developed separately right up to the present day.

Our interest, of course, is primarily in the training of the young person at his place of work in the tradition of the pre-industrial apprenticeship, because it was organized on quasi-familial lines. We will touch only briefly on school education in respect to its effects on pupils and on the situation in their families of origin.

Relics of domestic dependence in job training

With the decline of the guilds, the position of the young employed in crafts changed radically. In the eighteenth century mercantilist economics had attempted to undermine the guild rules that regulated training, rules that were hostile to competition and governed by corporate rigidity. Mid-nineteenth-century economics in Austria and Germany dismantled this structure completely. The system of trade licensing was abolished, and the principle of freedom of trade was introduced. The relationship between master and apprentice was now considered to be a private matter, and every master was free to employ as many apprentices as he wanted.

Whereas during the sixteenth, seventeenth and eighteenth centuries the master craftsman had rarely had more than three apprentices and journeymen, during the nineteenth century there was a marked increase in the number of apprentices and journeymen present in the households of the masters. In 1857 we find, for example, in the census of the Austrian town of Stein, a master shoemaker with no fewer than eight journeymen in his household. At the same time, in the Vienna suburb of Schottenfeld, there was a turner with only one journeyman but with 11 apprentices between the ages of 12 and 17 years. This example of *Lehrlingszüchterei* (hoarding of apprentices) highlights the economic significance of the young as a cheap labour force that enabled the crafts to meet the increasing pressure of industrial competition.

The first wave of industrialization was characterized, on the whole, by a very rapid increase in the number of unskilled labourers, among them many children and adolescents. The comprehensive, practical job qualifications that guild training had tried to provide were replaced by requirements that corresponded with the new industrial mode of production: discipline, diligence, speed, stamina in work that had become increasingly alienating.

Although young people employed in factories were protected by regulations laid down in the middle of the nineteenth century (work was restricted to 12 hours a day for those under 16, for example) the situation of apprentices in the crafts remained unchanged. They often had to work longer hours than did young factory hands. After their actual day's work was over, they often had to undertake tasks involving cleaning and transport. This resulted in frequent accidents and damage to their health.

The only way in which many small businesses could counter the growing pressure of manufacturing industry was to exploit the cheap labour provided by apprentices. A 1905 report by the Austrian trade inspectors says that the existence of small businesses was based on their having apprentices. Many masters began to work for factories on a commission basis. Apprentices in the factories themselves received no comprehensive training but were set, as soon as possible, to the business of production, performing the simple tasks into which mechanical production was divided.

Even the conservative policy pursued in Austria and Germany at the end of the nineteenth century – a policy that favoured the middle classes but tried to restrain the excesses of heavy industry – did little to improve the position of apprentices. At the turn of the century an apprentice in a craft was still subject to the 'protective power' of his master; that is to say, the 'fatherly authority' of the master was considered by contemporaries to be as legitimate as the authority of the father. An Austrian trade regulation of 1907 actually states: 'A minor apprentice is subject to the fatherly authority of his master.'

The legal right to quasi-paternal authority and correction led very easily to physical maltreatment. Physical correction was a traditional element of domestic education and was regarded as one of the few means available for making young people work harder. Artisans short of capital could not usually afford to offer material incentives. It was typically among craftsmen in those trades that had to bear the brunt of the competition of the new manufacturing industry that threats and actual physical violence are found to have been most widespread – among cobblers, joiners and tailors.

Apprentices often ran away from the brutality of masters and journeymen. Corporations of masters, however, established bans similar to those that constrained runaway servants in the country, and these made it impossible for other masters to employ such apprentices. Since their parents often lived some distance away, in the countryside or in another town, apprentices could hardly count on them for support.

The way in which apprenticeships were arranged sometimes resembled a regular slave trade. There are reports of traders who went about the country to collect 'redundant' children, who were then offered to masters in towns for a commission. The majority of apprentices in Vienna came from the Czech or other Slavic territories of the Austrian Empire and were taken on by masters for board and lodging alone. This quasi-familial arrangement facilitated the exploitation of the young, since the master could often make them work into the night without anybody noticing.

Only about 10 per cent of apprentices were allowed to stay on as journeymen after serving their apprenticeships. The other 90 per cent were sacked immediately at this point, in order to circumvent the obligation to pay them higher wages that journeymen earned. The victims tried to make a living as day labourers or went into factories, where their need to find work helped to keep wages down. In 1925 within the clothmaking trade, for example, there were 12,000 apprentices in Austria but only 800 journeymen in employment. These figures prove that the apprentice was taken on principally to provide cheap labour, and that the laws that tried to remedy this were largely ineffectual.

The rising cost of living in the household of the master reduced the extent to which the apprentice was integrated into the master's family. (Nevertheless, the practice still persists today, typically in households that are able to keep the cost of living down, such as those in the catering industry.) In almost all other trades the former quasi-familial integration of the apprentice was replaced by an increasingly detached relationship between apprentice and master, anticipating the later capitalist relationship of employer and employed.

Elements of domestic dependence and of the quasi-paternal authority of the master must not be ignored, however. Structural features of on-the-spot job training that betray the modern relics of domestic labour can be seen in the extent to which the young are called upon to perform low-status work and in the exploitation of the work of the apprentice under the cover of training.

The trend towards privacy in the family and its consequences for the young

We will now consider the problems of youth in the family of today, the family that has lost almost all of its productive functions. Urbanization and industrialization have separated the work place from the family home. In contrast to the situation prevalent among farmers and artisans, whose young have always regarded the family as a place of learning and of service, the family has now become a refuge, as we have noted, where youngsters live and recuperate in order to recover physical and psychic energy that is to be used at school and in their professional lives.

The situation of the young in the contemporary family can be grasped in a preliminary way by considering the following two factors: the emergence of paid labour and the development of the service industry, which have offered the young an opportunity to obtain work outside the house, together with the growing importance of education, which keeps young people dependent on the family for a longer time. The first have made the young less dependent on the family in social and economic matters; the latter has lengthened the youthful phase of dependency in the parental home.

When we remember that in the past most children left their families of origin early, whether they were the non-inheriting children of farmers or the children of artisans, it becomes clear that schooling, which now forces so many of the young to stay with their parents for so long, has resulted in the families of the more wealthy classes becoming more private and the relationship between parents and children being charged with more emotion. This was evident in the seventeenth and eighteenth centuries, when moral and educational writers began to point out that parents had the duty personally to assume responsibility for the improvement of their children's education. City councils were required to build more schools, so that children and teenagers could attend schools near the houses of their parents.

There is a clear connection between the intensification of the schooling of the young and the increasing attention paid to the needs and problems of young people in their families of origin. It was only when school started to play a major role in the life of every individual (*Verschulung*: Ariès) that a hiatus was created for the young, a kind of 'social moratorium'. It was only with the delay of his entry into the sphere of productive work that a phase in the life of the individual was created – at first, admittedly, only in the case of the well-to-do – in which parents, teachers and tutors treated him with exceptional consideration. Guarding the adolescent from the immediate encroachment of the sphere of work allowed for a pedagogic approach to the formation of his personality and, consequently, the inception of 'adolescence' in the proper sense. In general, this encouraged the emotional loading of the relationship between parents and their children, if we leave out of consideration the effects of strict boarding-school discipline in its (often drastic) historical forms. Not only did schools begin to play a more important part overall, but learning and teaching also began to assume a role in the domestic sphere primarily of the educated middle-class families of lawyers, civil servants, doctors, scientists, teachers, clerics and so on. It was in their homes that a domestic sphere that was not as dominated by economic necessity was able to develop first.

Whereas those boys and girls who attended schools became more dependent on their parents because the length of time devoted to education was prolonged over the centuries, the young people of the lower classes, who started working at an early age, found it easier to get work outside the home. This did much to free them from the rigid system of parental control that had characterized the family as an economic enterprise. On the other hand, however, they lost the parental support and help that they had received before, embedded in the domestic group. When wage earning, bureaucracy and jobs in the service industry divided the sphere of family from the sphere of work, families lost much of their control over the work and leisure time of their children, who now worked outside the house. Growing economic independence and greater social and cultural freedom reduced the young person's obligation to do as he was expected to do or as the other members of his family did. The servant and the future heir to the farm, the apprentice and the journeyman in the artisan's household had their characters moulded and their conduct at work and at leisure regulated by the unlimited authority of the master of the house. Since young people now work outside the house, the family head is no longer the ultimate authority in matters of work. It is scarcely necessary to add that employers, supervisors, instructors and teachers now represent authority, and that nowadays there are even more subtle mechanisms of social control disciplining the young outside the family. With the spread of wage earning, the young person became increasingly subject to extrafamilial control, which was experienced mainly as the restraints and laws of the labour market.

Conflict within the family

The detachment of the young from the family is particularly marked where the attraction of specifically youthful pastimes is calculated to reduce parental influence. Thus the young labourer today develops outside interests and contacts, on the one hand with friends from his place of work and with other friends of his own age, on the other hand through a world pictured in films, on television and in magazines, which has a strong influence on youthful behaviour and opinions.

Whatever discipline and control parents exercise over their children is reduced in extent and effect in the course of their adolescence. The conflicts that arise as a result lead the young to retreat from their family of origin and its hierarchy of age, sex and function, and to attach themselves to their peers. The young organize themselves in formal and informal groups at school, at their place of work and in their free time, prompted by common opposition to parents, instructors and teachers, as well as to the adult world in general. They search for values and identification because they are unsure of the role they have to play, and they therefore adopt the subculture of their own generation, which seems to give them the self-esteem and fulfilment that they seek.

When we compare the present-day situation of the young in the family with that of earlier times, we find that relationships and influences from outside the family (that is, those of school, work and peer groups) have become much more important. The small family of today no longer forms an educational community in itself. Only in a minority of families, preoccupied with religion and politics, are distinct values and attitudes taught. In the lower classes of the population particularly, the young are generally not guided in cultural and social matters. It is true that in the lower classes practical problems of life are discussed, members of the family do consult each other and some parental control is exercised, but subjects of political, ideological and religious importance are rarely raised between parents and children (Pelikan).

Parental control over children attending secondary schools is generally stricter than the parental control over apprentices and wage earning children. Nevertheless, here too controversial topics are generally avoided, and conflicts are often latent. This is particularly so where standards of value and of relationship prevailing at school or in the peer group are not the same as those of the parents.

Loss or intensification of family functions?

By contrast with families of farmers and artisans of an earlier period, in modern times the family is no longer in a position to instil into its offspring the attitudes and ideas that are necessary for their careers. In an industrial society based on performance, the social and economic position of the individual, his prestige and his standard of living, are inevitably determined by his efficiency. As the requisite attributes can be acquired only to a limited extent within the family, there is a tendency, among even the very young, to establish social contacts outside the family. To make their way in industrial society, young people of the present day have to learn much that they cannot learn at home – indeed, much that is opposed to familial patterns of behaviour (loving tenderness as against competition, for example).

Although we have established that the young live their lives and seek their status outside the family of origin, we must beware of making too facile a use of the sociological concept of loss of function. Historical development certainly indicates that industrial society poses new problems of upbringing and education for the family that were unknown in earlier times. It is true that by comparison with the professional qualifications conferred by the families of farmers and artisans, a loss of certain socializing functions has taken place. On the other hand, the significance to the individual of the emotional security of the home and his ability to recover there, both physically and mentally, from strain at school and at work has increased markedly, and this we must regard as an intensification of family function that is of direct concern to the young. (However, it must be said that the family frequently cannot fulfil the excessive demands imposed on it in this respect.)

At the same time, stronger emotional ties forged by structural change in the family may also represent a danger for the young person in connection with the development of his personality. The extension of the schooling phase and the intensified emotional ties between parents and children have led in increasing measure to over-organization and overprotection. The family ties of the adolescent are maintained to such a degree that they often impede the development of an independent personality. The human being is subjected to a continuous socializing process, which in the youthful phase inculcates values and standards opposed to those of the family, and this requires a reorientation of the young. The family of origin, with its rigid control mechanisms and intense emotional envelopment, therefore exercises a negative influence after a certain age has been reached. The young person must stand his ground in the extra-familial world (school, job, leisure time) if he does not want to be called a mother's darling or home-bird. In addition, the independence and emancipation of the young person become evident when he is no longer fully subordinate to his parents in making decisions but has become autonomous to some extent. Only then is he able to adopt a relatively independent attitude towards his parents that is free from tension.

Relics of the past in today's family life

The overall release of the family from productive functions has certainly had positive effects on the situation of the young. It has permitted the partial removal of restrictions on the free choice of occupation and of marriage partner and the creation of specifically youthful pastimes, and it has made possible a greater measure of intra-familial independence for adolescents.

But where this release from functions has not taken place – that is, where families still function as units of production – we find considerable limitations on the choice of occupation and of marriage partner even today. This happens both in farming families and in craft and commercial family businesses. Conflict between the generations may be particularly marked because of the specific conditions imposed by the economic needs of the family enterprise. Inheritance, marriage and the transfer of the enterprise are still, as before, the main causes of conflict between parents and children. Parents often impose their wishes on the young, who have to submit to the needs of the family enterprise in their choice of suitable marriage partners and in preparing themselves for taking over the business. Little understanding is shown of a child's desire to follow another occupation. When the family is still basically a family enterprise, the young have, as a rule, less independence than those in families entirely freed from productive functions. Where there is an overriding need to make the family business profitable, there is no emancipation of the young person from traditional bonds of domestic dependence, and the desire to develop his personality is pushed into the background.

In families that no longer form the basis of farming or artisan enterprises, these traditional causes of conflict – inheritance, marriage and business – naturally no longer exist. In these cases the causes of tension between parents and children lie mainly in the exercise of parental control over the children and in different ways of life and standards of value that result from the fact that the young nowadays generally choose different occupations from those of their fathers, are educated outside the home and have friends and acquaintances other than those of their parents. There are also causes of conflict that may be explained by the retention of traditional parental control. For example, the sex life of the young person is still frequently restricted by his parents (or perhaps we should say they attempt to restrict it). And this happens even when the young are regarded largely as responsible beings at school and at work. This is undoubtedly a relic of the historical role played by parents in controlling their children's choice of partner in sex and marriage, as the economic necessities of the farming or artisan enterprise dictated.

The socio-cultural and economic changes that we have described and better means of contraception have rendered such restrictions on the young less necessary. From the historical point of view, parental restrictions in sexual matters may therefore be seen as a cultural lag.

Historical trends in the relationship between generations

The history of the young within the family is, as we have seen, the history of their partial emancipation from family dependence and lack of autonomy. It is in this respect also the history of the growing possibilities for the development of social manifestations of youth as an independent socio-cultural phenomenon. The development of youth, in this sense, is the result of a structural opposition between family and domestic group on the one hand and between local communities and society on the other.

The adolescent has been exposed, to an increasing degree, to a multitude of competing influences opposed to the basically uniform patterns of socialization within the family and domestic group and within the relatively homogeneous local community. The fact that in pre-industrial society the adolescent was restricted to a few tightly organized groups from which he could not escape as a rule gave rise to a relatively fixed set of attitudes, ideas and norms. The specialization, differentiation and organization of the institutions responsible for the socialization of the adolescent provoked clashes between sets of values – for instance, a contradiction between the aims of socialization in the family and at school. Growing professional and regional mobility has accorded the adolescent greater opportunity to live according to his own wishes. At the same time, he has experienced growing uncertainty in attempting to get his bearings in a more and more complicated system of values.

The growth of the range of choices open to the individual adolescent in the course of history has been the emancipatory by-product of a complex process by which more and higher professional qualifications have been required by industrial society. The prolongation of the phase of youth as a period during which the adolescent is partly freed from productive labour in order to improve his qualifications through training at school or place of work is a development inherent in the process of industrialization. At the same time, the development of youth groups at schools and training centres, leisure-time groups and so on has led to the development of a parallel juvenile culture. The habits and interests of juveniles have reached a high level of particularity and autonomy not previously present even among youth groups such as brotherhoods of journeymen or village fraternities, which sometimes stood in opposition to adult society.

Today this parallel culture of the young covers nearly all fields of life. The young have generation-specific manners, sports, entertainments, fashion, literature, music and language. Values and aspects of the youth culture often meet with the opposition of members of their families of origin and provide, as we have said, a relatively recent potential for conflict in the family. This appears to be functional in the process of the detachment of adolescents from their families of origin and their going out into society that is necessary in universalistic societies.

The particularistic societies of pre-industrial times did not experience such a clash of values between generations. The values of the young and the old were basically the same. In those days it was above all the economic struggle associated with the succession to the farm or restrictive guild rules that led to tension between the generations.

In modern industrial societies the economic problems of distribution have been transferred from individual families to the nation, from the smallest to the largest unit of social collaboration. They arise in the context of old-age pension schemes, social security, perhaps also in discussions about claims for age-related salaries, without affecting the relationship between parents and children within the family. Thus the quality of the generational conflict has changed. What was once a socio-economic conflict about redistribution and succession has turned into a conflict of values. The structural opposition of familial forms of domination and life inherited from history on the one hand, and the ways of communication practised at school, place of work and leisure-time groups on the other, have intensified inter-generational differences in values and behaviour.

The young and the need for democratic behaviour

The progressive transition of youthful social contacts from those with the family of origin to those with peer groups, school friends and work mates signifies less dependence on authority based on age or position and the creation of social connections which, by contrast with the constraints and domination typical of the patriarchal family, are characterized by greater equality and co-operation. Participation in formal and informal youth groups opens up for the young the possibility of associating with others on a basis of equality, which was impossible or difficult in the traditional family, with its hierarchical relationships. But, as has been shown, relationships within the family have also changed in the same direction, mainly by release from the objective obligations of the family business.

Psychology and psychoanalysis tell us that relationships of authority and of equality entail corresponding moral attitudes. Through association with persons of authority, duties of submission, obedience and conformity are instilled, whereas a sense of reciprocity and justice is created mainly by relationships of equality. From this point of view, we must welcome unreservedly the loss of certain functions by the family and the fact that, on the one hand, the young look to their peer groups for their standards and, on the other, there is at least a moderate trend towards partnership within the family.

It is true that subcultures of youth created by historical development are exposed to the growing danger of commercialization because of the aggressive courting of the young by business interests. It cannot be denied that the pressures of industrial society compel people towards efficiency and productive work through a repressive school and educational system. But, in essence, the obvious historical trend towards living within, and being orientated towards, peer groups seems to be a necessary premise of the development of democratic attitudes and, with it, the permanent democratization of society.

SELECT BIBLIOGRAPHY

Allerbeck, Klaus and Rosenmayr, Leopold (eds.), *Aufstand der Jugend? Neue Aspekte der Jugendsoziologie*, Munich, 1971.

Ariès, Philippe, *Centuries of childhood: a social history of family life*, New York, 1962.

Bernfeld, Siegfried, 'Über eine typische Form der männlichen Pubertät', *Imago*, 9 (1923).

Deenen, Bernd van, *Die bäuerliche Familie im sozialen Wandel*, Bonn, 1969.

Demos, John and Demos, Virginia, 'Adolescence in historical perspective', *Journal of Marriage and the Family* 31 (1969), pp. 632ff.

Eisenstadt, S. N., *Von Generation zu Generation. Altersgruppen und Sozialstruktur*, Munich, 1966.

Feilzer, Heinrich, *Jugend in der mittelalterlichen Ständegesellschaft*, Vienna, 1971.

Friedeburg, Ludwig von (ed.), *Jugend in der modernen Gesellschaft*, Cologne/Berlin, 1971.

Gillis, John R., *Youth and history. Tradition and change in European age relations, 1770 to the present*, New York, 1974.

Kreutz, Henrik, *Youth and social change: a methodological review of European youth research 1960—1970*, Vienna, 1973.
Soziologie der Jugend, Munich, 1974.

Kühn, Arthur, 'Jugend und sozialer Wandel. Kritische Anmerkungen zu neueren, konflikttheoretischen Perspektiven der Jugendsoziologie', *Soziale Welt* 23 (1972), pp. 129ff.

Laslett, Peter, 'Age at menarche in Europe since the 18th century', *Journal of Interdisciplinary History* 2, 2 (1971), pp. 221ff.

Linde, Hans, 'Persönlichkeitsbildung in der Landfamilie', *Soziale Welt* 10 (1959), pp. 297ff.

Litt, Theodor, *Das Verhältnis der Generationen ehedem und heute*, Wiesbaden, 1947.

Lüschen, Günther and Koñig, René, *Jugend in der Familie. Überblick zur wissenschaftlichen Jugendkunde*, vol. 3, Munich, 1966.

Mannheim, Karl, 'Das Problem der Generationen', *Kölner Vierteljahrsheft für Soziologie* 2 and 3 (1928). Reprinted in L. von Friedeburg (ed.), *Jugend in der modernen Gesellschaft,* Cologne/Berlin, 1971, and recently in Martin Kohli (ed.), *Soziologie des Lebenslaufs*, Darmstadt/Neuwied, 1978.

Mitterauer, Michael, 'Jugendgruppen' in *Jugend im historischen Wandel. Beiträge zur historischen Sozialkunde* 6 (1976).

Möller, Helmut, *Die kleinbürgerliche Familie im 18. Jahrhundert. Verhalten und Gruppenkultur*, Berlin, 1969.

Muchow, Hans Heinrich, *Jugend und Zeitgeist. Morphologie der Kulturpubertät*, Reinbek, 1962.
Jugendgenerationen im Wandel der Zeiten, Vienna, 1964.

Neidhardt, Friedhelm, *Die junge Generation. Jugend und Gesellschaft in der Bundesrepublik*, Opladen, 1970.

Neidhardt, Friedhelm, *et al. Jugend im Spektrum der Wissenschaften. Beiträge zur Theorie des Jugendalters*, Munich, 1970.

Pelikan, Jürgen, *Jugend und Familie: Probleme der Konzeptualisierung und Messung* (dissertation, University of Vienna), Vienna, 1970.

Planck, Ulrich. *Landjugend im sozialen Wandel*, Munich, 1970.

Riedel, Manfred, *Wandel des Generationsproblems in der modernen Gesellschaft*, Düsseldorf/Cologne, 1969.

Rössler, Wilhelm, *Jugend im Erziehungsfeld*, Düsseldorf, 1957.

Rosenmayr, Leopold, *Familienbeziehungen und Freizeitgewohnheiten jugendlicher Arbeiter*, Vienna, 1963.
'Schwerpunkte der Jugendsoziologie' in René König (ed.), *Handbuch der*

empirischen Sozialforschung, vol. 7, 2nd edn, Stuttgart, 1976 (1969), pp. 218ff.

Rosenmayr, Leopold, Köckeis, Eva and Kreutz, Henrik, *Kulturelle Interessen von Jugendlichen*, Vienna/Munich, 1966.

Schelsky, Helmut, *Die skeptische Generation*, Düsseldorf/Cologne, 1963.

Tanner, James M., *Wachstum und Reifung des Menschen*, Stuttgart, 1962.

Tenbruck, Friedrich H., *Jugend und Gesellschaft. Soziologische Perspektiven*, Freiburg, 1965.

Wissell, Rudolf, *Des alten Handwerks Recht und Gewohnheit*, Berlin, 1929.

6

Marriage, Reproduction and Sexuality

Sexuality as a subject for historians

Human sexuality differs from animal sexuality mainly in that it is almost entirely free from the compulsion of a periodical sexual urge. Among human beings sexual intercourse is not governed by a rigid, biologically determined rutting cycle. Fluctuations in sexual desire and differences in sexual behaviour among human beings should rather be seen in a social context, as responses to social rather than biological stimuli. The continuous presence of sexual impulses has to be managed and controlled. Since human sexuality is largely socially determined, the adaptation of people to the social system prevalent at any given time is achieved to a large extent through the disciplining of their sexuality.

The sexual relationships of men and women are not necessarily linked with begetting. It is true, of course, that we have only recently succeeded in availing ourselves consistently and deliberately of the opportunities that this inherent potential of human sexuality offers.

Most of the insecurity that is so typical of these matters at the present time arises from the fact that the relationship between male and female is characterized more and more by a widening gulf between social sexuality and procreation. The means of preventing unwanted pregnancies are constantly being improved, while the intrinsic socio-cultural value of sexual relationships is recognized to an increasing extent. Hence the need to reconsider and to modify traditional standards and patterns of behaviour.

All branches of social science that deal with human sexual relationships must take account of their history. And it is the task of the social historian to undertake research into the historical and social conditions governing the genesis of our standards of sexuality and to find out how they have changed. He has to determine whether former norms and relationships have been transformed by social, economic and cultural changes, or whether they have become inadequate to meet the social situation today. He has also to ask whether the patterns of sexual behaviour adapted to our present situation allow for a maximum of human fulfilment (through its liberation from unwanted pregnancy, for instance) or whether sexuality is still accompanied by exploitation for material ends, if in novel ways.

As the following survey of the historical development of marriage and sexuality over the last few centuries will show, there is an obvious connection between human sexual relationships and the social and economic conditions in which people live. If we take a view of the concept of reproduction that is broad enough to include both procreation and the physical and psychological reproduction of the individual and of his labour power, then we can conceive of all forms of human sexuality as an integral part of social reproduction and of the social relationships into which human beings enter as part of the production relations of their daily life and work.

In general, therefore, it may be said that the quality of human sexual relationships finally depends on the relations of production and on the state of development of productive forces. Hence in what follows we shall demonstrate how the conditions of work in traditional European society, in the peasant household economy and the artisan's shop, governed sexual and reproductive relationships. We shall have to show, for example, what sort of connection existed between sexuality and work in the family of the industrial labourer and of the salaried employee. We shall concentrate on the influence that the requirements of work and the social conditions that arose from the social organization of labour have on social and sexual relations between the sexes.

Marriageability and mate selection in pre-industrial times

Before industrialization brought wage labour to the masses in Central Europe, large numbers of people lived in families that were domestic economic enterprises. The peasant family, the artisan family, the family of the noble landowner were all places both of social reproduction and of economic production. Even those who could not establish their own families lived and worked in the domestic groups of others, and were subject to their laws and rules.

Social ties, the relationship between the sexes and the roles of husband and wife were determined by the requirements and opportunities of the family's form of production. Choice of a marriage partner was controlled primarily not by love and affection but by social and economic needs associated with the care of dependants and the continuation of the family enterprise or of the lineage. Sexual suitability was not, as a rule, the decisive factor in this kind of mate selection.

In all classes in pre-modern Europe the choice of a marriage partner was very much controlled and influenced by the immediate family, by relatives and by neighbours because the marriage partner could be of overriding importance to the family labour unit in the domestic economy. He or she might be the future head of the family or of a gentle or noble house, as well as the source of capital in the shape of a dowry or of rights of inheritance. Indeed, the choice of partner could affect the entire circle of relatives, as well as social, political and class interests. Selection of spouses was narrowed because of the socio-economic role to be played by the future spouse, a role which demanded of him or her a class-specific socialization.

To ignore the limitations established by social class or group would have meant running a social and economic risk for all the members of the family. Apart from the restriction on individual freedom of choice exercised by family interests, the landlord or the lord of the manor, the guilds and later the state tried to influence choice of marriage partner and marital relationships. Landlords and lords of the manor were concerned that the composition of persons of the farming families should be such as to ensure the effective working of the property assigned to them. In Austrian and Central European regions farming widowers and widows were either urged to remarry quickly or forced to give up the management of the farm. The choice of successor to the dead or retired farmer was determined, if possible, by ability.

But since land, the most important means of production in a farming community, could not be increased at will, some of the population was necessarily denied the prospect of founding a family. If a person wanted to enter into matrimony he had, as a rule, to obtain the permission of the landlord. Persons without means who had no hope of acquiring a farm or a cottage in the foreseeable future were often forbidden to marry. In Central Europe this applied above all to servants and day labourers in rural areas and to journeymen in towns.

The policy of restricting the marriage of servants and day labourers in these areas goes back to the sixteenth century. In many Tyrolean parishes the clergyman was forbidden by law to marry indigent persons without a marriage permit issued by the local judiciary or the local authorities. In Bavaria this was attempted for the first time in 1553 by the *Landes und Polizey Ordnung*. This provided, among other things, that servants who married illegally, ran away from their masters and sought refuge in the so-called *Winkelherbergen* (refuges for vagrant and impecunious people) should be caught and taken back to the farm from which they had absconded.

In the seventeenth century this policy was reinforced. Married servants were forbidden to enter these refuges or to become day labourers. Many tried to find shelter in the towns. The Bavarian state law of 1616 therefore laid down that people without means should be forbidden to find refuge in the towns.

It was not till the second half of the eighteenth century that doubts were expressed about this sort of population policy. It was recognized that it was not possible to mitigate the much lamented scarcity of servants if the very classes of the population from among whose offspring servants and day labourers were largely recruited were prevented from marrying. Joseph II therefore inserted in the letters patent abolishing serfdom (1781) a clause stipulating that the lord of the manor was allowed to refuse permission to marry only when there were particular reasons for refusal.

But in the first half of the nineteenth century legislation preventing marriage, which thus had been put aside by enlightened absolutism, was again enforced in the Austrian Empire. In 1820 the Tyrol and Vorarlberg, provinces of Austria, established a *politischen Ehekonsens* (political marriage permit), without which servants, journeymen, day labourers and inmates could not marry. In addition, the political authorities were empowered to refuse a marriage licence to those persons who 'were in receipt of poor relief or who were beggars, and to those who had no steady livelihood and were of no fixed abode'. This political marriage permit was only abolished in 1921 in Austria, after the existing restrictions on the ability to marry had already been cancelled by the Federal Constitution of 1920.

We cannot know for certain how the prohibition to marry affected the love life and sexual relationships of impecunious persons. Sex before and outside marriage was quite common and was looked upon to some extent as natural and understandable. The cause lay in the very conditions of the family as an economic unit: the overriding importance to the peasant family of having children imposed on the wife the social duty of bearing children. In some regions she was cast out by her husband or was, at any rate, held in little esteem, if she was unable to have children. In some areas it was therefore quite usual for a young farmer to test his future wife's fecundity before marriage. If she became pregnant, there was nothing to stand in the way of a wedding. This form of pre-marital sexual intercourse was called 'testing' or 'trying out' by contemporaries. It is clear that this type of pre-marital relationship and its socially recognized function had its effect on all non-marital sexual intercourse. In particular regions very little shame was attached to having an illegitimate child, as will be seen from the following description by a civil servant of the Mürztal in Upper Styria in 1802:

The feeling of shame experienced by a fallen girl is so slight and is so little supported by public opinion, that wenches often boast of being robbed of their virginity and, rocking their infants in their arms, mock those who have given no proof of their fertility. When it comes to marrying, girls who have not been pregnant stand in danger of being put in the shade by those who have. For a bridegroom prefers a bride already endowed with children who will soon provide the house with work people. The bridegroom will usually adopt illegitimate children, even when he is not the father, as is often the case, or when he already has his own legitimate children.

This report derives from a region where, because of the rise of the iron industry, there was already a scarcity of servants. The self-assurance of the unmarried mother may have been founded on her knowledge that in spite of having one or more children, she could obtain a post as maidservant. The general shortage of servants forced the farmers to be tolerant and strengthened the hands of men and maids in their attempt to improve their position. In many districts servants insisted on sleeping in the barn and not the house in order to enjoy an undisturbed sex life. Men- and maidservants themselves decided where they should go into service the following year so that they might remain with their sexual partner.

Many did not trust themselves to say this for fear that their being lovers might become known to the authorities and that they might therefore be separated. This was a considerable worry for the farmers, who tried to discover by devious means which of the girls the farm servant loved and wanted to have for his own. When he had discovered this he would try to persuade the girl to enter into service with him. (Description of Thal Neuberg im Mürzthale Steyermarks, 1802)

Statutory decrees and rules governing service seemed to have had little effect. The tone in which the civil servant quoted above spoke of the 'fallen woman servant is certainly significant. He was aware of the economic importance of her illegitimate children as future servants and he showed himself remarkably tolerant, by contrast with the usual Jeremiads about a decline in morals.

Even if the maid servant who has been seduced has her children with her, she will not stop working for the farmer, nor will she stop caring for the children. There is the instance of the girl who became pregnant seven times; she now has seven excellent sons who are in great demand as farm servants. She has brought them all up herself and has also carried out her work as a servant. Although both she and the children have had to be fed by the farmer, she has never been in danger of not being able to work.

It must be remembered that the incidence of illegitimacy in Austria was very high indeed by European standards. In the early 1800s the illegitimacy ratio in the province of Styria amounted to 11.2 per cent. It rose considerably in the following decades and reached its highest point in the year 1870, at 27.8 per cent. (This can be contrasted, for example, with a ratio in England at that time of just over 5 per cent.) By 1910 the Austrian ratio had fallen again to 24.1 per cent. It is thought that the reason for this development, which took place in nearly all the Austrian provinces, may have been the enormous changes that were occurring in the agrarian sector. Fallow land was being brought under cultivation; potatoes, maize and clover were being grown; there was an increase in the number of cattle being reared. As a result, there was greater need for workers and a wider range of foodstuffs. The introduction of the potato, for instance, made it possible to feed between three and four times as many people from the same acreage of land. But since the productivity of the Austrian farm labourer hardly increased at all, it was only possible to keep up the rapid expansion of the agricultural production by using additional workers.

This may be the reason why the peasants did not take steps to prevent extramarital sexual intercourse between servants and were willing to take in their illegitimate children. It was probably the real cause of the rise in illegitimacy in these decades in this area.

Technical innovations in the second half of the nineteenth century, labour-saving devices such as new ploughing, sowing, threshing and straw-cutting machines and the use of the scythe instead of the sickle reduced the number of people employed in agriculture, and the earlier trend was reversed. Part of the landless country population migrated to the industrial centres that had recently come into existence. The number of farm servants declined more sharply than the changes in agriculture warranted, and servants' wages rose in the 1870s and 1880s. As a result, the scarcity of domestic servants again became acute.

In 1882 an investigation by the Styrian *Landtag* (legislative chamber) established the fact that on the large farms of Upper Styria children of unmarried servants were always welcome:

The property-owning farming population gladly keep the children of servants in the house; they care for them as so-called foster children, even when the mother later leaves their service. . . . For in the large households the children are not much of an expense and later give cheap and devoted service to the house.

The problem of illegitimate children in Austria was therefore primarily a question of the supply of food and the demand for labourers. Children born out of wedlock were not necessarily an indication of immorality or the degradation of the lower classes, but rather the result of a temporary or permanent inability to marry and of the opportunity to sustain extramarital relationships.

The quality of marital sexuality in pre-industrial times

From the scant information we have been able to gather about the structure of the family, it is, of course, difficult to form any idea of the quality of marital relationships and particularly of the standard of marital sexuality. We do have some knowledge of the differences in ages between marriage partners, which was often considerable in pre-industrial times, to the extent that the lifecycles of the two spouses were not synchronous. This was true particularly in the case of widows who were heading the households and enterprises of former artisans and commercial people and of those remarrying in country and farming districts.

For an artisan's widow remarriage, often to a younger journeyman employed in the family enterprise, represented the only form of care in old age. There were no such things as pension rights in the society in which she lived. And for the journeyman who was not the son of a master, marrying the master's widow was often the only way of achieving the status of master.

In farming circles too, economics dictated that the central roles of master and mistress of the house should be filled if at all possible, and remarriage, sometimes to a much younger or older partner, was quite usual.

Among the lower classes in the towns – above all, among day labourers and masons, carpenters, stone breakers and other less well respected traders – great differences between the ages of spouses were to be found also. In Salzburg in 1794 more than half of all carpenters' wives were considerably older than their husbands. Austrian towns, by comparison with those in Western Europe, appear to have had a much higher proportion of wives who were older than their husbands. Compared with England, there were many more cases of marriages in which one partner was more than ten years older than the other.

It is clear that modern notions of love and eroticism cannot be applied indiscriminately to such conditions. A life without luxury or even comfort, typified by hard labour and a long working day, would probably not encourage sexual passion within marriage. Even in the nineteenth century kissing and caressing were rare among married peasants. Heinrich Rauscher reports on family relationships in the Waldviertel of Lower Austria:

Relationships between members of the family lack tenderness; people converse soberly and matter-of-factly with each other. They are loath to show their feelings, as it is assumed to be a sign of weakness and affectation. Only very young children are kissed and fondled. Relationships between spouses appear cold. (p. 22)

And Karl Renner writes about peasant relationships in Güssing, Burgenland, at the end of the nineteenth century:

Expressions of tenderness in family life so well-known to us (kissing, embracing, fondling a child in one's lap and so on), were considered unseemly, not only between brothers and sisters, but also between parents and children. . . . (p. 272)

Such references point to a connection between the harshness of working life and the loving quality of the relationship between husband and wife and between parents and children. Their relationships must be seen in a psycho–genetic context.

In farming circles, on the other hand, it must always have been possible, at any rate for the man, to find some compensation if he was not able to satisfy his sexual needs within marriage. There were nearly always single persons living on the farmsteads as servants, day labourers and inmates. But the married woman was in a much weaker position. Extramarital sex would have been very difficult for her, in the first place because of the social risk that she might run and, secondly, because of her frequent pregnancies and lactation periods. It may be assumed that she herself would hardly have laid claim to the satisfaction of her sexual desires.

The separation of love and marriage in the privileged classes

Among members of the higher classes of society, the relationship between marriage and sexual life was quite different from that among peasants and craftsmen. The lifestyle of the elite was not restricted by scarcity of food and hard labour. From quite early times, members of the nobility entertained a hedonistic and aesthetic notion of love, which could flourish unhampered by economic needs and pressures. This applied above all to extramarital love. Among the members of the nobility who lived in towns and had connections with the court there developed a dichotomy between 'chaste' love within marriage and extramarital, erotic love. Love was not considered to be a precondition of marriage. Christianity decreed that spouses should enter into this relationship once they were married. They were cautioned against marrying for love and against excessive married love. Among the French and Italian court nobility especially, marriage was seen as a prudent economic arrangement and love as an erotic, sexual relationship, and the two were considered irreconcilable. Nobles, who were financially privileged, were in a position to pursue their lovelives outside marriage, and such extramarital liaisons hardly affected the durability of marriage itself. Such circumstances were regarded as perfectly natural: a noble lady without lovers must be unattractive; a noble gentleman without mistresses must be either impotent or bankrupt.

The illegitimate child was viewed favourably when its father was highly placed. This was a consequence of the veneration of blood, which held that the characteristic attributes and the social status of the nobleman could be inherited. Every noble gentleman was therefore entitled (indeed, it was sometimes considered to be his right) to rape any girl from a lower social class who pleased him.

The young nobleman could collect sexual experiences on his grand tour through the most important cities of Europe. Courtesans and noble widows taught him fine manners to grace his treatment of the female sex; chamber maids and serving wenches enriched his experience. Only noble marriageable candidates were forbidden him, for they had to enter into marriage as virgins.

Since early times soldiers and students enjoyed special sexual privileges. Hairdressers, milliners, tailors and domestic servants, because they were constantly in contact with the noble upper classes, adopted a notion of marriage and sexual morals that was modelled on theirs. This produced similarities in social behaviour, but also a certain disorientation in social and sexual relationships, for the grandiose ideas of aristocratic love were quite out of keeping with the material conditions of lower–class living.

The development of love, marriage and the bourgeois model of the family

In the train of urbanization and industrialization came a greater variety of opportunities for trades and ways of subsistence that could be practised outside the house and away from the family. The separation of home from work place caused the family to become more private. People lived increasingly with members of their immediate family and no one else. This gave rise to more intense, and probably more emotional, family relationships. Around the middle of the eighteenth century more people began to see marriage as a 'union of souls'.

The dualism of marriage and sensuality was first overcome by the educated classes. People moralized about love, and bourgeois marriage for money was condemned. This new idea of marriage and the family found its clearest expression in the period of Romanticism. For the first time, broad sections of the population regarded the family as fundamental, and home became increasingly an intimate haven, closed to outsiders. At the same time, there was a greater appreciation of the emotional and sexual relationship between marriage partners. Greater restrictions were imposed on the individual in connection with sexual matters, and there was a growing discrimination against pre- and extramarital relationships.

In a society that was becoming more and more complex, there was increasing differentiation of social roles. This meant that people were more dependent on each other, which in turn imposed a greater need for self-restraint and self-control in order that the close union of those living together should not be put at risk. The 'man of restraint', a complete master of himself, was held up to the adolescent as a model that he should strive to emulate. The sensuality and spontaneity of the individual were relegated from the public to the intimate sphere, where parents tended to conceal their sexual and carnal life from their children. With the confinement of sexual–erotic relationships to the intimate sphere of married life, the lack of sexual and emotional satisfaction could endanger a marriage. On the other hand, exacting subjective–emotional and sexual–erotic demands made on the marriage partner increased the susceptibility of marriage to all sorts of strain.

For the first time a private, domestic sphere developed on a large scale in the families of lawyers, civil servants, doctors, scientists, teachers and clerics as we have remarked. It was here that family life ceased to be dominated by the dictates of the domestic economy. A new sentimentality between spouses and a new relationship towards the child took their place. We encounter the first instances of a family type centred on the mother, because at this level of society the husband's occupation took him out of the house more and more, and he was therefore separated from wife and children all day long.

Whereas the farmer's and the master's wife played a decisive part in the production of goods for sale and for everyday consumption in the domestic eonomy, the middle-class woman was the first to be restricted to the tasks of private reproduction. The upper middle class considered even housework unfit for the wife and left it to servants. All that remained for the wife to do was to give birth to and rear her children, and also partly to educate them. As a result of the ideological glorification of these functions in society's image of the woman as a mother, she has been effectively tied to this role to the present day.

This was also the kernel of a new middle-class ideology of the family, which had become necessary to more and wider strata of the population in which the division of labour between husband and wife of the former domestic economy had become impracticable. The economic demands of the 'whole house' had to be substituted by a new concept of the family that would perpetuate the traditional dominance of the husband in the now 'private' family. The development of the ideology of the character of the sexes around 1800 may have been an important means to this end. A wave of dictionary entries, philosophical treatises and magazines helped to propagate the idea that the woman's place was in the home, with her children, and that this was a consequence of her nature. The man's place was in the world outside. On the farm and in the artisan's household, roles had been allocated in a particularistic way that was related to specific modes of production, but now definitions of the male and the female character, claiming universalistic validity, were devised. The aim was to define not the role of the farmer's or the master's wife, but the role of woman and of man in general. Passivity and emotionalism were ascribed to the woman, rationalism and activity to the man.

Middle-class family ideology based on this concept of sex-specific nature proved effective far beyond the middle classes. It spread relatively fast among the lower middle class and also, in the early twentieth century and in a somewhat modified form, among the industrial proletariat, despite its completely different economic and cultural conditions.

In the nineteenth century public interest in the family increased, as is clear from contemporary political discussion. The population at large, the state and even industrial enterprises were often characterized metaphorically by the expression 'family'. The family, it was always claimed, was the foundation of society – of bourgeois society. State and Church showed great concern for the sex life of the individual and for the morals of the people. Love, which the Romantics were the first to regard as the pivot of a marriage, took on the character of a moral duty. The interest of the absolute state in marriage and the family was reflected in a renewed assertion of the 'holiness' of the family (and it must be remembered that the absolute state ruled over the whole of Central and Eastern Europe). An entry in the 1834 edition of the *Brockhaus encyclopaedia*, for instance, states: 'The family is the most natural, the oldest and the holiest institution of mankind.' The idyll of happy family life was constantly presented as a model; the family was represented as a harmonious unit, free of strife. Woman was confined expressly to the family, hence participation in political action was generally denied to her. 'The wife does not live for herself, but only in and with the family' (Riehl).

Not until the second half of the nineteenth century did tendencies towards emancipation from this repressive family system begin to make themselves felt. The fight for the rights of women and children began to shatter the myth of the 'holy family'. Since the turn of the century psychoanalysis and psychotherapy have brought into the open the conflict and spiritual malaise lying dormant within the family.

Marriage and sex among the early industrial working classes

It is true that the development that we have described applied only to those social classes who lived in relative affluence and were thus able to secure familial privacy for themselves. It did not apply to the relationships among working people in the first phase of industrialization, since their housing and work conditions allowed for no intensification of privacy and emotional life. Bourgeois sex norms applied to these people to a far lesser extent; Wilhelm Reich speaks of the 'physical robustness' and 'natural sex inclinations' of the proletariat.

By comparison with the present day, the number of married labourers in Central Europe was very low. Age at marriage was high, and the possibility of founding a family was confined to those employed in a few of the more profitable occupations. In the Viennese district of Gumpendorf, for instance, only 19 per cent of male and female workers were married in 1857. Roughly a third of all workers there could never afford to marry or have a family. A large part of the labour force, therefore, lived in a state of consensual union. This is understandable when one considers that more than 50 per cent of the labourers at that time did not have their own dwellings but had to live as sub-tenants in barrack-like workmen's quarters provided by their employer. Sometimes they could only rent a bed for a few hours.

Cottage industry, which was quite widespread even in the late nineteenth century, principally in the textile industry, made it easier for workers to found a family. Husband and wife usually worked together. The wife could combine her household chores and her wage earning, frequently at the cost of her health, because she often tried to make an additional income by sewing, washing and so on. Here the family was a social form for the organization of survival, permitting the spouses to scrape through and save themselves and their children from starvation.

It was not before the 1870s that opportunities for marrying and rearing a family underwent any marked or general improvement. The proportion of married workers in Vienna increased from 20 per cent to 30 per cent between 1869 and 1890.

At the beginning of the Industrial Revolution the very existence of a worker's household was based on the contribution of every able member of the family to the domestic economy. As industrialization proceeded, individual wage earning grew common, along with the separate integration of family members into industrial production. This brought about the separation of work from family life among workers, too. Both aspects of the production of the working force, its daily work as well as the rearing of children, had now become the foremost task of the worker's family.

In spite of the fact that the wife frequently had a job, it was the husband who continued to assume the traditional role of breadwinner in the worker's family. His participation in the tasks of familial production (the preparation of meals, taking care of the children and so on) was generally negligible. If the wife could not perform some of the familial services necessary to the daily production of the labour force because of her occupation outside the house, the family had to buy these services on the market. The expenses thus incurred made many working women try to reduce wage earning outside the house as much as possible or to find work that could be carried out at home. As soon as the husband made enough money to feed all his family, his wife often stayed at home for good. The middle-class ideology about woman's 'destiny' as housewife and mother was thus adopted by the working class wherever it was economically feasible.

The struggle of the working class for socio-political progress brought about improvements in the family conditions of working people. As a result of better material conditions, they attempted to model their lives on middle-class standards, which involved the confinement of sex within marriage.

Sex in the consumer society: new constraints, new freedoms

In all classes and sections of traditional Central European society that were constituted by house and family units, there were relationships of personal dependence – in the households of lords of the manor, in those of farmers, of artisans and of shopkeepers. Everywhere the head of the household had authority not only over the conduct of the family undertaking but also over the way of life of his servants and workers, and therefore over their love lives and sexual relationships. The farmer demanded diligence and application from his servants, and he watched over their morals. Apprentices and journeymen were subject to the all-embracing, paternalistic authority of their master, even in their relationships outside their place of work. The system of production attempted to govern the work and the lives of these people in the framework of the family enterprise. The authority of the noble landlord, the farmer or the master craftsman had to uphold specific group norms and the discipline of labour. The civil servant of the Upper Styria estate of Neuberg whom we cited above describes the pressure exercised by the domestic group and the village community:

Everything depends on the farmer or the *Maier* (the foreman of the servants) who is the first to start work. If he is energetic and persevering, then all the others follow suit. He who does not do this is taunted by all the others; he is not respected, and at meetings, games and feasts is not exactly treated with contempt but receives little attention. But if the leading workman himself is lazy, then so are all his co-workers; they have no shame to fear and there is no one to ridicule them.

This system of discipline therefore functioned within the hierarchy of small groups whose members could be supervised. Those who did not conform were treated with contempt, were laughed at or mocked, were made to feel ashamed of themselves and were likely to suffer loss of prestige in the group and in the village community.

With the socialization and the rationalization of production in the course of industrialization, this direct control over the individual became less effective. The qualities of workmen who were adequate for industrialized production processes could no longer be subjected to outside control. After a transitional period (in which supervision, for example, was the task of factory overseers), the apparatus of manufacture, factories and management became increasingly difficult to oversee and control. From then on control was necessarily inherent in the psyche as an ideology of performance that the individual would find more difficult to sabotage than control from outside.

Mature capitalism not only requires that the individual should be able to work; it also needs him as a consumer, so that the volume of goods demanded may increase. We note the same sort of dualism in sexual relationships. On the one hand, sex is offered as a commodity: the amusement industry, from the cinema to the sex shop, profits from the sexual frustration of its customers. Advertising makes use of the readiness of the public to be stimulated by associating with sex many of the products offered on the market. On the other hand, the dream worlds of an aesthetic lifestyle in luxurious surroundings evoked by the advertisers cannot be realized by the average person caught up in the daily grind. The hard, nerve-shattering world of labour disciplines and impoverishes people's sex life. Those belonging to the middle classes, ambitious to achieve success in their professions, exhaust their energies in the daily battle. In many work places the people suffer from deadening labour conditions. Loss of creativity and a stunted sex life frequently result. Yet the individual feels compelled to perform efficiently in matters of sex. The commercialization of sexual desires produces a world in which sexuality is thought of in terms of material, quantifiable categories. It provokes physical and psychological disturbances such as would not have been known to pre-industrial society.

In present-day Central Europe, social development has made it possible for practically everyone to start a family and thus to enjoy marital sex. Legal impediment now prevents only marriages between near relatives and between minors. The influence of economic pressure on the choice of partners, on marriage and on remarriage has been greatly reduced. Nowadays it is only found where it is important to secure the family property or where the family is still a productive unit (in family enterprises and farms, for example).

In spite of the general disappearance of legal and economic obstacles to marriage, it should not be assumed that the choice of marriage partners is at present entirely free from economic and social determinants. Although the notion of the ideal love match may be seen as an important element of social change, marriages are generally contracted between people in similar social, economic and cultural circumstances. The workman usually chooses his wife from among labouring groups; the intellectual chooses his mainly from academic circles.

The decrease in socio-economic impediments to marriage in highly industrialized societies has been accompanied by increased opportunities for marital dissolution. There is an evident connection between the frequency of divorces and the question of whether the family is or is not the economic unit of production. In pre-industrial society, the choice of a marriage partner, conjugal life and the relationship between parents and children had to conform with the economic exigencies of the 'whole house'. This was manifest in the requirement that a man should be married if he wanted to run a farm or to ply a craft, and in the fact that the dissolution of marriages was virtually impossible. In general, however, the duration of a marriage was relatively short because of the high age at marriage and the lower life expectancy. It often happened that the father or the mother did not survive the infancy of their last-born child. This led to a high rate of remarriage. Most of the people who lived to an old age had married more than once. Because of the relatively short duration of marriages and the different expectations of their marriage partners, the desire to dissolve a marriage was probably less common than it is today.

Even today the rate of divorce is much lower where the family is still the unit of production – that is, particularly in farming and to some extent in the trades. The shared ownership of the means of production and the need to cope together with the work load in farming and in trading family businesses probably reduces the readiness to contemplate a divorce because of the consequent economic disadvantages for both partners. In addition to this, there is an ideological gloss to the demands of the family economy, in that divorced people are discriminated against more in rural areas than in towns.

In cases in which the family is no longer the unit of production and one or both marriage partners earn a living outside the home, there is a far greater chance of divorce should conflict arise. It appears that those marriages in which the wife herself has a job dissolve most readily. In Austria the marriages of female salaried employees end in separation or divorce more often than those of female workers. The economic feasibility of divorce and the consequent willingness to contemplate it seem to be more developed among female salaried employees.

The number of divorces has risen generally in the last two decades. One in every seven marriages that were contracted 20 or 30 years ago in Austria ended in a divorce, whereas the rate among more recent marriages is probably one in five. There is a significant connection between the frequency of divorce and the degree of urbanization. At the present time the divorce rate in Vienna is approximately twice as high as in the rest of Austria.

This increase in the frequency of divorce points to the growing fragility of the concept of marriage for life, which originated under quite different demographic conditions. The much shorter duration of marriages and the fact that their contraction was often dictated by necessity probably made it easier to live up to this ideal. For most people, divorce was impossible before the obligations and exigencies of the family economy were reduced and there was a substantial rise in real income in monetary economies. What one may conclude from the higher frequency of divorce, therefore, is above all that socio-cultural and economic obstacles to the dissolution of marriages have diminished.

It is not inconceivable that after a period during which marriages lasted longer as a result of demographic factors in the late nineteenth century, members of the highly industrialized societies of Western and Central Europe are once again contracting shorter, multiple marriages, the only difference being that these marriages are no longer dissolved by the premature death of a partner but rather by divorce.

Another result of the disappearance of the demands of the family economy and their effect on the choice of marriage partner and conjugal life is the fact that young people now tend to live together without being married. This is presumably because they want to be able to separate without trauma if their relationship should go wrong.

The reduction in the number of children per marriage has affected the quality of sexual life within marriage, which has become increasingly independent of procreation. The smaller number of pregnancies gives greater scope for sexual activity between marriage partners. Children now tend to be born during the early years of a marriage. A lower age at marriage, higher life expectancy and fewer births separated by shorter intervals have dramatically shortened the phase during which children are born and reared. (Those women who married between 1961 and 1965 gave birth to 90 per cent of the expected total of children, including those born before marriage, by the end of their first decade of marriage.) On the other hand, this has appreciably lengthened the phase of marriage after the departure of all the children. In pre-industrial times most married couples were practically at the end of their marriage when the youngest child had grown up; frequently one of the spouses was dead. Nowadays, however, marriage partners usually live together for at least 20 to 30 years after the departure of the youngest child, as we have noted. This 'empty nest' phase presents a serious challenge to most spouses. They are living alone again for the first time since the beginning of their marriage. New interests and occupations have to be found, where formerly the children were the focus of attention. The fact that many married women take a job at this stage is to be seen in this light as well.

On the other hand, there are signs that this critical phase of marriage should be formulated anew. Whereas in former times it was regarded as self-evident that at the end of her child-bearing period the older woman should return to an asexual phase, this is often questioned nowadays. The menopause is regarded less and less as a decisive period in a woman's life. She has usually given up her readiness to conceive long before this biological stage anyway, and her sexual energy is not limited by this event. The taboo on female sexuality after the climacteric has probably been conditioned by the fact that historically sex and procreation were regarded as identical. Until recently, the moral association between sexual experience and the intention to procreate, as encouraged by the Catholic Church, frequently led to the neglect of the sexual wishes of the woman when she was no longer able to conceive.

In the advanced phase of a marriage, this situation, which is a relatively recent one, entails special risks for the woman. On the one hand, she often feels threatened by massive advertising campaigns that make use of youthful beauties. On the other hand, after the completion of her task of bringing up her children, she may feel her energy revive and her sexual urge awaken again. For many ageing men, however, the continuation of sexual life is impossible in advanced old age. Wives therefore frequently channel their sexual energies into over-mothering grown-up children and grandchildren, or divert them into religious or social and charitable activities. The tendency to devote themselves entirely to the care of their ageing husbands is an expression of their sexual frustration. One speaks of 'over-protection' and of a 'matriarchy of the aged'. This is encouraged by the fact that when he has retired the husband often loses his self-esteem because he is no longer employed. He may also be in need of physical help at an earlier age than his wife.

In this rough sketch we have, of course, only been able to touch on some of the problems in the field of marriage and sex that present themselves from an historical point of view. In order to establish the interconnection between production, consumption and sexuality, we have refrained from dealing with other equally important questions. Obviously, we have not dealt adequately with the historical development of the relationships of authority in the family and in marriage or with the relationship between husband and wife. Our treatment of the various stages of historical development has not been sufficiently differentiated in time or in space. But the outline we have presented does at least establish the connection between sexuality and the basic social conditions of production and reproduction, and this should make sexuality easier to understand as a social phenomenon.

Knowledge of the socio-economic exigencies that formerly determined what was feasible among people in matters of sex enables us to regard the formation of social norms as neither natural nor, for that matter, arbitrary. The rejection of earlier norms and relationships that ran counter to personal happiness can only take place in the context of social relationships in general if it is to be taken up on a large scale. Experiments in forms of social and sexual living together that are in advance of social relationships in general can therefore only be practised by fringe groups. Their importance is not to be denied, however, for they demonstrate that different kinds of human sexual relationships are possible and thus make us aware of the fact that their nature is conditioned by the processes of social development.

SELECT BIBLIOGRAPHY

Bock, Gisela and Duden, Barbara, 'Arbeit aus Liebe – Liebe als Arbeit. Zur Entstehung der Hausarbeit im Kapitalismus' in *Frauen und Wissenschaft. Beiträge zur Berliner Sommeruniversität für Frauen,* Berlin, 1977, pp. 118ff.

Claessens, Dieter and Menne, Ferdinand W., 'Zur Dynamik der bürgerlichen Familie und ihrer möglichen Alternativen' in Günther Lüschen and Eugen Lupri (eds.), *Soziologie der Familie. Kölner Zeitschrift für Soziologie und Sozialpsychologie* 14 (1970), pp. 169ff.

Depauw, Jacques, 'Amour illégitime et société à Nantes aux XVIIIe siècle', *Annales E.S.C.* 27 (1972), pp. 1155ff.

Ehmer, Josef, 'Wohnen ohne eigene Wohung. Zur sozialen Stellung von Untermietern und Bettgehern' in L. Niethammer (ed.), *Wohnen im Wandel*, Wuppertal, 1979, pp. 132ff.

Familienstruktur und Arbeitsorganisation im frühindustriellen Wien, Vienna, 1980.

Elias, Norbert, *Über den Prozess der Zivilisation. Soziogenetische und psychogenetische Untersuchungen*, Berne, 1976 (1969).

Fehr, Hans, *Die Rechtsstellung der Frau und der Kinder in den Weistümern*, Jena, 1912.

Flandrin, Jean-Louis, 'Contraception, mariage et relations amoureuses dans l'Occident chrétien', *Annales E.S.C.* 24 (1969), pp. 1370ff.

Les amours paysannes (XVIe–XIXe siècle), Paris, 1975.

Familles. Parenté, maison, sexualité dans l'ancienne société, Paris, 1976.

'Represssion and change in the sexual life of young people in medieval and early modern times', *Journal of Family History* 2 (1977), pp. 196ff.

Foucault, Michel, *Sexualität und Wahrheit – Der Wille zum Wissen*, Frankfurt, 1977.

Habermas, Jürgen, *Strukturwandel der Öffentlichkeit. Untersuchungen zu einer Kategorie der bürgerlichen Gesellschaft*, Neuwied/Berlin, 1962.

Hajnal, J., 'European marriage patterns in perspective' in D. V. Glass and D. E. C. Eversley (eds.), *Population in History*, Chicago, 1965.

Haug, Wolfgang Fritz, *Warenästhetik, Sexualität und Herrschaft. Gesammelte Aufsätze*, Frankfurt, 1972.

Hausen, Karin, 'Die Polarisierung der "Geschlechtscharaktere". Eine Spiegelung der Dissoziation von Erwerbs- und Familienleben' in Werner Conze (ed.), *Sozialgeschichte der Familie in der Neuzeit Europas*, Stuttgart, 1976, pp. 365ff.

Held, Thomas, *Soziologie der ehelichen Machtverhältnisse*, Darmstadt, 1978.

König, René, *Die Familie der Gegenwart. Ein interkultureller Vergleich*, Munich, 1974.

Materialien zur Soziologie der Familie, Cologne, 1974.

Kula, Witold, 'La seigneurie et la famille paysanne en Pologne au XVIIIe siècle', *Annales E.S.C.* 27 (1972), pp. 949ff.

Lütge, Friedrich, *Die bayerische Grundherrschaft, Untersuchungen über die Agrarverfassung Altbayerns im 16.–18. Jh.*, Stuttgart, 1949.

Meillassoux, Claude, *Femmes, greniers et capitaux*, Paris, 1975.

Menne, Ferdinand W., *Kirchliche Sexualethik gegen gesellschaftliche Realität. Zu einer soziologischen Anthropologie menschlicher Fruchtbarkeit*, Munich, 1971.

Mitterauer, Michael, 'Auswirkungen von Urbanisierung und Frühindustrialisierung auf die Familienverfassung an Beispielen des österreichischen Raums' in Werner Conze (ed.), *Sozialgeschichte der Familie in der Neuzeit Europas*, Stuttgart, 1976, pp. 53ff.

'Zur familienbetrieblichen Struktur im zünftischen Handwerk' in *Wirtschafts- und sozialhistorische Beiträge (Festschrift für Alfred Hoffman)*, Vienna, 1979, pp. 190ff.

'Familienformen und Illegitimität in ländlichen Gebieten Österreichs', *Archiv für Sozialgeschichte* 19 (1979), pp. 123ff.

Rauscher, Heinrich, *Volkskunds des Waldviertels*, 1926.

Renner, Karl, *An der Wende zweier Zeiten*, Vienna, 1946.

Riehl, Wilhelm Heinrich, *Naturgeschichte des deutschen Volkes: Die Familie*, Stuttgart, 1961 (1854).

Sandgruber, Roman, 'Die Agrarrevolution in Österreich. Ertragssteigerung und Kommerzialisierung der landwirtschaftlichen Produktion im 18. und 19. Jahrhundert' in Alfred Hoffman (ed.), *Österreich-Ungarn als Agrarstaat (Sozial- und wirtschaftshistorische Studien* 10), Vienna, 1978.

Schelsky, Helmut, *Soziologie der Sexualität*, Hamburg, 1960.

Schwab, Dieter, *Grundlagen und Gestalt der staatlichen Ehegesetzgebung in der Neuzeit bis zum Beginn des 19. Jahrhunderts*, Bielefeld, 1967.

Shorter, Edward, 'Illegitimacy, sexual revolution and social change in modern Europe', *Journal of Interdisciplinary History* 2 (1971), pp. 237ff.

'Capitalism, culture and sexuality: some competing models', *Social Science Quarterly* 53 (1972), pp. 338ff.

' "La vie intime". Beiträge zu seiner Geschichte am Beispiel des kulturellen Wandels in den bayerischen Unterschichten im 19. Jahrhundert', *Soziologie und Sozialgeschichte (Kölner Zeitschrift für Soziologie und Sozialpsychologie)* 16, 1972, pp. 530ff.

'Der Wandel der Mutter-Kind-Beziehungen zu Beginn der Moderne', *Geschichte und Gesellschaft* 1 (1975), pp. 256ff.

The making of the modern family, New York, 1975.

Sieder, Reinhard, 'Strukturprobleme ländlicher Familien im 19. Jahrhundert', *Zeitschrift für bayerische Landesgeschichte* 41 (1978), pp. 173ff.

Taylor, Gordon R., *Im Garten der Lüste, Herrschaft und Wandlungen der Sexualität*, Frankfurt, 1970.

Ussel, Jos van, *Sexualunterdrückung. Geschichte der Sexualfeindschaft*, Reinbek, 1970.

Wikman, K. R. V., *Die Einleitung der Ehe: Eine vergleichende ethnosoziologische Untersuchung über die Vortufe der Ehe in den Sitten des schwedischen Volkstums (Acta Academiae Aboensis, Humaniora* II), Abo, 1937.

7

The Process of Ageing and the Changing Structure of the Family

Ageing: an historical theme

Nobody would deny that ageing is a subject that falls within the province of sociology, for many of the problems connected with it are of a social or socio-structural nature. But ageing should also be considered in the light of history, so that sociological notions about it may acquire a new dimension. A social history surely ought to be able to transcend the relatively narrow temporal scope of sociology and to reveal long-term trends and connections. It may be possible in this way to provide a more satisfactory interpretation of present-day problems and situations. The dynamic of historical change should also give us an understanding of the changes that we should try to bring about in the future.

Because little definitive research has so far been undertaken, we can offer only a provisional review of the problem. By making use of such results as have become available from sociological work, we shall attempt to see ageing in its socio-historical context. In order to outline the basis of this issue, we will have to look at the process of ageing in the light of historical changes in the role and behaviour of the ageing person in the social context and the effects that historical changes in his social environment have had on the process of ageing.

If we investigate the connection between problems of ageing and historical change in family and household structure, it becomes clear that ageing is determined less by the attainment of a certain number of years than it is by distinct breaks in the continuity of personal experiences, which are due to alterations in the relationship of the elderly person with his social environment in general and with his immediate social circle in particular. In our own day, however, it is not simply those members of the family who live together who are involved. The transformation brought about by urbanization and industrialization has assured that relationships between the old and their grown-up children have become, increasingly, social contacts maintained in spite of separation from the family home. 'Intimacy at a distance' is what Leopold Rosenmayr has termed it.

This is surely an indication that the institution of the family is of great importance both to those who are integral parts of it and to the old who live separated from the families of their children. From an historical point of view, the family of the young in which the old have a place has undoubtedly become less important. The present situation of the elderly in our society must be seen as a stage in an historical development that is closely connected with changes in the structure and function of the family.

To present this change as an opposition between pre-industrial and industrial family forms runs the risk of over-simplification. In making such a comparison, the family relationships of old people in the pre-industrial period are only too often idealized, although the available empirical data do not warrant any such assumption. Nevertheless, in the following pages we shall boldly attempt to contrast the problems of ageing in pre-industrial and in industrial society. In such a macro-historical presentation, industrialization and urbanization will necessarily be the focal points of our explanation for the most important changes in the situation of ageing and aged people.

Ageing is frequently described, and negatively evaluated, as the loss of personal relations, function and autonomy. The loss of personal relations is a consequence of the spatial separation of children from their parents, which causes an abrupt diminution of parental roles and activities, as it were. It is also said that the separation of the home from the work place and the loss of the family's productive function have reduced the importance and number of tasks carried out by the elderly. Because the family has handed over some of its former functions such as the greater part of the education of children to social institutions like kindergartens and schools, it has allegedly forfeited its autonomy. This has entailed a loss of function and prestige, particularly for older persons.

But it would be inaccurate to ascribe to the changing structure of the family only negative consequences for old people. The age structure of the population, as well as relationships specific to old age, have altered in such a way that we have to investigate very carefully how these changes have affected the quality of life of old people and the social meaning of ageing.

A longer lifespan and changes in the average age at which a woman bears her first and her last child have produced decisive changes in the family cycle and in the position of ageing people in the family. It is, therefore, impossible to draw precise conclusions without acquainting ourselves with the relevant historical data. Let us glance at some historical examples of changes in life expectancy, age at marriage and number of births, as well as at the length of time during which children remained in the family of origin and evidence of the presence of other persons within the household, together with their social consequences for ageing and aged people.

Causes of an increasing life expectancy

We have, unfortunately, little exact information about life expectancy at birth in pre-industrial Central Europe. For England it is now known precisely for every five-year period since 1541. Life expectancy at birth varied there between the late twenties and the mid-forties (Wrigley and Schofield). It has been accepted that the average length of life in the agrarian society of pre-industrial Central Europe was probably no higher than the early thirties. Not till the nineteenth century do we find more exact data for these regions.

The conspicuous increase in life expectancy shown in table 1 is not to be attributed exclusively, or even primarily, to advances in medicine. Economic development, social reforms, improvements in hygiene and in social welfare must all be seen as primary contributory factors. Apart from better medical treatment, improvements in diet helped to build up greater resistance to disease. Years of pestilence were generally also years of hunger. Famine, caused mainly by failure of crops, frequently could not be relieved by imported food-

Table 1
Development of average life expectancy in years

Age in years	Male population			Female population		
	1871–80	1967–69	increase	1871–80	1967–69	increase
Federal German Republic[1]						
0 (new-born)	35.6	67.4	31.8	38.5	73.5	35.0
5	49.4	64.5	15.1	51.0	70.3	19.3
30	31.4	40.9	9.5	33.1	46.0	12.9
60	12.1	15.1	3.0	12.7	18.8	6.1
80	4.1	5.3	1.2	4.2	6.0	1.8
Austria[2]						
0 (new-born)	30.4	66.6	36.2	33.1	73.7	40.6
5	45.3	63.9	18.6	46.5	70.6	24.1
30	29.7	40.5	10.8	30.5	46.3	15.8
60	11.8	15.2	3.4	11.7	19.1	7.4
80	4.1	5.2	1.1	3.9	6.1	2.2

[1]*Source*: G. Hohorst, J. Kocka and C. A. Ritter (eds.), *Sozialgeschichtliches Arbeitsbuch. Materialen zur Statistik des Kaiserreichs, 1870–1914*, Munich, 1975, pp. 33–4.
[2]*Source*: H. Helczmanovsky, 'Die Entwicklung der Bevölkerung Österreichs in den letztenhundert Jahren nach den wichtigsten demographischen Komponenten' in H. Helczmanovsky, (ed), *Beiträge zur Bevölkerungs- und Sozialgeschichte Österreichs*, Vienna, 1973, p. 136.

stuffs in Central Europe because of an underdeveloped transport system. Neighbouring agrarian regions did not produce enough to alleviate famine in the towns. Better transport, together with the agrarian revolution, which brought great improvements to the land economy, may be seen as preconditions for the decrease in mortality, providing the true basis for the growth in population of the nineteenth century.

The improvement in sanitary conditions was of particular benefit to the towns, where the danger of infection, which spread disease, was particularly acute because of bad drainage and impure drinking water. Because the towns were dependent for provisions on the surrounding countryside, they were very prone to crises. Accordingly, the life expectancy of their populations was lower than that of country people.

In Central Europe the decrease in mortality and the consequent rise in life expectancy seem to have begun in the last quarter of the eighteenth century. This did not apply in the same degree to all age groups: there were differences in mortality rates between men and women, infants and children, young adults and the elderly.

If one compares the increase in life expectancy of the new-born with that of 60-year-olds, it may be seen that for the former it was immeasurably higher than for the latter. The increase in life expectancy of the middle and higher age groups was less significant compared with that of the new-born. The new-born improved their chances of growing up considerably more than the adults improved their chances of growing very old.

In recent times, the proportion of adults and of the elderly in the population has increased markedly, more because of changes in fertility patterns than because of a higher life expectancy. As a result, fundamental changes in the relative proportions of different age groups have taken place.

As no overall figures are available for earlier times in Central Europe, we present for comparison in tables 2 and 3 three selected parishes from western Austria for which valid data for the seventeenth and eighteenth centuries have been obtained. They have been derived from documents that bear the title *status animarum* (descriptions of souls).

It is obvious that a rise of this order in the number of over-60s must have brought about an increase in those family types in which at least one person of the generation of grandparents lived together with the generation of parents when it was impossible for the genera-

Table 2
Age distribution (%) of the population in Austria, 1632–1970

Ages in years	Abtenau[1] (1632)	Dorfbeuern[2] (1671)	Zell/Ziller[3] (1779)	Austria (1900)	Austria (1951)	Austria[4] (1970)
0–15	37.3	34.0	31.3	29.7	22.9	24.4
15–60	57.1	59.1	60.1	60.8	61.4	55.2
60+	5.5	6.9	8.6	9.4	15.6	20.4

[1]*Source: Seelenbuch der Pfarre Abtenau, 1632*, Pfarrarchiv Abtenau (4112 persons).
[2]*Source: Catalogus Vivorum 1671*, Pfarrarchiv Michaelbeuern (882 persons).
[3]*Source: Liber animarum Parochiae Zellensis, Anno 1779*, Pfarrarchiv Zell am Ziller (2581 persons).
[4]*Source:* H. Helczmanovsky, 'Entwicklung der Bevölkerung Österreichs' in H. Helczmanovsky (ed.), *Beiträge zur Bevölkerungs- und Sozialgeschichte Österreichs*, Vienna, 1973, p. 134.

Table 3
Age distribution (%) of the population of the Federal German Republic,
1871–1970

Ages in years	1871	1900	1950	1970
0–15	34.3	34.8	23.3	23.2
15–65	61.0	60.3	68.2	63.6
65+	4.6	4.9	9.4	13.2

Source: G. Hohorst, J. Kocka and C. H. Ritter (eds.), *Sozialgeschichtliches Arbeitsbuch. Materialien zur Statistik des Kaiserreichs. 1870–1914*, Munich, 1975, p. 24.

tions to live separately, as was the case in rural Central Europe. During the nineteenth century, aggravated by the enormous acceleration in social change, tension and conflict between the generations became a mass phenomenon. This tension increased with a higher life expectancy. However, it must be appreciated that in preindustrial times slower progress in mastering the natural environment, which is evident in the more gradual changes in the conduct of household affairs, methods of cultivation and so on, and the consequent slow change of consciousness, produced no such patterns of values and behaviour specific to one generation as occur today.

The increase in the number of the sick and disabled old and the loss of prestige

Decrease in mortality is correlated with increase in morbidity. The impact of diseases resulting in death has been enormously reduced, so that more people have a chance to attain old age. Since a greater proportion of the elderly are old or very old, a greater proportion are ill. This frequently leads to loss of status, particularly in a society in which self-sufficiency, energy and aggression are the hallmarks of success. In the course of this development, the self-esteem of old people too, has become increasingly dominated by the association of illness with age. It is not age but illness that is the determining factor of feeling old.

Care of the elderly is more necessary now that an increasing proportion are old. But there is less opportunity to undertake the tasks within the family because their occupations take members of the family, especially women, away from home. However, the available demographic data should make us wary of exaggerating the function of large pre-industrial families in caring for their elderly members. To regard the pre-industrial agrarian family as a nursing home for the chronically ill and old appears unwarranted. Neither should it be presented as the ideal family devoted to the care of its members in order, for the most part, to promote certain social and political aims.

The problem of widowhood

Another aspect of the present-day problem of the elderly is the phenomenon of old women, mostly widows, living alone and in isolation. Historically, this is also a result of demographic change, which has reduced the number of children in the family, and its effect on the lifecycle of the family has been to lead to a longer evening of life for both spouses, but especially for the wife.

To illustrate conditions in the seventeenth and eighteenth centuries, we have again used the examples of the western Austrian parishes of Abtenau, Dorfbeuern and Zell am Ziller in table 4. To enable us to appreciate the change in the proportion of widowed in the adult population we decided to exclude all persons under 15 years of age.

Table 4 shows clearly that in pre-industrial times the proportion of widows could be twice as high as that of widowers. But because of the great difference in age between marriage partners, the proportion

Table 4
Sex-specific proportion (%) of widowed population between 15 and 99 years old

	Abtenau (1632)	Dorfbeuern (1671)	Zell/Ziller (1779)	Austria (1900)	(1969)
Widowers as proportion of total males	4	3	3.6	5	6
Widows as proportion of total females	8.7	7.6	10.5	11.6	22.5

Sources: As table 2.

Table 5
Age distribution of widowed males and females (%)

Age group	Abtenau (1632)		Dorfbeuern (1671)		Zell/Ziller (1779)	
	Widowed males	Widowed females	Widowed males	Widowed females	Widowed males	Widowed females
0–9						
10–19						
20–29	2.0	0.9	0	4.3	0	0
30–39	10.2	16.5	0	4.3	3.0	5.1
40–49	12.2	13.0	0	13.0	15.2	17.2
50–59	20.4	23.5	0	30.4	12.1	20.2
60–69	34.7	30.4	37.5	34.8	21.2	30.3
70–79	20.4	8.7	50.0	8.7	27.3	22.2
80–89	0	4.3	12.5	4.3	12.1	3.0
90–99	0	2.6	0	0	9.1	2.0
N	(49)	(115)	(8)	(23)	(33)	(99)

Source: As table 2.

of younger widows was larger (see table 5). There were also, although less frequently, married women who were older than their husbands. As we have remarked, this occurred particularly in artisan households, when the master's widow remarried or a daughter who had remained at home married a young journeyman so that the family enterprise might be maintained.

Similarly the great differences in age between spouses in rural areas were mainly due to the economic pressure to remarry. Heads of peasant households who were widowed, and sometimes widowed wives too, had to think of remarrying quickly because of the requirements of the domestic economy, as well as those of rearing the children. This compulsion to fill the central positions in the household that was a consequence of the needs of the domestic economy limited the scope of potential marriage partners immensely. For the daughters of artisans who wanted to continue the family enterprise, choice was confined to their father's journeymen, for instance. This often resulted in marriage partners being separated by what would to us seem a great difference in age.

The trend over the last two centuries has been a continuous decline of remarriage. This has been the consequence of a decrease in the social and economic importance of filling the central positions in the family, which has allowed for a greater number of 'incomplete' families. Increased length of marriage and a decrease in the number of remarriages are of great importance to the problem of ageing, and especially to the quality of the marriage partnership. These factors must be regarded as conditioning the growing intimacy of family life during the last two centuries.

It is understandable that in the course of this development emotional and social burdens should have been placed not only on the relationships between marriage partners but also on relationships between the generations. The loss of a life-time marriage partner or of a parent makes a deeper psychological impression today than would have been the case in pre-industrial times, when family connections were of comparatively short duration.

Care of the elderly in the multi-generational family

Lower age at marriage and a higher life expectancy have led to the creation of more multi-generational families. Even if the generations do not live together, the numbers of great-grandparents, particularly of great-grandmothers, are constantly increasing in modern industrial societies. Comparative research by Shanas and others into the situation of the old in Denmark, Britain and the United States has established that in all three countries there are substantial numbers of great-grandparents: 40 per cent of 65-year-olds in the United States had great-grandchildren, 22 per cent in Britain and 23 per cent in Denmark. This completely new phenomenon is referred to as the 'four-generation family' and also as the 'modified extended family'. It is a social structure made up of parents, children and other relatives who are closely associated in spite of the fact that as a rule they live apart from each other.

In this four-generational network – great-grandparents, grandparents, parents and children – the position of the grandparents is of particular interest. The third generation consists of both grandparents more frequently than was the case at the turn of the century. They are still relatively young and hardly need the help of their children. They are therefore more involved with their grandchildren, especially if the young mother is working, and their assistance may also be called upon by the fourth generation. Thus the relatively young grandparents occupy a helping position between their grand-children and their own parents.

In this social situation ageing has acquired a new quality. In pre-industrial times there was little chance of the formation of even a three-generational family, because of a lower life expectancy and a higher age at marriage. Accordingly, families in which both grand-parents were alive were rare. (In contrast with this situation in Cen-tral Europe, the Russian serf population is known to have married when both spouses were in their teens and the potential for complex households containing several generations was considerable.)

For Central Europe it would appear that the picture of the large pre-industrial family, 'great-grandmother, grandmother, mother and child' living together, is a myth, though if the generations of a family survived long enough to see each other, they did certainly live together more frequently than they do nowadays. For although in modern industrial societies early marriage and a higher life expec-tancy promote the formation of three- and even four-generational families, the generations do not usually form a communal household.

This leads us to consider the phenomenon of neo-locality, genera-tions of children and parents living apart from each other.

Neo-locality and 'post-parental comradeship'

The enormous increase in neo-locality in Austria and Central Europe during the nineteenth and twentieth centuries had its origin in urban-ization and industrialization, more particularly in the increase in liv-ing accommodation and occupational mobility. More people were able to start families because new occupations were created, which led to an increase in occupational opportunities. In the pre-industrial period, the ability to marry was confined for the most part to those who occupied the principal positions in agrarian and artisan enter-prises. The pre-industrial farming and craft household could nor-mally only feed and sustain the newly formed family of the inherit-ing child or the son- or daughter-in-law who took over.

Neo-locality – that is, the establishment of an independent house-hold by a child who married – followed naturally from the increas-ing employment opportunities that made it possible to start a family.

But unmarried children were also more inclined to live apart from their families of origin because they had a job and thus were independent.

Nowadays a young couple generally lives with parents only when the management of a family enterprise undertaking is passed directly from father to son, as was the rule in pre-industrial times, mainly in peasant families but sometimes in the trades and crafts as well. The term that we have come to use for this is the 'perennial family', by which we mean the overlapping of the generations and various transitional phases in the family cycle.

In modern times it has become the rule in most families that children leave the parental home when they are grown up, and this must be seen as a consequence of the historic process of releasing the family from its productive functions. The decline of the function of the family in allocating rank-specific social positions and status to its members may well be regarded as a structural change favouring the emancipation of the individual. By contrast with the 'perennial family', the frequent departure of children from the parental household produces the family cycle and, with it, the phenomenon of 'post-parental comradeship' (Rosenmayr). Nowadays this phase has become increasingly important to the elderly, although it scarcely occurred in the agrarian societies of pre-industrial Central Europe.

Apart from a higher life expectancy, the important factors that have prompted the development of this phase are a lower age at marriage, and the fact that the period during which the children are raised both starts and ends earlier. The younger the children are when they leave home, the longer the phase of post-parental comradeship. In addition, the number of children has decreased, and the intervals between births have become shorter by comparison with those of pre-industrial times, when surviving infants were separated by a longer timespan because of higher child mortality and perhaps also because of longer periods of lactation. The phase of child rearing therefore continued into the last years of the parents' life and frequently beyond the death of one of the parents.

In the course of demographic development fewer and fewer children have been born at shorter and shorter intervals. The phase of child rearing has become correspondingly briefer, and children have left the parental household earlier. Post-parental comradeship has been the result, and it can be evaluated against the background of historical development. Proposals for the solution of these present-day problems that are based on the pre-industrial large family fail to recognize the true relationships and associations that were prevalent in earlier times.

The isolation of the old: a recent phenomenon

Historically speaking, the isolation of the aged, like post-parental comradeship, is a relatively recent phenomenon. It is mainly a result of industrialization and urbanization, as shown by the striking proportion of people, especially women, living on their own in cities. In Vienna, for instance, more than 50 per cent of single (widowed, divorced or unmarried) women over 65 live in single-person households, as opposed to only 7 per cent of women over 65 in the rural population of Lower Austria (Rosenmayr). The perennial character of the peasant family and its links with the land tended to integrate the aged into the families of their children, an effect much more marked, of course, among peasant than among non-peasant families. Even today as much as 44 per cent of the rural population of Lower Austria aged 60 or over live in a household containing one of their married children. Among the non-peasant population of Lower Austria only 14 per cent of this age group live with one of their married children. In Vienna the proportion of parents over 60 living with one of their married children is as low as 3 per cent (Kaufmann).

In pre-industrial times, very few single people lived entirely on their own in the towns. This did not become a mass phenomenon until the nineteenth century. Most old people lived in very large households. It can be shown, for example, that in the Salzburg parish of Abtenau, which has already been drawn upon to illustrate conditions in the seventeenth century, the largest number of widowers occurred in ten-person households and the largest number of widows in eight-person households. These large pre-industrial domestic groups, however, were less frequently three-generational than today's peasant families. Their size was due primarily not to great numbers of children but to the number of persons living in the house as servants or inmates. Only when it is viewed in this light is the concept of the large pre-industrial family at all justifiable.

The reduction in the size of the household and family in the industrial era is to be explained mainly by the reduction in the number of persons belonging to these two groups. The number of inmates decreased during the seventeenth and eighteenth centuries and, after a temporary increase, the number of servants decreased after the middle of the nineteenth century.

These changes in the composition of the Austrian household naturally had serious consequences for the social position of the elderly. Whereas in pre-industrial times they generally lived with a large number of relatives and non-relatives, in the industrial period they have lived with far fewer people or entirely alone. For the household is now reduced to the nuclear family, and after the children have left home, the generations are separated from each other residentially. Old people therefore nearly always consort only with people of their own age now, whereas in pre-industrial times the old associated with people of different ages in the household. It must also be remembered that the composition of the rural domestic group was prone to continuous change. Servants moved practically every year and inmates usually every few years; sons and daughters were constantly leaving home to hire themselves out as men- and maidservants; foster children came and went. Thus elderly people probably had considerable experience of living with non-related persons early in their lives.

By contrast with this, the generations are now separated from each other in the 'empty nest' phase of the modern nuclear family, in which old people are reduced to associating with a small number of persons of their own age, often for long periods of time. Now that the home and the place of work are no longer the same, members of the family who go out to work are more dependent on the people they meet at work for their social contacts. But with retirement these contacts often lapse, thus increasing the isolation of old people. The consequence is that ageing people cannot get used to living with non-related persons. (Perhaps this explains their difficulties in adapting to living conditions in institutions that care for the elderly.)

Today most members of the family work outside the home, and it is often difficult, if not impossible, for them to look after elderly parents and relatives. The state is therefore increasingly involved in taking over the duties formerly carried out by the family; in order to fulfil this task, the state collects and administers financial contributions from the generation at work in the form of taxes, social security, pensions, insurance and so on.

Since the transfer of responsibility for the care of the elderly from the family to society has not been an autonomous historical development, independent of changes in the system of production, attempts to devise socio-political models that leave these social tendencies out of account are quite unacceptable, especially if they suggest solutions based on an idealized view of past methods of caring for the old. Nevertheless, the conservative interpretation of familial responsibility, insisting as it does that transfer of support from family to institutions is justified only in exceptional cases, cannot be repudiated without at the same time calling for a radical improvement in the organization of existing institutions for the old.

These historical changes in the family cycle and in demography underline the need for a comprehensive study of the problems of ageing. This study should not confine itself to a limited group of the aged but should strive to provide a social history of the various stages of the ageing process over the whole lifespan, a history analogous to the 'sociology of the stages of age' that Rosenmayr has proposed. Macro-historical comparison can show that we cannot assume the limits of old age to be precisely defined. Indeed, the same age measured in years has different consequences for the psychological, social and economic situation of old people in relation to time, class and culture. Hence, it is necessary to comprehend ageing as a whole social process, itself undergoing historical change. Only with the aid of such a comprehensive concept is it possible to understand clearly why society, through the attribution of social roles and positions, through legal norms, traditions and evaluations, has come to limit and define ageing according to time, class and culture, which in turn has given rise to different patterns of behaviour and problems among the ageing.

SELECT BIBLIOGRAPHY

Abel, Wilhelm, *Massenarmut und Hungerkrisen im vorindustriellen Europa*, Hamburg/Berlin, 1974.

Kaufmann, Albert, *Demographische Struktur und Haushalts- und Familienformen der Wiener Bevölkerung*, Vienna, 1971.

König, René, 'Die strukturelle Bedeutung des Alters in den fortgeschrittenen Industriegesellschaften' in René König, *Soziologische Orientierungen. Reden und Aufsätze*, Cologne, 1973, pp. 134ff.

Laslett, Peter, 'The history of aging and the aged' in Peter Laslett, *Family life and illicit love in earlier generations*, Cambridge, 1977, pp. 174ff.

Rosenmayr, Leopold, 'Schwerpunkte der Soziologie des Alters

(Gerosoziologie)' in René König (ed.), *Handbuch der empirischen Sozial-forschung*, vol. 7, 2nd edn, Stuttgart, 1976, pp. 218ff.

Rosenmayr, Leopold and Köckeis, Eva, *Umwelt und Familie alter Menschen*, Neuwied/Berlin, 1965.

Rosenmayr, Leopold and Rosenmayr, Hilde, *Der alte Mensch in der Gesellschaft*, Reinbek bei Hamburg, 1978.

Shanas, Ethel and Streib, Gordon F. (eds.) *Social structure and the family, generational relations*, Englewood Cliffs, NJ, 1965.

Shanas, Ethel, Townsend, P., Wedderburn, D., Milhøj, P., Friis, H. and Stehouwer, J., *Old people in three industrial societies*, New York, 1968.

Simmons, Leo, 'Aging in preindustrial societies' in C. Tibbitts (ed.), *Handbook of social gerontology – societal aspects of aging*, Chicago, 1960, pp. 62ff.

Tartler, Rudolf, *Das Alter in der modernen Gesellschaft*, Stuttgart, 1961.

Tews, Hans Peter, *Soziologie des Alterns*, Heidelberg, 1974.

Wrigley, E. A. and Schofield, R. S., *The population of England 1541–1871: a reconstruction*, London, 1981.

8

The Care of the Elderly and the Domestic Economy

Growing old is man's inevitable fate. Every society, past and present, has had to deal with the problem of the integration of ageing people. In the course of history the need and the opportunity to provide for the specific situation of the aged have changed according to the prevailing stage in the organization of labour.

In modern industrial society we are used to people no longer being compelled to work after a certain age. The date at which the person who has been in employment enters into retirement represents a decisive break. It marks the start of a clearly defined phase in his life, which is accompanied by particular economic and psychological problems. To us, therefore, old age is a specific phase in the individual's life cycle and is linked inseparably with retirement.

However, international labour statistics show that marking the starting point of the stage of being elderly by the date of retirement from work does not occur all over the world, even at the present time. Whereas the number of those over 65 who are gainfully employed is about 20 per cent in an industrial nation like the German Federal Republic, the comparative figure for semi-industrialized states is over 60 per cent and for predominantly agrarian states around 70 per cent. Such differences show the extent to which the process of industrialization brings about changed conditions for old people in modern times. This leads us to the subject of the historical development of present-day industrial nations.

The phase of old age in industrial society

There are two historical factors in particular that have given rise to the division between the work phase and the retirement phase in industrial society: higher life expectancy and change in the organization of work.

The first of these has not been brought about directly by industrialization, but rather by the modernization process that has run parallel with industrialization. The rise in average life expectancy has led to an ever-increasing proportion of the population reaching an age at which physiological processes reduce the capacity for work. In pre-industrial times many people died when they were quite young and still in full possession of their physical faculties, but since that time the percentage of ageing people in the total population has mounted steadily. The problem of retired people who are no longer able to earn their living because of their age has attained a new dimension with the enormous growth in the number of these people, which has necessitated general social solutions.

Even more important, apparently, is the second factor, the radical change in the structure of work, which now is quite different from that of pre-industrial times. Wage earners form the majority of the population today. The overwhelming predominance of those dependent on wages is, as we hope to show, by no means a consequence of industrialization alone. Factory workers are numerically very substantial indeed, but there too the overall modernization process must be considered as a determining cause. Because of the rapid increase in the number of people dependent on wages, traditional methods of caring for the elderly within the household or in institutions run by corporations have disappeared, and social insurance administered by the state has become indispensable. Statutory regulations have led to the introduction of a generally applicable age limit to working life. Retirement no longer depends on the individual's ability to work, but on his reaching a certain age. As far as wage earners are concerned, working life ends simultaneously for the whole age group. The organization of labour demands that an obligatory break in the individual's lifecycle occurs in a particular year, a phenomenon entirely unknown in pre-industrial societies.

The old in the pre-industrial working world

In the agrarian social order of pre-industrial times, the family household formed the predominant labour organization on the farmstead, in the household of the craftsman and in the merchant's house. Under these conditions, giving up work at a specific age was quite out of the question. The problem of the elderly retiring when they became partially or completely unable to work had to be solved in individual cases, of course. If an old person was gradually eased out by the rearrangement of the work load within the group, then he would experience no abrupt break in his life. Such a break would only take place if old age brought a complete change in familial roles, as, for example, when the farm was handed over to a new master, or if a farmer or master left the household altogether. It was not only the master of the house, as manager of the family enterprise, who was closely concerned in such changes, but to some extent the mistress of the house as well, because of the close connection between these two roles.

An investigation into the conditions governing loss of position by the master of the house in old age should not be confined to those households in the pre-industrial social order that produced goods in a narrow sense, the households of peasants and artisans. In those days the whole social structure was based on the house, with the master at its head, including the royal or princely court as the house of the ruler. In all these houses the position of the master was bound up with certain duties that were carried out partly within the house and partly outside it. Since it was by no means certain that the ageing master of the house could meet these obligations, the question of his position was of general importance.

Princes and nobles

In advanced old age the ruler could be partly freed from his duties by the appointment of a co-regent, which implied settling the issue of succession. The elderly ruler might find it particularly difficult to carry out the duty of leading his army into battle in person, though this did not necessarily mean that he was incapable of ruling. Ways of deputizing in military and other matters fell in the first place to the heir apparent, so that the ruler would be able to carry out his duties into advanced old age. In general, the prince could continue to rule until the end of his life: only rarely did he give up his position voluntarily.

In the Middle Ages the ruler who had abdicated usually retired to a monastery. This was a tradition followed from the time of the Carolingians onwards: Karlmann entered Montecassino in 747, and the Emperor Charles V spent the evening of his life in the Spanish monastery of San Geronimo de Yuste. There were also rulers who were forced to retire to a monastery not because of old age but because they were deposed. Voluntary or enforced retirement to a monastic community deprived a ruler of the right to bear arms: this meant a loss of responsibility and prevented the ruler from regaining his throne. Widowed princesses frequently retired to a convent where they received in old age the care that befitted their position.

The nobleman enjoyed his position as master of the house for life in the same way as the prince. He too had to deal with the problem of carrying out his military duties when he had become physically incapable of doing so. Rendering military service to the king was his primary task, for according to medieval tradition, his function as lord of the manor was to give shelter and protection to his people. Military power was therefore of fundamental importance to the social position of the nobility. However, it was precisely because of their role as warriors that many nobles did not attain a great age. Their relatively low life expectancy is established by demographic analysis, but it cannot be attributed only to death in battle or in private feuds. Epidemics were also of great consequence, for they frequently broke out during military campaigns and often carried off whole armies, as happened during the Middle Ages when German kings marched on Rome.

It has been established that nobles of advanced age still took part in military expeditions on occasion, but as a rule the old were no longer required to render military service. This did not affect their status, however, for the noble vassal also had to render 'counsel and aid' to his lord, and this he could continue to do by participating in the provincial assemblies and in the meetings of the prince's council. Changes took place in military organization during the later Middle Ages, however. There was the payment of wages to the soldiery, and above all the raising of a standing army in the seventeenth century. The duty of the nobility to render military service, therefore, became less and less important. For those Austrian and European nobles who decided to give up their life-long occupation as master of the house at an early age, there was really only one expedient in the Catholic areas: to take holy orders. Many a nobleman gave up his house and status as a layman and entered a religious house. This change of place and status is interesting because it was to be the cornerstone of a way of caring for the elderly that has played a role to the present day.

Care of the old in a monastery or hospital

The early Middle Ages provide many instances of nobles entering monasteries, to which they donated all their possessions, and so being received into religious communities. Security of maintenance for the rest of their lives does not seem to have been their only motive – it was probably not even the primary one. The motive was rather the attainment of eternal salvation through the renouncement of worldly pleasures. However, the donation of one's property to a monastery always ensured provision for old age.

As an analogy with this donation of goods and retirement to a monastery, we find the development of donations to a hospital. This took place with the rise of hospitals from the thirteenth century onwards. Originally, as we have noted, hospitals were not refuges for the sick but generally dispensed care and hospitality. The hospital was a religious community too. On being taken into a brotherhood, the beneficiary lost his independence. In the course of time, admission to this new domestic community assumed the character of an arrangement for old age. The applicant was no longer required to donate all his possessions but only such a proportion as was regarded as an adequate recompense for services rendered. Thus the right to maintenance in the institution by voluntary donation took on the character of a contractual agreement.

A decisive step in the development of this process took place in the late Middle Ages, when people were no longer forced to join the religious community of a monastery or hospital. The donation of a certain amount of property entitled the donor to be regularly supplied with goods or money for the duration of his life. Instead of being cared for in the house, he received a regular pension. Donations had been replaced by annuity agreements for life, and what was originally conceived of as provision for life and salvation for eternity by the surrender of self and property had ended up by being a purely business arrangement.

Such life annuity contracts could now be concluded not only with religious bodies but also with other institutions, such as town councils or corporations, which offered the guarantee of a permanent entitlement to a pension. The result of the change to a monetary arrangement was that the wealthy classes as well as the aristocracy attempted to introduce the taking up of annuities as a provision for old age. This custom developed mainly in the cities, where it was adopted by those who had the necessary means at their disposal. With the loss of the personal character of the donation, the pension rights could also be transferred to a third person. Such rights were purchased mainly as suitable security for the surviving wife, in order to ensure her independence from children and relatives in old age. As a result, old women lived alone in the towns from quite an early period.

Forms of old-age insurance other than the life annuity developed in the towns because of particular financial conditions. We may mention the funds of guilds and fraternities that were fed by the regular contributions of their members. Such contributions were transacted on the legal basis of donations to the Church. Fraternities placed property in special Church funds to be used for various community purposes, with the aim of caring for members of the brotherhood unable to work and for their widows and orphans. It is significant that such forms of insurance applied only in case of disablement in old age. Unlike the life annuity, it could not be used in order to secure rest without labour.

The care of the elderly farmer

In the country economic conditions were not sufficiently well developed to enable the peasants to provide financial support for their old people, as many people in the towns did during the Middle Ages. A different method of caring for the elderly was therefore practised among farming people in Austria and in Central Europe. It deserves special attention because the peasantry constituted a large proportion of the pre-industrial population in this region as everywhere else. The institution is encountered under various names, such as: *Altenteil* (old person's portion), *Ausgedinge* (stipulated right [to maintenance]), *Auszug* (departure, removal [from the farm]), *Ausnahm, Austrag, Leibzucht, Leibgedinge, Viertel* (fourth part), *Narem = Nahrung* (support, maintenance).

There is, however, general agreement about the purpose of the institution described in these different ways. The 'old person's portion' was a lawfully regulated form of care, within the framework of the household community, for the old farmer and/or his wife, together with those children who were still minors at the retirement of the parent. The old farmer therefore generally continued to live with the family. The legal arrangement was laid down in the transfer agreement. The farmer handed over his house and, with it, his position as master of the house to his successor, usually one of his sons, who then had to make sufficient provision for the old farmer and for those who went with him into retirement. This meant, in the first place, that he was regularly provided with foodstuffs, unless he continued to eat at the table of his successor. The old person's portion was therefore usually provided in kind.

The peasant economy was, in essence, an economy without money, so that the provision of care for the elderly was only feasible within the household. Providing in kind would have been impossible over a distance, for this would have involved payment in cash and the proximity of a market at which to buy food with this money. Neither existed in the rural areas of this region in pre-industrial times and it was, therefore, an economic necessity for the old farmer, alone or with his wife, to remain within the house after handing it over. The agreement to make payments in cash is only met with in more recent times, and then only in neighbourhoods near to towns, where the economy was served by a good transport system, where there were vineyards and where a monetary economy had been generally adopted.

Apart from providing food, the transfer agreement arranged for accommodation for the old people. This could take one of several forms, depending on the situation of the peasant family. In those parts of the country where scattered farms or *Weilersiedlungen* (hamlets), predominated, old people frequently retired to a small house reserved for them in the immediate neighbourhood of the farm. In village settlements it was usually not possible to build such cottages for the old. However, certain rooms in the farm were reserved for the old couple, as, for example, the so-called *Stübl* (little room) in the northern part of Lower Austria. Frequently the person handing over could only be assured of a special corner within the communal family room. In many regions the old person was also given a plot of land for his own use, provided that he was still capable of cultivating it. Handing over the farm was not necessarily followed by total exclusion from the farmer's family as a production unit. The old farmer could continue to co-operate as long as he was willing and able.

The origin of the retirement agreement

The organization of work on the farmstead did not make retirement absolutely necessary. Where men- and maidservants or grown-up children were available, the old farmer could hand over to them work that he no longer had the strength to do without having to give up his position as master of the house. In some regions of the country the farmer remained in charge until he reached an advanced age, and the farm was handed over only in exceptional circumstances, as in certain parts of the Tyrol or Salzburg, for example. In other areas transferring the farm was the rule. Those handing over varied considerably in age. Some went into retirement in their early fifties, particularly those on richer farms which were in a position to carry such an economic burden for a long time. But as a rule the transfer did not take place until the farmer was about 60 years old. Diminishing physical strength was by no means always the only reason for giving up the management of the farming enterprise. Whether and when it was handed over depended on a number of factors, and local traditions played an important role. This leads us to consider the origins of the retirement custom, which are by no means entirely clear.

Retirement arrangements may be traced back to the early Middle Ages. Seignorial rights may have played a significant role in their origin. In considering the development of the institution, it must be assumed that there could have been no agreement, free from outside influence, between the person who retired and his successor, until the former owned the farm as property. This was impossible until the lord of the manor had given up his overlordship. It is true that hundreds of years earlier there had been large territories in Central Europe with free peasant inheritance, where the lord did not influence the transfer of the farm. However, the origin of retirement rights goes back to the time when the lord was in a position to interfere to great effect when the farm property changed hands. Therefore the retirement of the old farmer was unlikely to have been, in its origin, a voluntary matter.

The transfer and management of the farm

During the Middle Ages the serfs among the peasant population who lived on a farm could be moved away or exchanged without their having a say in the matter. But even when the personal freedom of the peasant was recognized, there were certain restricted forms of tenure that made it possible for the landlord to make a new appointment to the farmer's position at a suitable point in time. There was, for example, the *Freistiftrecht*, which restricted the lease of the farm to only one year. Naturally, frequent changes were not in the landlord's interest because these would endanger the orderly conduct of business and consequently the tributes rendered to him by the farm. But even with such restricted forms of tenure, in practice the property remained under the same ownership over long periods of time and was bequeathed to a son.

The appointment of a new farmer did not, as a rule, mean that the old farmer was actually expelled from his property. If he had conducted the business well, he was given the right to a place to live and to eat, as were his wife and any children who were still under age. As a result, the old farmer and his family would live with his successor to the property, who might be a son or some other relative or perhaps someone who was not even related to them. In seventeenth-century Austrian documents one frequently finds references to retired old people who did not bear the same name as the owner of the farm. The fact that the old farmer remained on the farm does not always mean that he was being cared for within the framework of the family community. Old people who lived together with non-relatives were quite frequent in the agrarian society of pre-industrial times.

The landlord became concerned about a new appointment to the farm when the current owner was no longer able to conduct the business efficiently because of old age, although he might not be entirely incapable of carrying on. If a grown-up son seemed likely to be better able to manage the farm than his ageing father, the landlord might consider making a change. This might also happen if the farmer was widowed, for the role of the housewife was of central importance to the economy of the farming enterprise. Too long a retirement was not very desirable for the landlord either because of the burden it placed on the farm. Retirement was a widespread institution in those places where the landlord exercised a considerable influence over appointments on farms. And in these districts retirement retained its importance as the farmer's customary right, even when the landlord's influence had declined. On the other hand, arrangements for the farmer's old age portion were less in evidence in places where the right to inherit had obtained for a long time. The interest of the old farmer in retaining his position as master of the house for as long as possible triumphed over eventual economic disadvantages.

With the rationalization of seignorial organization in early modern times the effectiveness of the farmer's management of the domestic economy became of greater importance to the landlord. These economic changes may well have played a part in the spread of retirement rights. Another quite different outside influence came with the newly ordered military organization of the eighteenth century. Many farmers decided to hand over the farm at an early age so that their sons might be excused from military service. This may well have led to parents and grandparents living in retirement at the same time. The rise in life expectancy in the nineteenth century also increased the number of retirement arrangements for the old. In earlier times there was frequently no need to hand over the farm because of old age, for the farmer often died while still in full possession of his physical faculties. Orphans who survived the farmer were occasionally a greater problem than grown-up sons, who would have welcomed the transfer, since they wished to become independent and to marry. In the nineteenth century the situation changed radically. In many places the number of retirements doubled within a few decades.

Generations living together

It was only with the increase in the number of retirements that the multi-generational family became a dominant feature of rural areas of Central Europe. It was by no means the historical form of the family as such, as the conservative social historians of the nineteenth century would have us believe. They held it up as a model of the right way of caring for the elderly in emerging industrialized society. Folklorists, family sociologists and social historians have adopted this ideologically biased picture.

By dwelling so much on the virtues of the three-generational family, they ignored the disadvantages of the retirement rights associated with it. The conflict between father and son before the transfer of the property was one of the difficulties, together with the legal battles over the conclusion of the arrangement and its provisions, and the psychologically difficult situation of the old farmer in the household community after the loss of his position as master of the house. As we have remarked, the often petty regulations of the retirement agreement indicate that the generations did not always live together harmoniously. The old farmer, for instance, was given permission in writing to enter by the front door, to use a certain chair and so on.

Peasant proverbs illustrate the experiences of the old: 'To hand over is no longer to live', 'To sit on the children's bench is hard for the old', 'Do not take your clothes off before you go to sleep.' The description of retirement as *Ableben* (to give up living) is an expression of this feeling. It was used in southern Burgenland and in some districts of the Steiermark. The loss of status in one's own eyes and in the eyes of others was to some extent balanced by the uninterrupted integration of the aged into the community he was used to. He was taken care of when the need arose and was allowed to occupy himself for as long as he was able. Retirement rights may well have been the best solution to the problem of caring for the elderly, given the economic conditions in the country in earlier times. But the cohabitation of different generations is certainly not to be seen as the only way of dealing with the problem of ageing.

Providing for care in old age in agrarian society was a difficulty not only for the old farmer himself but also for his wife, whose fate was largely dependent on that of her husband. When he handed over the farm, she went with him into retirement. If he kept the farm until the end of his life, she could, after his death, arrange for her own retirement. If there was a considerable difference in age between the widow and the deceased husband, which might happen if it was a second or third marriage, then she might have to put up with a very long period of retirement. If she had a partial claim to the property, she could retain her position as housewife by entering into a new marriage. Remarrying as a means of caring for the widow was quite common in Austria and Central Europe in pre-industrial times in farming, as well as in town circles.

Servants and inmates

The need to look after men- and maidservants in old age hardly posed a problem in the society of the pre-industrial period. Statistics derived from seventeenth- and even eighteenth-century sources show that service was a temporary phase in a person's life: only a few men- and maidservants over 30 years of age were to be found in the countryside. Many became independent as farmers or farmers' wives. Most of the others would also marry and then live as inmates on a farm. We must not think of the farm servants of former times as remaining single for all their lives, at least not according to the evidence of Austrian documents. At 40 years of age practically the whole population was either married or already widowed.

Aged inmates presented the most difficult problem in the countryside. They mostly ran small businesses, or worked as day labourers, timberworkers, carters and so on. As payment for their right to live on the farm, they helped at those times when there was a need for additional workers, above all at harvest time. The basis of subsistence for the maintenance of the family of an *Inwohner* was extremely slender, and times of crisis presented a special danger. This was particularly true as they grew old.

The farmer's means of caring for the retired were not available to them. When they were unable to work, they were either taken into a farmer's household for the rest of their lives as an act of mercy, or they were handed on from household to household in the community. (This custom, also found in Scandinavia, especially Norway, has so far never been found in England.) In the seventeenth and eighteenth centuries these rural paupers posed a considerable social problem. An attempt was made to solve it either by forbidding people to marry if they had no house or by setting them up as cotters, which supplied them with a minimum of provisions. But cotters could not rely on being cared for in old age by the specific peasant institution of retirement rights.

With the increase in the number of day labourers, the problem of potential elderly dependents of wage earners appeared on a massive scale. And this applied not only to day labourers employed on the land but also to the men employed in the forests, in transport, in shipping and, above all, in the mines. The case of miners is discussed below.

The artisan in old age

There was no solution comparable with the farmer's retirement arrangement for the old craftsman in the cities of Austria and Central

Europe in pre-industrial times. There were several reasons for this.

In the first place, most crafts could be practised throughout life, as far as the required physical strength was concerned. The problem of releasing the old master from work was not as great in artisan enterprises as it was on the farms. Secondly, accommodation in the cities was more cramped than in the country, so that it was not easy to set aside a separate room for the old master craftsman and his wife. Lastly, to care for the old in the way dictated by an economy based on the land, which would have tied them to the house, was neither possible nor necessary in familial artisan enterprises. The craftsman, unlike the farmer, did not produce the foodstuffs needed for survival. On the other hand, through his market connections he did have money at his disposal, so that care of the elderly outside the household might be accomplished by such an expedient as buying a place in a hospital in the town. Again, the craftsman was not dependent on a landlord; unlike the farmer, he could not be forced to give up his position as head of the family and master of the house. When he eventually did give up work, it was not done at the insistence of the landlord.

Under these very different conditions it was exceptional to find the same family circumstances as those in which old and young farming couples lived together with their children. Three-generational families did occur, though not often. They occurred, for instance, when the widow of the master lived in the household community. It was characteristic of the conditions of the crafts that widows took care of themselves by remarrying, frequently journeymen younger than themselves. By contrast with the farmer's widow, the artisan's widow could be financially provided for. If her husband had left her an adequate income, her livelihood in old age was secured. It was already becoming possible for her to receive a life annuity, as well as contributions from the fraternity associations. Of course, the town also offered opportunities for the widowed woman to earn some money by sewing, spinning, stitching, washing, cleaning and carrying water, although this would not be sufficient to provide her with a living. In old age widows in towns did not, as a rule, live in isolation. They often dwelt as members of a household with non-related persons or with other widows.

Journeymen in the city who finally achieved the status of master craftsman did not have to face the problem of old age. But as the guilds of master craftsmen became exclusive in the late Middle Ages, journeymen had to wait for a longer and longer time before they could become independent; indeed, they sometimes did not achieve this goal at all. If ageing journeymen were not kept by their masters in their households, they had to look for outside employment as day labourers.

To work for wages by the day was one way for old people to eke out a scanty livelihood. The man who had not achieved independence by attaining the mastership or a similar position and the man who could not remain in his master's house as journeyman or servant in old age had no other means of securing a livelihood. As the position of servant in the town increasingly lost its temporary character as a stage in his lifecycle, those who lost their jobs were driven to earning a daily wage, which was a highly uncertain and insecure source of income. Old age and poverty became synonymous for those people.

Wage earning in the pre-industrial world

In the pre-industrial cities of these regions of traditional Europe, people who spent their entire lives working for a daily wage certainly existed. Wage labour did not make its first appearance with industrialization. There were the labourers in building, who were especially numerous in the princely capitals of the Baroque period. There were those employed in transport, such as carters, keepers of pack-horses, messengers and boat crews, and there were the many employees of the city itself, those in subordinate positions such as constables, nightwatchmen and ushers. It was generally accepted that all those who were employed in these jobs should, like the craftsmen, continue to be so until the end of their lives. There was no security for old age, however: the families of such persons were seldom in a position to provide it. Those who were unable to work had to rely on public charity. In the course of time, religious and municipal relief organizations became unable to cope with the increase in the number of the city's poor. Begging was therefore the only solution.

Life expectancy in pre-industrial towns was generally low, especially among the lower classes. Surviving widows of day labourers and other city wage earners therefore presented a serious problem for those who had to care for them. Remarriage was no solution for the widows of labourers, as it was for artisans' widows, for they had nothing to contribute to a marriage. As a rule, their children could

not look after them, for at their father's death the children themselves
were often still in need of care. True, there were more opportunities
for townswomen than for women in the country to earn something
extra, but not enough to provide lasting security.

In pre-industrial times in the Central European region wage-
earning was most fully developed in mining, which was a large-scale
industry in a world of small-scale family enterprises as early as the
Middle Ages. The social situation of mine workers was therefore in
many respects comparable with that of factory workers in modern
industry. Care for those unable to work because of illness or old age
had to be provided accordingly. Dangerous working conditions in
the mines might incapacitate the miner and force him to retire early.
His family, since it did not function as a productive unit, was not in a
position to protect or to provide for him. Fellowship associations had
to undertake this task. As an extension of the fraternities to which
the miners regularly contributed, there were special miners' funds.
Because of the conditions obtaining in mining, these insurance
arrangements soon reached a stage of development that anticipated
by several hundred years many of the principles of modern social
security. A fixed age of retirement was not introduced until the
second half of the nineteenth century, however. Until that time, in
mining, as in many other parts of the pre-industrial working world,
only sickness in old age justified retirement from work.

Wage earning in industry

With industrialization, wage earning became a mass phenomenon.
By contrast with craft methods of production, large-scale factory
production involved employment outside the home. It also involved
payment of the individual, regardless of his family situation. The
level of wages did not allow the industrial labourer to save enough to
compensate him for the loss of employment in sickness or old age.
Neither was it possible for his family to do so. He was also denied the
artisan's traditional participation in types of insurance constructed
entirely on the basis of individual contributions to the guild fraternities. In the end, the problem of old age and sickness had to be
solved by the state. But it was only after a considerable delay that the
state reacted to the changed conditions in the organization of labour
caused by industrialization.

Imperial Germany was the first country in which old-age insurance was regulated by law. Bismarck initiated proposals to deal with social insurance in 1889, and in 1891 legislation was passed making old age and sickness insurance compulsory, entitling wage earners to draw a pension at 70 years of age. It was not until 1916 that the age limit for workers was reduced to 65 years, as had been the case for employees. The labourer's widow was not included in the insurance at the outset. As late as 1911 legislators justified this omission by stating that widows of labourers 'could well be expected to work', whereas widows of employees 'could not adapt so easily to many types of work'.

Austria-Hungary followed Germany's example a little later, with legislation for workers' accident and sickness insurance, and was later still with old-age insurance. Voluntary pension funds supported by the state had existed for some time in England and in other Western European countries, but it was not until 1908 that the old person's entitlement to social insurance was laid down by British law. In Britain too 70 years was fixed as the age of retirement. In 1910 France introduced compulsory insurance for all wage earners.

Civil servants and white-collar workers

Wage earning had its origins only partly in the industrialization process, although it was the most important. Greater bureaucratization also had much to do with its becoming predominant. In the public sector, this led to the foundation of the Civil Service. In the secondary and tertiary industries, bureaucratization created a class of white-collar workers. The government bureaucracy had its origin in the service of the royal house. As long as such offices were not the only source of income and were not held for life, there was no need to provide for the position of former office holders or to care for them in old age. With the extension of government departments in early modern times, the problem became more acute. Earlier attempts at a solution had been modelled on Church officialdom. A younger man was attached to a functionary when he became elderly and unable to carry out his duties. These he then handed over partly or wholly to the young assistant, with whom he shared the income of his post by mutual agreement. Sometimes the assistant was a son, a son-in-law or some other person of his choice.

The principle of retaining a post for life and of being dismissible only under certain circumstances became general among civil servants in the period of enlightened absolutism in Germany and Austria. At the same time it was realized that pension arrangements had to be made for old age and illness, and lower royal servants were pensioned off in old age. Provision for widows depended on the charity of the ruler and developed only gradually into a legal right. Civil servants did not receive a pension as of right when they reached a certain age, but only when they were no longer able to work because of illness and old age. In these circles too, old age entirely relieved of any obligation to work was at first unknown.

Assistants in the great merchant houses were the precursors of modern salaried employees. The position of a merchant's assistant was originally held by a young man for a limited number of years, a temporary phase in his life, as was all service in former times. He always had the opportunity of becoming independent, as indeed did some of the employees of the earlier entrepreneurs. The mechanization of industrial production and the expansion of enterprise in the nineteenth century necessitated a considerable increase in the salaried employee group. To become independent was now generally impossible. A development took place similar to that which had taken place in the crafts and in industry especially: a temporary, age-specific period of service gave way to permanent employment dependent on a salary. With this development, arrangements for the care of the aged became necessary. Austria-Hungary was the first country to introduce legalized pension insurance for salaried employees in 1906. The German Empire followed in 1911 and other European countries at short intervals. A retirement age of 65 years was adopted on the introduction of pension insurance for employees.

Effects on wage earning

Industrialization and bureaucratization have made wage earning the predominant way of earning a living in the modern world, and this seems to be a continuing development. The number of those in receipt of a wage or salary rises constantly, while the number of those who are independently employed perpetually shrinks. The family enterprise, which in the pre-industrial period represented the dominant form of labour organization, is now largely confined to the continually diminishing agrarian sector. In modern industrial society, the overwhelming majority of families have no productive function.

Many of the present-day social problems of old people must be seen in the light of this historical development. The decrease of family enterprises and the transition to forms of employment outside the household have led to a separation of the place of work from the home and to the family's becoming more private. The employed man in old age has been affected by this emergence of privacy in a different way from the housewife.

For the man, departure from public and professional life and the start of retirement represent a definitive break, a situation which did not exist under pre-industrial conditions of work. The sudden change and the interruption of social contacts made in the course of a professional career often bring psychological problems in their wake. To make new contacts in old age is not easy. The person leaving his life at work is faced with the difficult task of finding new fulfilment in the familial privacy of his retirement.

This privacy has always limited the wife's opportunities to establish personal relationships. The social bonds of old people have been established in earlier phases of their lives. Therefore the housewife will have difficulty in making new contacts in old age. She enjoys a higher life expectancy than the man and will therefore experience a longer period of widowhood, and this will entail the risk of isolation.

With the gradual spread of wage-earning, there is greater opportunity for young people to begin their working lives at an early age and to become independent of their parents. By contrast with conditions in the pre-industrial family enterprise, this means that generations living at the same time have their separate homes. The neo-locality of children brings about the 'empty nest' phase in the family cycle. Such a phase, with both parents or one surviving parent remaining behind, could occur in cities in the pre-industrial period, but it did not become a general feature of society until more recent times. Here again, it is the change in the economic structure that has led to the isolation and loneliness of the aged.

The change in the structure of employment has also brought about a change in the social evaluation of the old. Professional status and social worth are closely connected. When men continued to work all their lives, as most of them did until late in the nineteenth century, there was no loss of self-esteem in old age. On the contrary, greater experience or a rise to a higher professional post could lead to an increase in prestige in later life. This might happen to the old master in his craft and to the senior civil servant. Being pensioned off, on the other hand, now means departure from the working world and a loss of social esteem. Retirement frequently causes a drop in social standing, since prevalent standards of value are based on employment and on professional status.

A socio-political model based on past family forms?

Problems of old age in the contemporary world cannot be solved by a return to the family forms of the past. A vanished social order in which the position of old people was less precarious cannot furnish us with models for the improvement of present–day conditions. The social context within which they prevailed is irretrievably lost.

The separation of work- from living-place, and with it the contrast between the public, professional world and the private world of the family, is the irreversible result of historical development. But it is highly questionable whether the model of familial intimacy should remain restricted to the narrowing circle of the nuclear family. The problem of isolation in old age might become less acute if in earlier phases of the cycle the small family could live less within itself.

Generations co-residing on the farmstead can assuredly no longer provide us with a valid model for the care of the elderly. To represent the care for the elderly as above all the duty of the children is an anachronistic relic of a time when there were no solutions other than those to be found within the framework of the family. But a reconsideration of our ideas along these lines should not lead us to transfer individual responsibility to anonymous institutions either.

The constant increase in the number of old-age pensioners is a social reality in our world. It does not help to bemoan the loss of prestige that they suffer now because they have been forced to give up work. It is an open question, however, whether we are justified in applying to those no longer actively employed standards of value based on work performance. It cannot be the aim of a study of the position of the aged in the past to revive historical conditions. What must be uppermost in our minds is the need to understand the historical origins of today's problems concerning the old. If such an attempted explanation is the first to displace anachronistic and obsolete values, attitudes and ideas, then historical analysis will have contributed to the solution of present-day problems.

SELECT BIBLIOGRAPHY

Baumert, Gerhard, 'Changes in the family and the position of older persons in Germany', *International Journal of Comparative Sociology* 1 (1960), pp. 202ff.

Berkner, Lutz Karl, 'The stem-family and the developmental cycle of the peasant household: an eighteenth-century Austrian example', *American Historical Review* 77 (1972), pp. 398ff.

'Inheritance, land tenure and peasant family: a German regional comparison' in Jack Goody *et al.* (eds.), *Family and inheritance*, Cambridge, 1976, pp. 71ff.

Demleitner, Josef, 'Hofübergabe und Heirat im bayerischen Alpenvorland', *Volk und Volkstum* 3 (1938), pp. 54ff.

Fick, Ludwig, *Die bäuerliche Erbfolge im rechtsrheinischen Bayern (Münchener volkswirtschaftliche Studien)*, Stuttgart, 1895.

Hintze, Otto, *Der Beamtenstand (Vorträge der Gehe-Stiftung zu Dresden 3)*, Dresden, 1911.

Homans, George, *English villagers of the thirteenth century*, Cambridge, 1941.

Horáček, C., *Das Ausgedinge. Eine agrarpolitische Studie mit besonderer Berücksichtigung der böhmischen Länder (Wiener staatswissenschaftliche Studien 1)*, Vienna, 1904.

Kretschmer, Ingrid and Piegler, Josef, 'Ausgedinge' in *Österreichischer Volkskunde-Atlas*, 2/18 Commentary, 1965.

Mitterauer, Michael, 'Zur Familienstruktur in ländlichen Gebieten Österreichs im 17. Jahrhundert' in Heimold Helczmanovszki (ed.), *Beiträge zur Bevölkerungs- und Sozialgeschichte Österreichs*, Vienna, 1973, pp. 167ff.

'Vorindustrielle Familienformen. Zur Funktionsentlastung des "ganzen Hauses" im 17. und 18. Jahrhundert', *Wiener Beiträge zur Geschichte der Neuzeit* 2 (1975), pp. 123ff. (= Michael Mitterauer, *Grundtypen alteuropäischer Sozialformen*, Stuttgart, 1979, pp. 35ff.).

'Auswirkungen von Urbanisierung und Frühindustrialisierung auf die Familienverfassung an Beispielen des österreichischen Raums' in Werner Conze (ed.), *Sozialgeschichte der Familie in der Neuzeit Europas*, Stuttgart, 1976, pp. 53ff.

'Zur familienbetrieblichen Struktur im zünftischen Handwerk' in *Wirtschafts- und sozialhistorische Beiträge (Festschrift für Alfred Hoffmann)*, Vienna, 1979, pp. 190ff. (= Michael Mitterauer, *Grundtypen alteuropäischer Sozialformen*, Stuttgart, 1979, pp. 98ff.).

Ogris, Werner, *Der mittelalterliche Leibrentenvertrag (Wiener rechtsgeschichtliche Arbeiten* 6), Vienna, 1961.

Piepenbroek, J., *Die Entwicklung des Altenteils oder Leibzucht unter besonderer Berücksichtigung von Westfalen*, Münster, 1926.

Planck, Ulrich, *Der bäuerliche Familienbetrieb zwischen Patriarchat und Partnerschaft*, Stuttgart, 1964 (excerpts as 'Die Eigenart der Bauernfamilie und die bäuerliche Familienverfassung' in Heidi Rosenbaum (ed.), *Seminar: Familie und Gesellschaftsstruktur*, Frankfurt, 1978, pp. 195ff.).

'Agrarsoziologische Überlegungen zur Hofübergabe', *Mitteilungen für die Praxis* 33 (1967), pp. 89ff.

Rosenmayr, Leopold, 'Schwerpunkte der Soziologie des Alters' in *Handbuch der empirischen Sozialforschung*, vol. 7, 2nd edn, Stuttgart, 1976 (1967), pp. 218ff.

Rosenmayr, Leopold and Rosenmayr, Hild, *Der alte Mensch in der Gesellschaft*, Reinbek, 1978.

Runde, Christian L., *Die Rechtslehre von der Leibzucht oder dem Altenteiler auf deutschen Bauerngütern nach gemeinen und besonderen Rechten*, Oldenburg, 1805.

Schmidt, Karl, *Gutsübergabe und Ausgedinge. Eine agrarpolitische Untersuchung mit besonderer Berücksichtigung der Alpen- und Sudetenländer*, Vienna, 1920.

Schultze, Alfred, 'Die Rechtslage des alternden Bauern nach den altnordischen Rechten', *Zeitschrift der Savigny-Stiftung für Rechtsgeschichte, Germanistische Abteilung* 51 (1931), pp. 258ff.

Sering, Max, *Erbrecht und Agrarverfassung in Schleswig-Holstein*, Berlin, 1908.

Weber, H., *Der deutsche bäuerliche Übergabevertrag als vorweggenommene Erbfolge in den Hof. Ein Beitrag zu Geschichte der bäuerlichen Hofübergabe*, Berlin, 1941.

Weiland, Hans Georg, *Die geschichtliche Entwicklung des bäuerlichen Altenteils und seine Regelung nach dem Reichserbhofgesetz*, Emsdetten, 1939.

General Bibliography

This bibliography contains only those works on the social history of the family that have appeared in English, French and German. The scope of the books and articles that are included is confined to Europe, and as regards historical periods, it is limited to the Middle Ages and modern times. Publications related to other social sciences have been selected only in so far as they also take account of the historical dimension. Work on the bibliography finished in January 1981.

The one journal that deals exclusively with questions of the social history of the family is the *Journal of Family History*. Other historical periodicals that frequently dedicate their pages to family topics are the *Journal of Interdisciplinary History*, the *Journal of Social History*, the *Annales: Economies – Sociétés – Civilisations (Annales E. S. C.)* and the *History of Childhood Quarterly*. An historico–demographic view of family topics is adopted principally in *Annales de Démographie Historique, Population, Population Studies* and *Local Population Studies*. An historical treatment of family issues and the status of women is frequently to be found in the *Journal of Marriage and the Family*, the *Journal of Comparative Family Studies, The Family Coordinator, Feminist Studies* and *Signs, Journal of Women in Culture and Society*.

The bibliography is divided into five main sections. Section 1 covers bibliographies and reviews. Section 2 is devoted to works on theoretical and methodological questions. Section 3, which includes surveys and temporally or regionally comprehensive studies, is subdivided into the following categories: (a) general; (b) wife and mother; (c) husband and father; (d) children and adolescents in the family; (e) the aged in the family; (f) the family cycle; (g) natality, nuptiality and historical demography; (h) sexuality; (i) marriage and divorce; (j) family law and inheritance; (k) the home; (l) relatives. Section 4 is devoted to works on the medieval family. Section 5 covers the modern family and is subdivided into six categories: (a) the British Isles; (b) France; (c) Central Europe; (d) Scandinavia; (e) Eastern and South-Eastern Europe; (f) the Mediterranean region.

Section 1: Bibliographies and reviews

Aldous, Joan, and Dahl, Nancy, *International bibliography of research in marriage and the family*, vol. 2, *1965–1972*, Minneapolis, 1974.

Aldous, Joan, and Hill, Reuben, *International bibliography of research in marriage and the family*, vol. 1, *1900–1964*, Minneapolis, 1967.

Berkner, Lutz-Karl, 'Recent research on the history of the family in Western Europe', *Journal of Marriage and the Family* 35 (1973), pp. 395ff.

Burch, Thomas K., 'Household and family demography: a bibliographic essay', *Population Index* 45/2 (1979), pp. 173ff.

Erickson, Carolly, and Casey, Kathleen, 'Women in the Middle Ages: a working bibliography', *Medieval Studies* 37 (1975), pp. 340ff.

Freedman, Ronald, *The sociology of human fertility: an annotated bibliography*, New York, 1975.

Lopez, Manuel D., 'A guide to the interdisciplinary literature of the history of childhood', *History of Childhood Quarterly* 1 (1973–4). pp. 463ff.

Ludlow, William L., *A syllabus and a bibliography of marriage and the family*, New Concord, Ohio, 1951.

Milden, James Wallace, *The family in past time: a guide to the literature*, New York, 1977.

Shaw, Robert K., *Bibliography of domestic economy in English*, Albany, New York, 1901.

Sheehan, Michael M., *Family and marriage in medieval Europe: a working bibliography*, Vancouver, 1976.

Soliday, Gerald, *et al.* (eds.) *History of the family and kinship: a select international bibliography,* New York, 1980.

Walle, E. Van de, and Kantrow, L., 'Historical demography: a bibliographical essay', *Population Index* 40 (1974), pp. 611ff.

Section 2: Theoretical and methodological questions

Akerman, Sune, 'An evaluation of the family reconstitution technique'. *Scandinavian Economic History Review* 25 (1977), pp. 160ff.

Alexander, Sally, and Davin, Anna, 'Feminist history', *History Workshop* 1 (1976), pp. 4ff.

Anderson, Michael, 'The study of family structure' in Edward Anthony Wrigley (ed.), *Nineteenth-century society*, Cambridge, 1972, pp. 47ff.

Bardis, Panos D., 'Synopsis and evaluation of theories concerning family evolution', *Social Science* 38 (1963), pp. 42ff.

'Family forms and variations historically considered' in Harold T. Christensen (ed.), *Handbook of marriage and the family*, Chicago, 1964, pp. 403ff.

Berkner, Lutz Karl, 'The use and misuse of census data for the historical analysis of family structure', *Journal of Interdisciplinary History* 5 (1975), pp. 721ff.

Boocock, Sarane Spence, 'Historical and sociological research on the family and the life cycle: methodological alternatives' in John Demos and Sarane Spence Boocock (eds.), *Turning points: historical and sociological essays on the family* (supplement to *American Journal of Sociology* 84), Chicago/London, 1978, pp. 366ff.

Braun, Rudolf, 'Historische Demographie im Rahmen einer integrierten Geschichtsbetrachtung: Jüngere Forschungsansätze und ihre Verwendung', *Geschichte und Gesellschaft* 3 (1977), pp. 525ff.

Bullough, Vern L., 'Sex history: a virgin field', *Journal of Sex Research* 8 (1972), pp. 101ff.

Burch, Thomas K., 'Some demographic determinants of average household size: an analytical approach', *Demography* 7 (1970), pp. 61ff.

'The size and structure of families: a comparative analysis of census data', *American Sociological Review* 32 (1967), pp. 347ff.

'Comparative family structure: a demographic approach', *Estadística* 26 (1968), pp. 285ff.

Burch, Thomas K., and Murray, Gendell, 'Extended family structure and fertility: some conceptual and methodological issues', *Journal of Marriage and the Family* (Minneapolis.) 2/32 (1970), pp. 227ff.

Burguière, André, 'La démographie' in Jacques Le Goff and Pierre Nora (eds.), *Faire de l'histoire*, vol. 2, Paris, 1974, pp. 74ff.

Cajanov, A. V., *The theory of peasant economy*, ed. D. Thorner, B. Kerblay and R. E. F. Smith, Homewood, Ill., 1966.

Christensen, Harold T., 'Development of the family field of study' in Harold T. Christensen (ed.), *Handbook of marriage and the family*, Chicago, 1964, pp. 3ff.

Conze, Werner, 'Sozialgeschichte der Familie. Neuere Literatur – Probleme der Forschung', *Vierteljahrschrift für Sozial- und Wirtschaftsgeschichte* 65 (1978), pp. 357ff.

'Die Familie der Gegenwart in geschichtlicher Sicht', *Jahrbuch der Heidelberger Akademie der Wissenschaften für das Jahr 1978*, Heidelberg, 1979, pp. 87ff.

Easterlin, Richard A., 'Towards a socio-economic theory of fertility' in S. J. Behrman *et al.*, *Fertility and family planning: a world view*, Ann Arbor, 1969, pp. 127ff.

Elder, Glen H. Jr, 'Approaches to social change and the family' in John Demos and Sarane Spence Boocock (eds.), *Turning points: historical and sociological essays on the family* (supplement to *American Journal of Sociology* 84), Chicago/London, 1978, pp. 1ff.

Gaunt, David, 'Household typology: problems – methods – results' in Sune Akerman *et al.* (eds.), *Chance and change: economic and social studies of historical demography in the Baltic area*, Odense, 1978, pp. 69ff.

Gavazzi, Milovan, 'Die Erforschung der Mehrfamilien Südosteuropas in den letzten Dezennien' in Klaus Detlev Grothusen (ed.), *Südosteuropa und Südosteuropa-Forschung*, Hamburg, 1976, pp. 133ff.

Gillis, John R., 'Youth history: progress and prospects', *Journal of Social History* 7 (1973), pp. 201ff.

Goode, William Josiah, 'The theory and measurement of family change' in Eleanor H. Sheldon and Wilbert E. Moore (eds.), *Indicators of social change: concepts and measurements*, New York, 1968, pp. 295ff.

Goodman, Leo A., *et al.* 'Family formation and the frequency of various kinship relations', *Theoretical Population Biology* 5 (1974), pp. 1ff.

Goubert, Pierre, 'Historical demography and the reinterpretation of early modern French history: a research review', *Journal of Interdisciplinary History* 1 (1971), pp. 37ff.

Greenfield, Sidney, M., 'Industrialization and the family in sociological theory', *American Journal of Sociology* 67 (1961), pp. 312ff.

Hammel, Eugene A., and Laslett, Peter, 'Comparing household structure over time and between cultures', *Comparative Studies in Society and History* 16 (1974), pp. 73ff.

Hareven, Tamara K., 'The history of the family as an interdisciplinary field', *Journal of Interdisciplinary History* 2 (1971), pp. 399ff.

'Die Familie in historischer Perspektive. Laufende Arbeiten in England und den Vereinigten Staaten', *Geschichte und Gesellschaft* 1 (1975), pp. 370ff.

'Introduction: the historical study of the family in urban society', *Journal of Urban History* 1 (1975), pp. 259ff.

'The family cycle in historical perspective: a proposal for a developmental approach', in Jean Cuisenier (ed.), *The family life cycle in European societies*, The Hague, 1977, pp. 339ff.

Harris, Barbara J., 'Recent work on the history of the family: a review article', *Feminist Studies* 3 (1976), pp. 159ff.

Hausen, Karin, 'Familie als Gegenstand historischer Sozialwissenschaft', *Geschichte und Gesellschaft* 1 (1975), pp. 171ff.

'Historische Familienforschung' in Reinhard Rürup (ed.), *Historische Sozialwissenschaft*, Göttingen, 1977, pp. 59ff.

Henry, Louis, 'Historical demography', *Daedalus* 97 (1968), pp. 385ff.

Herrmann, Ulrich, 'Empfehlungen zum Studium der Geschichte der Familienerziehung' in K. Mollenhauer (ed.), *Die Familienerziehung*, Munich, 1975, pp. 207ff.

Hornstein, Walter, and Flitner, Andreas, 'Neuere Literatur zur Geschichte des Kindes- und Jugendalters', *Zeitschrift für Pädagogik* 11 (1965), pp. 66ff.

Imhof, Arthur E., 'Généalogie et démographie historique en Allemagne', *Annales de Démographie Historique* (1976), pp. 77ff.

  'Historical demography as social history: possibilities in Germany', *Journal of Family History* 2 (1977), pp. 305ff.

  Einführung in die historische Demographie, Munich, 1977.

Kanter, Rosabeth Moss, 'Families, family processes and economic life: toward systematic analysis of social historical research' in John Demos and Sarane Spence Boocock (eds.), *Turning points: historical and sociological essays on the family* (supplement to *American Journal of Sociology* 84), Chicago/London, 1978, pp. 316ff.

Kelly-Gadol, Joan, 'The social relations of the sexes: methodological implications of women's history', *Signs* 1 (1976), pp. 809ff.

Keniston, Kenneth, 'Psychological development and historical change', *Journal of Interdisciplinary History* 2 (1971), pp. 329ff.

Knodel, John, 'Ortssippenbücher als Quelle für die historische Demographie', *Geschichte und Gesellschaft* 1 (1975), pp. 288ff.

Knodel, John, and Shorter, Edward, 'The reliability of family reconstitution data in German village genealogies (*Ortssippenbücher*)', *Annales de Démographie Historique* (1976), pp. 115ff.

König, René, 'Alte Probleme und neue Fragen in der Familiensoziologie', *Kölner Zeitschrift für Soziologie und Sozialpsychologie* 18 (1966), pp. 1ff.

Kooy, G. A., 'Urbanization and nuclear family individualization: a causal connection?', *Current Sociology* 12 (1963–64), pp. 13ff.

Lasch, Christopher, 'The family and history', *New York Review of Books*, 13 November 1975, pp. 33ff.; 27 November 1975, pp. 37ff.; 11 December 1975, pp. 50ff.

Laslett, Peter, 'The comparative history of household and family', *Journal of Social History* 4 (1970), pp. 75ff.

  'Introduction: the history of the family' in Peter Laslett and Richard Wall (eds.), *Household and family in past time*, London, 1972, pp. 1ff.

  'La famille et le ménage: approches historiques', *Annales E. S. C.* 27 (1972), pp. 847ff.

  'Familie und Industrialisierung: eine "starke Theorie" ' in Werner Conze (ed.), *Sozialgeschichte der Familie in der Neuzeit Europas*, Stuttgart, 1976, pp. 13ff.

Lee, Ronald Demos, 'Methods and models for analyzing historical series of births, deaths and marriages', in Ronald Demos Lee (ed.), *Population patterns in the past*, New York, 1977, pp. 337ff.

Levy, Marion J., 'Aspects of the analysis of family structure' in Ansley J. Coale *et al.*, *Aspects of the analysis of family structure*, Princeton, 1965, pp. 1ff.

Linde, Hans, 'Familie und Haushalt als Gegenstand bevölkerungsgeschichtlicher Forschung. Erörterung eines problembezogenen und materialorientierten Bezugsrahmen' in Werner Conze (ed.), *Sozialgeschichte der Familie in der Neuzeit Europas*, Stuttgart, 1976, pp. 32ff.

Macfarlane, Alan, *Reconstructing historical communities*, Cambridge, 1977.

Mackenroth, Gerhard, *Bevölkerungslehre. Theorie, Soziologie und Statistik der Bevölkerung*, Berlin, 1953.

Marciano, Teresa Donati, 'Variant family forms in a world perspective', *The Family Coordinator* 24 (1975), pp. 407ff.

McGregor, Oliver Ross, 'Some research possibilities and historic materials for family and kinship study in Britain', *British Journal of Sociology* 12 (1961), pp. 310ff.

Mendels, Franklin, 'Recent research in European historical demography', *American Historical Review* 75 (1970), pp. 1065ff.

Ming-Kalman, Wanda, 'A theory of European household economy during the peasant-to-worker transition', *Ethnology* 17/2 (1978), pp. 183ff.

Mitterauer, Michael, 'Familiengrösse – Familientypen – Familienzyklus. Probleme quantitativer Auswertung von österreichischem Quellenmaterial', *Geschichte und Gesellschaft* 1 (1975), pp. 226ff.

'Zur Problematik des Begriffs "Familie" im 17. Jahrhundert' in Heidi Rosenbaum (ed.), *Seminar: Familie und Gesellschaftsstruktur*, Frankfurt, 1978, pp. 73ff.

Modell, John, 'Economic dimensions of family history', *The Family in Perspective* 6 (1974), pp. 7ff.

Mogey, J. M., 'Contribution of Frédéric Le Play to family research', *Marriage and Family Living* 17 (1955), pp. 310ff.

'Residence, family, kinship: some recent research', *Journal of Family History* 1 (1976), pp. 95ff.

Ogburn, W. F., and Nimkoff, N. B., *Technology and the changing family*, Boston, 1955.

Ortigues, Edmund, 'La psychanalyse et les institutions familiales', *Annales E. S. C.* 27 (1972), pp. 1091ff.

Pfeiffer, Gerhard, 'Familiengeschichte und Soziologie', *Blätter für fränkische Familienkunde* 10 (1972–73), pp. 270ff.

Plakans, Andrejs, 'The study of social structure from listings of inhabitants', *Journal of Family History* 4 (1979), pp. 87ff.

Rapp, Rayna, *et al.*, 'Examining family history', *Feminist Studies* 5 (1979), pp. 174ff.

Reiter, Rauna R. (ed.), *Toward an anthropology of women*, New York, 1975.

Rogers, Susan Carol, 'Woman's place: a critical review of anthropological theory', *Comparative Studies in Society and History* 20/1 (1978), pp. 123ff.

Rosaldo, Michelle Z., 'Women, culture and society: a theoretical overview' in M. Z. Rosaldo and L. Lamphere (eds.), *Women, culture and society*, Stanford, 1974, pp. 17ff.

Rosenbaum, Heidi, 'Zur neueren Entwicklung der historischen Familienforschung', *Geschichte und Gesellschaft* 1 (1975), pp. 210ff.

'Die Bedeutung historischer Forschung für die Gegenwart – dargestellt am Beispiel der Familiensoziologie' in A. Lüdtke and H. Uhl (eds.), Kooperation der Sozialwissenschaften, vol. 2, Stuttgart, 1977, pp. 178ff.

Familie als Gegenstruktur zur Gesellschaft. Kritik grundlegender theoretischer Ansätze der westdeutschen Familiensoziologie, 2nd edn, Stuttgart, 1978 (1973).

'Einleitung' in Heidi Rosenbaum (ed.), *Familie und Gesellschaftsstruktur. Materialen zu den sozioökonomischen Bedingungen von Familienformen*, Frankfurt, 1974, pp. 7ff. (extended version Frankfurt 1978, pp. 9ff,),

Ryan, Mary P., *et al.*, 'Examining family history', *Feminist Studies* 5/1 (1979), pp. 174ff.

Saveth, Edward Norman, 'The problems of American family history', *American Quarterly* 21 (1969), pp. 311ff.

Schaub, Walter, 'Sozialgenealogie – Probleme und Methoden', *Blätter für deutsche Landesgeschichte* 110 (1974), pp. 1ff.

Schmidt, Karl, 'Zur Problematik von Familie, Sippe und Geschlecht, Haus und Dynastie beim hochmittelalterlichen Adel', *Zeitschrift für die Geschichte des Oberrheins* 105 (1957), pp. 1ff.

Schofield, Roger S., 'La reconstitution de la famille par ordinateur', *Annales E. S. C.* 27 (1972), pp. 1071ff.

'Representativeness and family reconstitution', *Annales de Démographie Historique* (1972), pp. 121ff.

Schwägler, Georg, *Soziologie der Familie. Ursprung und Entwicklung*, Tübingen, 1970.

Shore, Miles F., 'The child and historiography', *Journal of Interdisciplinary History* 6 (1976), pp. 495ff.

Skolnick, Arlene, 'The family revisited: themes in recent social science research', *Journal of Interdisciplinary History* 5 (1975), pp. 703ff.

Skolnick, A. S., and Skolnick, J. H., *Family in transition: rethinking marriage, sexuality, child rearing and family organization*, Boston, 1971.

Smelser, Neil J., and Halpern, Sydney, 'The historical triangulation of family, economy and education' in John Demos and Sarane Spence Boocock (eds.), *Turning points: historical and sociological essays on the family* (supplement to *American Journal of Sociology* 84), Chicago/London, 1978, pp. 288ff.

Somerville, C. John, 'Toward a history of childhood and youth', *Journal of Interdisciplinary History* 3 (1972), pp. 439ff.

Spitzer, Alan B., 'The historical problem of generations', *American Historical Review* 78 (1973), pp. 1353ff.

Stewart, A., et al., 'Coding categories for the study of child rearing from historical sources', *Journal of Interdisciplinary History* 5 (1975), pp. 687ff.

Thompson, E. P., 'Happy families: review of Lawrence Stone: *The family, sex and marriage in England 1500–1800', New Society*, 8 September 1977, pp. 499ff.

'Under the rooftree', *Times Literary Supplement*, 4 May 1973, pp. 485ff.

Tilly, Charles, 'The historical study of vital processes' in Charles Tilly (ed.), *Historical studies of changing fertility*, Princeton, 1978, pp. 3ff.

Tilly, Louise A., 'The social sciences and the study of women: a review article', *Comparative Studies in Society and History* 20/1 (1978), pp. 163ff.

Tyrell, Hartmann, 'Probleme einer Theorie der gesellschaftlichen Ausdifferenzierung der privatisierten modernen Kernfamilie', *Zeitschrift für Soziologie* 5 (1976), pp. 393ff.

'Historische Familienforschung und Familiensoziologie. Versuch einer Zwischenbilanz der historischen Familienforschung und Kritik eines Forschungsprogrammes', *Kölner Zeitschrift für Soziologie und Sozialpsychologie* 29 (1977), pp. 677ff.

Vann, Richard T., 'History and demography', *History and Theory* 9 (1969), pp. 64ff.

Vinovskis, Maris, 'From household size to the life course: some observations on recent trends in family history' in Allan Bogue and Jerome Clubb (eds.), *History and the social sciences* (special issue of *American Behavioral Scientist*), 1980.

'The field of early American family history: a methodological critique', *The Family in Historical Perspective: An International Newsletter* 14 (1971), pp. 141ff.

Walter, Emil J., 'Kritik einiger familien-soziologischer Begriffe im Lichte der politischen Arithmetik des 18. Jahrhunderts', *Schweizerische Zeitschrift für Volkswirtschaft und Statistik* 97 (1961), pp. 64ff.

Wehler, Hans Ulrich (ed.), 'Historische Familienforschung und Demographie', *Geschichte und Gesellschaft* 1/2 and 3 (1975), pp. 171ff.

Weinstein, Fred, and Platt, Gerald M., *The wish to be free: society, psyche and value change*, Berkeley, 1969.

Wells, Robert, 'Family history and demographic transition', *Journal of Social History* 9 (1975), pp. 1ff.

Wrigley, Edward A., *Population and history*, New York, 1969.

'Population, family and household' in Charles Martin Ballard (ed.), *New movements in the study and teaching of history*, Bloomington, 1970, pp. 93ff.

'Some problems of family reconstitution using English parish register material: an example of Colyton', *Proceedings of the Third International Conference of Economic History*, Paris, 1972, pp. 199ff.

'Reflections on the history of the family', *Daedalus* 106/2 (1977), pp. 71ff.

(ed.), *An introduction to English historical demography*, New York, 1966.

Section 3: Surveys and temporally or regionally comprehensive studies

(a) GENERAL

Anderson, Michael, 'Family and class in nineteenth-century cities', *Journal of Family History* 2 (1977), pp. 139ff.

'Sociological history and the working-class family: Smelser revisited', *Social History* 3 (1976), pp. 317ff.

Ariès, Philippe, 'The family and the city', *Daedalus* 106/2 (1977), pp. 227ff.

Armens, Syen M., *Archetypes of the family in literature*, Seattle, 1966.

Begemann, Helmutt, *Strukturwandel der Familie. Eine sozialtheologische Untersuchung über den Strukturwandel von der patriarchalischen zur partnerschaftlichen Familie*, Hamburg, 1960.

Berg, J. H. van den, *Metabletica. Über die Wandlungen des Menschen. Grundlinien einer historischen Psychologie*, Göttingen, 1960.

Berkner, Lutz Karl, 'Rural family organization in Europe: a problem in comparative history', *Peasant Studies Newsletter* 1 (1972), pp. 145ff.

Bock, Gisela, and Duden, Barbara, 'Arbeit aus Liebe – Liebe als Arbeit. Zur Entstehung der Hausarbeit im Kapitalismus' in *Frauen und Wissenschaft. Beiträge zur Berliner Sommeruniversität für Frauen*, Berlin, 1977, pp. 118ff.

Brunner, Otto, 'Das "ganze Haus" und die alteuropäische "Ökonomik",' *Zeitschrift für Nationalökonomie* 13 (1950), pp. 114ff; reprinted in Otto Brunner, *Neue Wege der Sozialgeschichte*, Göttingen, 1956, pp. 33ff.

Burgess, Ernest, *et al.*, *The family: from institution to companionship*, 3rd edn, New York, 1963 (1945).

Dubnoff, Steven, 'Gender, the family and the problems of work motivation in a transition to industrial capitalism', *Journal of Family History* 4 (1979), pp. 121ff.

Egner, Erich, *Entwicklungsphasen der Hauswirtschaft (Göttinger Wirtschafts- und Sozialwissenschaftliche Studien* 1), Göttingen, 1964.

'Epochen im Wandel des Familienhaushalts' in F. Oeter (ed.), *Familie und Gesellschaft*, Tübingen, 1966, pp. 57ff.; reprinted in Heidi Rosenbaum (ed.), *Seminar: Familie und Gesellschaftsstruktur*, Frankfurt, 1978, pp. 92ff.

Elias, Norbert, 'Zum Zusammenhang von Triebkontrolle und Familienformen bzw. Gesellschaftsstruktur (excerpts from *Über den Prozess der Zivilisation*, vol. 1, Basle, 1939) in Heidi Rosenbaum (ed.), *Seminar: Familie und Gesellschaftsstruktur*, Frankfurt, 1978, pp. 152ff.

Engels, Friedrich, *Der Ursprung der Familie, des Privateigentums und des Staates*, 4th edn, Stuttgart, 1892.

Famille et société (special edition of *Annales E. S. C.*, no. 4/5), 1972.

Flandrin, J.-L., *Families in former times: kinship, household and sexuality*, Cambridge, 1979.

Familles. Parenté, maison, sexualité dans l'ancienne société, Paris, 1976.

Forster, Robert, and Ranum, Orest (eds.), *Biology of Man in History: Selections from the Annales*, Baltimore, 1975.

Friedmann, Harriet, 'World market, state and family farm: social basis of household production in the era of wage labor', *Comparative Studies in Society and History* 20/4 (1978), pp. 545ff.

Fromm, E., *et al.* (eds.), *Studien über Autorität und Familie. Forschungsberichte aus dem Institut für Sozialforschung*, Paris, 1936.

Goldschmidt, Walter, and Kunkel, Evelyn Jakobsen, 'The structure of the peasant family', *American Anthropologist* 73 (1971), pp. 1058ff.

Goode, William, *World revolution and family patterns*, Glencoe, Ill., 1963.
   'The processing of role bargaining in the impact of urbanization and industrialization on family systems', *Current Sociology* 12 (1963–64), pp. 1ff.

Goody, Jack, 'The Evolution of the Family' in Peter Laslett and Richard Wall (eds.), *Household and family in past time*, Cambridge, 1972, pp. 103ff.

Production and reproduction: a comparative study of the domestic domain, Cambridge, 1976.

Habakkuk, H. J., 'Family structure and economic change in nineteenth century Europe', *Journal of Economic History* 15 (1955), pp. 1ff.

Habermas, Jürgen, *Strukturwandel der Öffentlichkeit. Untersuchungen zu einer Kategorie der bürgerlichen Gesellschaft*, Neuwied/Berlin, 1962.

Hareven, Tamara K., 'Modernization and family history: perspectives on social change', *Signs: Journal of Women in Culture and Society* 2 (1976), pp. 190ff.

(ed.), *Family and Kin in Urban Communities 1700–1930*, New York, 1977.

Hobsbawm, Eric J., 'Vom Zusammenhang von Erwerbsleben und bürgerlicher Familienstruktur' (excerpts from *Die Blütezeit des Kapitals*, Munich, 1977) in Heidi Rosenbaum (ed.), *Seminar: Familie und Gesellschaftsstruktur*, Frankfurt, 1978, pp. 404ff.

Klippel, Diethelm, 'Entstehung und Strukturwandel der modernen Familie', *Fam. RZ* 25 (1978), pp, 558ff.

Lasch, Christopher, *Haven in a heartless world: the family besieged*, New York, 1977.

Laslett, Barbara, 'The family as a public and private institution: an historical perspective', *Journal of Marriage and the Family* 35 (1973), pp. 480ff.

Laslett, Peter, 'Characteristics of the Western family considered over time', *Journal of Family History* 2 (1977), pp. 117ff.; reprinted in Peter Laslett, *Family life and illicit love in earlier generations*, Cambridge, 1977, pp. 12ff.

Laslett, Peter, and Wall, Richard (eds.), *Household and family in past time*, Cambridge, 1972.

Latham, J., *Happy families: growing up in the eighteenth and nineteenth centuries*, London, 1974.

Le Play, Frédéric, *Les ouvriers européens*, 6 vols., Paris, 1855.

Les ouvriers des deux mondes, 4 vols., Paris 1857–62.

L'organisation de la famille selon le vrai modèle signalé par l'histoire de toutes les races et de tous les temps, Paris, 1871.

Lupri, Eugen, 'Industrialisierung und Strukturwandlungen in der Familie', *Sociologia Ruralis* 5 (1955), pp. 57ff.

Manheim, Ernst, 'Beiträge zu einer Geschichte der autoritären Familie' in E. Fromm *et al.* (eds.), *Autorität und Familie*, Paris, 1936, pp. 523ff.

Medick, Hans, 'Die proto-industrielle Familienwirtschaft' in Peter Kriedte, Hans Medick and Jürgen Schlumbohm, *Industrialisierung vor der Industrialisierung*, Göttingen, 1975, pp. 90ff.

'The proto-industrial family economy: the structural function of household and family during the transition from peasant society to industrial capitalism', *Social History* 1 (1976), pp. 291ff.

'Zur strukturellen Funktion von Haushalt und Familie im Übergang von der traditionellen Agrargesellschaft zum industriellen Kapitalismus: die protoindustrielle Familienwirtschaft' in Werner Conze (ed.), *Sozialgeschichte der Familie in der Neuzeit Europas*, Stuttgart, 1976, pp. 254ff.

Mitterauer, Michael, 'Der Mythos von der vorindustriellen Grossfamilie' in Heidi Rosenbaum (ed.), *Seminar: Familie und Gesellschaftsstruktur*, Frankfurt, 1978, pp. 128ff.

'Funktionswandel der Familie' in Erika Weinzierl und Karl Stadler (eds.), *Geschichte der Familienrechtsgesetzgebung in Österreich (Justiz- und Zeitgeschichte* 3), Vienna, 1978, pp. 155ff.

Grundtypen alteuropäischer Sozialformen, Stuttgart, 1979.

'Faktoren des Wandels historischer Familienformen' in Helge Pross (ed.), *Familie wohin?*, Reinbek, 1979.

Mitterauer, Michael, and Sieder, Reinhard, *Vom Patriarchat zur Partnerschaft*, 2nd edn., Munich, 1980 (1977).

Mousnier, Roland, *La famille, l'enfant et l'éducation en France et en Grande-Bretagne du XVIe au XVIIIe siècle*, Paris, 1975.

Nahrstedt, W., *Die Entstehung der Freizeit*, Göttingen, 1972.

Oeter, Ferdinand (ed.), *Familie und Gesellschaft*, Tübingen, 1966.

Pillorget, René, *La tige et le rameau. Famille anglaise et francaise XVIe–XVIIIe siècle*, Paris, 1979.

Plakans, Andrejs, 'Peasant families east and west: a comment on Lutz K. Berkner's "Rural Family Organization in Europe: A Problem in Comparative History",' *Peasant Studies Newsletter* 2 (1973), pp. 11ff.

Planck, Ulrich, 'Die Eigenart der Bauernfamilie und die bäuerliche Familienverfassung' (excerpts from *Der bäuerliche Familienbetrieb zwischen Patriarchat und Partnerschaft*, Stuttgart, 1964) in Heidi Rosenbaum (ed.), *Seminar: Familie und Gesellschaftsstruktur*, Frankfurt, 1978, pp. 195ff.

Pleck, Elizabeth, 'Two worlds in one: work and family', *Journal of Social History* 10 (1976), pp. 178ff.

Rabb, T. K., and Rotberg, R. I., *Family in history: interdisciplinary essays*, New York, 1973.

Rao, L. J., 'Industrialization and the family: a world view', *International Journal of Sociology of the Family* 3 (1973), pp. 179ff.

Rosenberg, Charles E. (ed.) *The Family in History*, Philadelphia, 1975.

Schultz, Alwin, *Das häusliche Leben der europäischen Kulturvölker vom Mittelalter bis zur 2. Hälfte des 18. Jahrhunderts*, Munich, 1903.

Schwab, Dieter, 'Familie' in *Geschichtliche Grundbegriffe, Historisches Lexikon zur politisch-sozialen Sprache in Deutschland* 2, Stuttgart, 1975, pp. 253ff.

Shorter, Edward, *The making of the modern family*, New York, 1975.

Sjoberg, Gideon, 'Familial organization in the preindustrial city', *Marriage and Family Living* 18 (1956), pp. 30ff.

Smelser, Neil, 'Sociological history: the industrial revolution and the British working-class family', *Journal of Social History* 1 (1967), pp. 17ff.

Stekl, Hannes, 'Hausrechtlich Abhängige – das Gesinde', *Beiträge zur historischen Sozialkunde* 5 (1975), pp. 34ff.

Thirsk, Joan, The family', *Past and Present* 27 (1964), pp. 116ff.

Thomas, Keith, 'Work and leisure in pre-industrial societies', *Past and Present* 29 (1966), pp. 50ff.

Thurnwald, Richard, *Die menschliche Gesellschaft*, vol. 2, *Werden, Wandel und Gestaltung von Familie, Verwandtschaft und Bünden im Lichte der Völkerforschung*, Berlin, 1932.

Townsend, Peter, *The family of three generations in Britain, the United States and Denmark*. Report to the Sixth International Congress of Gerontology, Copenhagen, 1963.

Trumbach, Randolf, Europe and its families: a review essay of Lawrence Stone, *The Family, Sex and Marriage in England 1500–1800*', *Journal of Social History* 13 (1979), pp. 136ff.

Weber, Max, 'Die Familien- und Arbeitsgemeinschaften' (excerpts from *Zur Geschichte der Handelsgesellschaften im Mittelalter*) in Heidi Rosenbaum (ed.), *Seminar: Familie und Gesellschaftsstruktur*, Frankfurt, 1978, pp. 63ff.

Weber-Kellermann, Ingeborg, 'Kontinuität und Familienstruktur: W. H. Riehl und das Problem der Geschichtlichkeit von Primärgruppen' in H. Bausinger and W. Brückner (eds.), *Kontinuität, Geschichtlichkeit und Dauer als volkskundliches Problem*, Berlin, 1969, pp. 143ff.

Die deutsche Familie. Versuch einer Sozialgeschichte, Frankfurt, 1974.

Die Familie. Geschichte, Geschichten und Bilder, Frankfurt, 1976.

(b) WIFE AND MOTHER

Angenot, Marc, *Les champions des femmes: examen du discours sur la supériorité des femmes 1400–1800*, Montreal, 1977.

Ankarloo, Bengt, 'Agriculture and women's work: directions of change in the west, 1700–1900', *Journal of Family History* 4 (1979), pp. 111ff.

Branca, Patricia, 'A new perspective on women's work: a comparative typology', *Journal of Social History* 1/2 (1975), pp. 129ff.
Women in Europe since 1750, London, 1978.

Bridenthal, Renate, and Koonz, Claudia, *Becoming visible: women in European history*, Boston, 1977.

Briffault, Robert, *The mothers: the matriarchal theory of social origins*, 2nd edn, 3 vols., New York, 1960 (1927).

Bullough, Vern L., *The subordinate sex: a history of attitudes toward women*, Urbana, 1973.

Bunkle, Phillida E., 'Sentimental womanhood and domestic education, 1830–1870, *History of Education Quarterly* 14 (1974), pp. 13ff.

Carroll, Bernice A., *Liberating women's history*, Urbana, 1976.

Coulson, M., *et al.*, 'The housewife and her labor under capitalism: a critique', *New Left Review* 89 (1975), pp. 59ff.

Cowan, Ruth Schwartz, 'A case study of technological and social change: the washing machine and the working wife' in Mary Hartman and Lois W. Banner, *Clio's consciousness raised: new perspectives on the history of women*, New York, 1974, pp. 245ff.

Delamont, Sara, and Duffin, Lorna (eds.) *The nineteenth century woman*, New York, 1978.

Femme, La, Recueils de la Société Jean Bodin 11–13 (1959).

Hausen, Karin, 'Die Polarisierung der "Geschlechtscharaktere". Eine Spiegelung der Dissoziation von Erwerbs- und Familienleben' in Werner Conze (ed.), *Sozialgeschichte der Familie in der Neuzeit Europas*, Stuttgart, 1976, pp. 363ff.
'Technischer Fortschritt und Frauenarbeit im 19. Jahrhundert. Zur Sozialgeschichte der Nähmaschine', *Geschichte und Gesellschaft* 4 (1978), pp. 148ff.

Herlihy, David, *Women in medieval society*, Houston, 1971.

Kuhn, Anette, and Schneider, Gerhard (eds.), *Frauen in der Geschichte*, Düsseldorf, 1978.

McBride, Theresa, *The domestic revolution: the modernization of household service in England and France, 1820–1920*, New York, 1976.

McDougall, Mary Lynn, 'Working Class Women during the Industrial Revolution, 1780–1914' in Renate Bridenthal and Claudia Koonz (eds.), *Becoming visible: women in European history*, Boston, 1977, pp. 255ff.

Meillassoux, Claude, *Femmes, greniers et capitaux*, Paris, 1975.

Oakley, Ann, *Woman's work: the housewife, past and present*, New York, 1974.

Rainwater, Lee, 'Mothers' contribution to the family money: economy in Europe and the United States', *Journal of Family History* 4 (1979), pp. 198ff.

Rowbotham, Sheila, *Hidden from history: rediscovering women in history from the seventeenth century to the present*, New York, 1974.

Scott, Joan W., and Tilly, Louise A., 'Women's work and the family in nineteenth-century Europe', *Comparative Studies in Society and History* 17 (1975), pp. 36ff.

Secombe, Wally, 'Housework under capitalism', *New Left Review* 83 (1974), 3ff.

Shorter, Edward, 'Women's work: what difference did capitalism make?', *Theory and Society* 3 (1976), pp. 513ff.

'Female emancipation, birth control and fertility in European history', *American Historical Review* 78 (1973), pp. 605ff.

'Der Wandel der Mutter-Kind-Beziehungen zu Beginn der Moderne', *Geschichte und Gesellschaft* 1 (1975), pp. 256ff.

Sullerot, Evelyne, *Histoire et sociologie du travail*, Paris, 1968.

(ed.), *Le fait féminin*, Paris, 1978.

Tilly, Louise A., *et al.*, 'Women's work and European fertility patterns', *Journal of Interdisciplinary History* 6 (1976), pp. 447ff.

Tilly, Louise A., and Scott, Joan W., *Women, work, and family*, New York, 1978.

Weber, Marianne, *Ehefrau und Mutter in der Rechtsentwicklung. Eine Einführung*, Tübingen, 1907.

Whyte, Martin King, *The status of women in preindustrial societies*, Princeton, 1978.

(c) HUSBAND AND FATHER

Connor, Paul, 'Patriarchy: Old World and New', *American Quarterly* 17 (1965), pp. 48ff.

Ehmer, Josef, 'Entstehung und Wesen des bürgerlichen Patriarchalismus', *Beiträge zur historischen Sozialkunde* 8 (1978), pp. 56ff.

Hartmann, Heidi, 'Capitalism, patriarchy and job segregation by sex', *Signs* 1 (1976), pp. 137ff.

Mogey, John M., 'A century of declining paternal authority', *Marriage and Family Living* 19 (1957), pp. 234ff.

Schochet, G. J., *Patriarchalism and political theory*, Oxford, 1975.

Tellenbach, Hubertus (ed.), *Das Vaterbild in Mythos und Geschichte*, Stuttgart, 1976.

(ed.), *Das Vaterbild im Abendland*, 2 vols., Stuttgart, 1978.

Wais, Kurt K. T., *Das Vater–Sohn Motiv in der Dichtung bis 1880*, Berlin/Leipzig, 1931.

Wittfogel, Karl A., 'Wirtschaftsgeschichtliche Grundlagen der Entwicklung der Familienautorität' in E. Fromm *et al.*, *Autorität und Familie*, Paris, 1936, pp. 473ff.

(d) CHILDREN AND ADOLESCENTS IN THE FAMILY

Anderson, John E., 'Child development: an historical perspective', *Child Development* 27 (1956), pp. 181ff.

Ariès, Philippe, *L'enfant et la vie familiale sous l'ancien régime*, 2nd edn, Paris,

1973 (1960) (*Centuries of childhood: a social history of family life*, New York, 1962.)

Armengaud, André, 'L'attitude de la société à l'égard de l'enfant au XIXe siècle', *Annales de démographie historique* (1973), pp. 303ff.

'La famille et l'enfant en France et en Angleterre du XVIe aux XVIIIe siècle', *Aspects démographiques*, Paris, 1975.

Braun, Samuel J., and Edwards, Esther P., *History and theory of early child-hood education*, Worthington, 1972.

Brim, Orville G., 'A History of Education for Child Rearing' in *Education for Child Rearing*, New York, 1959, pp. 321ff.

Cloer, Ernst, 'Ausgewählte systematische Fragestellungen der Geschichte der Kindheit und der historischen Familien- und Sozialisationsfor-schung', *Neue Sammlung* 18 (1978), pp. 519ff.

Demos, John, 'Developmental perspectives on the history of childhood', *Journal of Interdisciplinary History* 2 (1971), pp. 315ff.

Demos, John, and Demos, Virginia, 'Adolescence in historical perspective', *Journal of Marriage and the Family* 31 (1969), pp. 632ff.

Elkar, Rainer S., 'Das Kind in der Familie – Einige Bemerkungen zur hist-orischen, Familienforschung', *Sozialwissenschaftliche Informationen für Unterricht und Studium* 8/1 (1979), pp. 2ff.

Flandrin, J.-L., 'L'attitude à l'égard du petit enfant et les conduites sexuelles dans la civilisation occidentale', *Annales de démographie historique* (1973), pp. 143ff.

'Enfance et société', *Annales E. S. C.* (1964), pp. 322ff.

Giesen, Josef, *Europäische Kinderbilder. Die Soziale Stellung des Kindes im Wandel der Zeit*, Munich, 1966.

Giehler, W., and Lüscher, K., 'Die Soziologie des Kindes in historischer Sicht. Hinweise auf neuere Literatur', *Neue Sammlung* 15 (1975), pp. 442ff.

Gillis, John, *Youth and History. Tradition and Change in European Age Rela-tions, 1770 to the Present*, New York, 1974.

Graf, Friedrich Wilhelm, 'Geschichte der Individualisierung. Neuere Literatur zum Strukturwandel von Kindheit und Familie', *Zeitschrift für evangelische Ethik* 4 (1978), pp. 309ff.

Herrmann, Ulrich, 'Probleme und Aspekte historischer Ansätze in der Sozialisationsforschung' in Klaus Hurrelmann and Dieter Ulich (eds.), *Handbuch der Sozialisationsforschung*, Weinheim/Basel, 1980, pp. 227ff.

Horkheimer, Max, 'Die Erziehungsleistung der bürgerlichen Familie' (excerpts from *Studien über Autorität und Familie. Forschungsberichte aus dem Institut für Sozialforschung*, Paris, 1936) in Heidi Rosenbaum (ed.), *Familie und Gesellschaftsstruktur*, Frankfurt, 1978, pp. 425ff.

Illick, Joseph, 'Kindererziehung in England und Amerika im siebzehnten Jahrhundert' in Lloyd de Mause (ed.), *Hört ihr die Kinder weinen*, Frank-furt, 1977, pp. 422ff.

Johansen, Erna M., *Betrogene Kinder. Eine Sozialgeschichte der Kindheit*, Frankfurt, 1978.

Langer, William L., 'Infanticide: a historical survey', *History of Childhood Quarterly* 1 (1974), pp. 353ff.

Linde, Hans, 'Persönlichkeitsbildung in der Land-Familie', *Soziale Welt* 10 (1959), pp. 297ff.; reprinted in Heidi Rosenbaum (ed.), *Seminar: Familie und Gesellschaftsstruktur*, Frankfurt, 1978, pp. 215ff.

Lorence, Bogna W., 'Parents and children in eighteenth century Europe', *History of Childhood Quarterly* 2 (1974), pp. 1ff.

Lüscher, K., 'Die Entwicklung der Rolle des Kindes' in K. Hurrelmann (ed.), *Sozialisation und Lebenslauf*, Reinbek, 1976, pp. 129ff.

Mause, Lloyd de, 'The evolution of childhood', *History of Childhood Quarterly* 1 (1974), pp. 503ff.

(ed.), *The history of childhood*, New York, 1974.

Minge-Kalman, Wanda, 'The Industrial Revolution and the European family: the institutionalization of "childhood" as a market for family labor', *Comparative Studies in Society and History* 20/3 (1978), pp. 454ff.

Mitterauer, Michael, 'Jugendgruppen' in *Jugend im historische Wandel. Beiträge zur historischen Sozialkunde* 6 (1976), pp. 34ff.

Modell, John. 'Social change and transitions to adulthood in historical perspective', *Journal of Family History* 1 (1976), pp. 7ff.

Neumann, Robert Paul, 'Masturbation, madness and the modern concepts of childhood and adolescence', *Journal of Social History* 8 (1975), pp. 1ff.

Robertson, Priscilla, 'Das Heim als Nest: Mittelschichten-Kindheit in Europa im neunzehnten Jahrhundert' in Lloyd de Mause (ed.), *Hört ihr die Kinder weinen*, Frankfurt, 1977, pp. 565ff.

Schorsch, A., *Images of childhood: an illustrated social history*, New York, 1979.

Senn, Milton J. E., 'Changing concepts of child care: a historical review', New York Academy of Medicine, *The March of Medicine* 17 (1955), pp. 83ff.

Sieder, Reinhard, 'Historische Reflexionen zur Stellung des Kindes in der Familie' in Erika Weinzierl and Karl Stadler (eds.), *Geschichte der Familienrechtsgesetzgebung in Österreich (Justiz und Zeitgeschichte* 3), Vienna, 1978, pp. 82ff.

Vischer, Eberhard, *Jugend und Alter in der Geschichte*, Basle, 1938.

Weber-Kellermann, Ingeborg, *Die Kindheit. Kleidung und Wohnen, Arbeit und Spiel. Eine Kulturgeschichte*, Frankfurt, 1979.

(e) THE AGED IN THE FAMILY

Anderson, Michael, 'The impact on the family relationships of the elderly of changes since Victorian times in governmental income–maintenance provision' in Ethel Shanas and Marvin B. Sussman (eds.), *Family bureaucracy and the elderly*, Durham, 1977, pp. 36ff.

Brubaker, Timothy H., and Sneden, Lawrence E. (eds.) *Aging in a changing family context*, special issue of *The Family Coordinator* 27 (1978).

Cavan, Ruth Shonle, 'Roles of the old in personal and impersonal societies' in *Aging in a changing family context*, special issue of *The Family Coordinator* 27 (1978), pp. 315ff.

Chudacoff, Howard, and Hareven, Tamara K., 'Family transition into old age' in Tamara K. Hareven (ed.), *Transitions*, New York, 1978, pp. 217ff.

'From the empty nest to family dissolution: life course transitions into old age', *Journal of Family History* 4 (1979), pp. 69ff.

Goody, Jack, 'Aging in non-industrial societies' in J. R. Birren, E. Shanas and R. Binstock (eds.), *Handbook of Aging and the Social Sciences*, New York, 1976.

Hareven, Tamara K., 'The last stage: historical adulthood and old age', *Daedalus* 105 (1976), pp. 13ff.

Johansen, Hans Christian, 'The position of the old in the rural household in traditional society', *Scandinavian Economic History Review* 24 (1976), pp. 129ff.

König, René, 'Die strukturelle Bedeutung des Alters in den fortgeschrittenen Industriegesellschaften' in René König, *Soziologische Orientierungen. Reden und Aufsätze*, Cologne, 1973, pp. 134ff.

Laslett, Peter, 'The history of aging and the aged' in Peter Laslett, *Family life and illicit love in earlier generations*, Cambridge, 1977, pp. 174ff.

Simmons, Leo, 'Aging in preindustrial societies' in C. Tibbits (ed.), *Handbook of social gerontology – societal aspects of aging*, Chicago, 1960, pp. 62ff.

Stearns, Peter N., *Old age in European society*, New York, 1976.

'Old women: some historical observations', *Journal of Family History* 5 (1980), pp. 44ff.

Thomas, Keith, 'Age and authority in early modern Europe', *Proceedings of the British Academy* 62 (1976), pp. 205ff.

(f) THE FAMILY CYCLE

Cuisenier, Jean (ed.), *The family life cycle in European societies (Le cycle de la vie familiale dans les sociétés européennes)*, The Hague, 1977.

Demos, John, and Boocock, Sarane Spence (eds.), *Turning points: historical and sociological essays on the family* (supplement to the *American Journal of Sociology* 84), Chicago/London, 1978.

Durall, Evelyn M., *Family development*, 4th edition, Philadelphia, 1971.

Elder, Glen H., 'Family history and the life course', *Journal of Family History* 2 (1977), pp. 279ff.

'Family history and the life course' in Tamara K. Hareven (ed.), *Transitions*, New York, 1978, pp. 17ff.

Engerman, Stanley, 'Economic perspectives on the life course' in Tamara K. Hareven (ed.), *Transitions*, New York, 1978, pp. 271ff.

Foner, Anne, 'Age stratification and the changing family' in John Demos and Sarane Spence Boocock (eds.), *Turning points: historical and sociological essays on the family* (supplement to *American Journal of Sociology* 84), Chicago/London, 1978, pp. 340ff.

Goody, Jack (ed.), *The Developmental Cycle in Domestic Groups*, Cambridge, 1958.

Haines, Michael R., 'Industrial work and the family cycle, 1889–1890' in Paul Uselding (ed.), *Research in Economic History*, Vol. 4, Greenwich, Conn., 1980.

Hareven, Tamara K., 'The family as process: the historical study of the family cycle', *Journal of Social History* 7 (1974), pp. 322ff.

'Family time and industrial time: family and work in a planned corporation town, 1900–1924', *Journal of Urban History* 1 (1975), pp. 365ff.

(ed.), *Transitions: the family and the life course in historical perspective*, New York, 1978.

'Historical changes in the life course and the family' in J. Milton Yinger and Stephen J. Cutler (eds.), *Major social issues: a multidisciplinary view*, New York, 1978, pp. 338ff.

Laslett, Peter, 'Le cycle familial et le processus de socialisation: charactéristiques du schéma occidental considéré dans le temps' in Jean Cuisenier (ed.), *The family life cycle in European societies*, The Hague, 1977, pp. 317ff.

Levine, Robert A., 'Comparative notes on the life course' in Tamara K. Hareven (ed.), *Transitions*, New York, 1978, pp. 287ff.

Mitterauer, Michael, and Sieder, Reinhard, 'The developmental process of domestic groups', *Journal of Family History* 4 (1979), pp. 257ff.

Rosenmayr, Leopold, 'Die menschlichen Lebensalter in Deutungsversuchen der europäischen Kulturgeschichte' in L. Rosenmayr (ed.), *Die menschlichen Lebensalter. Kontinuität und Krisen*, Munich, 1978.

Uhlenberg, Peter R., 'Changing configurations of the life course' in Tamara K. Hareven (ed.), *Transitions*, New York, 1978, pp. 65ff.

(g) NATALITY, NUPTIALITY AND HISTORICAL DEMOGRAPHY

Anderson, O. W., 'Infant mortality and social and cultural factors: historical trends and current patterns' in E. G. Jaco (ed.), *Patient, physicians and illness*, New York, 1958.

Bergues, H., et al., *La prévention des naissances dans la famille. Ses origines dans les Temps Modernes* (Institut national d'études démographiques, *Cahiers et Documents* 35), Paris, 1960.

Burguière, André, 'De Malthus à Max Weber: le mariage tardif et l'esprit d'entreprise', *Annales E. S. C.* 27 (1972), pp. 1128ff.

Coale, Ansley J., 'The decline in fertility in Europe from the French Revolution to World War II' in Samuel J. Behrmann *et al.* (ed.), *Fertility and family planning: a world view*, Ann Arbor, 1969, pp. 3ff.

Cohen, Joel E., 'Childhood mortality, family size and birth order in pre-industrial Europe', *Demography* 12 (1975), pp. 35ff.

Cutright, Philippe, 'Historical and contemporary trends in illegitimacy', *Archives of Sexual Behaviour* 2 (1972), pp. 97ff.

Drake, Michael, 'Age at marriage in the pre-industrial West' in Frank Bechhofer (ed.), *Population growth and the brain drain*, Edinburgh, 1969, pp. 196ff.

Dupâquier, Jacques, 'De l'animal à l'homme: le mécanisme autorégulateur des populations traditionelles', *Revue de l'Institut de Sociologie* (1972), pp. 177ff.

Easterlin, Richard A., 'The economics and sociology of fertility: a synthesis' in Charles Tilly (ed.), *Historical Studies of Changing Fertility*, Princeton, 1978, pp. 57ff.

Engerman, Stanley, 'The study of the European fertility decline', *Journal of Family History* 2 (1976), pp. 244ff.

Flandrin, Jean-Louis, 'Contraception, marriage et relations amoureuses dans l'Occident chrétien', *Annales E. S. C.* (1969), pp. 1370ff.

L'église et le contrôle des naissances, Paris, 1970.

Gaskin, Katharine, 'Age at first marriage in Europe before 1850: a summary of family reconstitution data', *Journal of Family History* 3 (1978), pp. 23ff.

Hainal, J., 'European marriage patterns in perspective' in David Victor Glass and D. E. C. Eversley (eds.), *Population in History*, Chicago, 1965, pp. 101ff.

Heer, David M., 'Economic development and the fertility transition', *Daedalus* (1968), pp. 447ff.

Himes, Norman E., *Medical history of contraception*, Baltimore, 1936.

Imhof, Arthur E., 'Die Bevölkerungsentwicklung in den Agrargesellschaften des Ancien Régime', *Schweizerische Zeitschrift für Geschichte* 24 (1974), pp. 225ff.

Knodel, John, 'Family limitation and the fertility transition from the age patterns of fertility in Europe and Asia', *Population Studies* 31 (1977), pp. 219ff.

'Breast-feeding and population growth', *Science* 198 (1977), pp. 1111ff.

Laslett, Peter (ed.), *Bastardy and its comparative history*, London, 1980.

Lee, W. Robert, 'Introduction: population growth, economic development and social change in Europe 1750–1970' in W. Robert Lee (ed.), *European Demography and Economic Growth*, New York, 1979, pp. 10ff.

Matossian, M. K., and Schafer, W. D., 'Family, fertility and political violence, 1700–1900', *Journal of Social History* 11 (1977), pp. 137ff.

Mattessich, Paul W., 'Childlessness and its correlates in historical perspective: a research note', *Journal of Family History* 4 (1979), pp. 299ff.

Medick, Hans, 'Strukturen und Funktionen der Bevölkerungsentwicklung im protoindustriellen System' in Peter Kriedte, Hans Medick and Jürgen Schlumbohm, *Industrialisierung vor der Industrialisierung*, Göttingen, 1978, pp. 155ff.

'Bevölkerungsentwicklung, Familienstruktur und Proto-Industrialisierung', *Sozialwissenschaftliche Informationen* 3 (1974), pp. 33ff.

Ranum, Orest, and Ranum, Patricia (eds.), *Popular attitudes toward birth control in pre-industrial France and England*, New York, 1972.

Shorter, Edward, *et al.*, 'The Decline in non-marital fertility in Europe, 1880–1940', *Population Studies* 25 (1971), pp. 375ff.

Smith, Daniel Scott, 'A homeostatic demographic regime: patterns in West European family reconstitution studies' in Ronald Demos Lee (ed.), *Population Patterns in the Past*, New York, 1977, pp. 19ff.

Tietze, Christopher, 'History of contraception methods', *Journal of Sex Research* 1 (1965), pp. 69ff.

Tilly, Charles (ed.), *Historical studies of changing fertility*, Princeton, 1978.

Walle, Étienne van de, 'Marriage and marital fertility', *Daedalus* 97 (1968), pp. 486ff.

et al., 'The decline of non-marital fertility in Europe, 1880–1940', *Population Studies* 25 (1971), pp. 375ff.

(h) SEXUALITY

Bullough, Vern, *Sexual variance in society and history*, New York, 1976.

Cutright, Philippe, 'The teenage sexual revolution and the myth of an abstinent past', *Family Planning Perspectives* 4 (1972), pp. 24ff.

Flandrin, Jean-Louis, 'Repression and change in the sexual life of young people in medieval and early modern times', *Journal of Family History* 2 (1977), pp. 196ff.

Foucault, Michel, *Histoire de la sexualité*, Paris, 1976.

Gillis, John P., 'Servants, sexual relations and the risks of illegitimacy in London, 1801–1900', *Feminist Studies* 5/1 (1979), pp. 142ff.

Lasch, Christopher, 'Ideology of sexual emancipation and its domestication, 1900–1935', *Katallegete* 5 (1975), pp. 19ff.

Lewinsohn, Richard, *History of sexual customs*, New York, 1959.

Noonan, John T. Jr, *Empfängnisverhütung. Geschichte ihrer Beurteilung in der katholischen Theologie und im kanonischen Recht*, Mainz, 1969.

Pfürtner, Stephan H., *Kirche und Sexualität*, Reinbek bei Hamburg, 1972.

Phayer, J. M., *Sexual liberation and religion in nineteenth century Europe*, London, 1977.

Saller, Karl, 'Sexualität und Sitte in der vorindustriellen Zeit' in Ferdinand Oeter (ed.), *Familie und Gesellschaft*, Tübingen, 1968, pp. 113ff.

Shorter, Edward, 'Illegitimacy, sexual revolution and social change in modern Europe', *Journal of Interdisciplinary History* 2 (1971), pp. 237ff.

'Sexual change and illegitimacy: the European experience' in Robert Bezucha (ed.), *Modern European social history*, Lexington, 1972, pp. 231ff.

'Capitalism, culture and sexuality: some competing models', *Social Science Quarterly* 53 (1972), pp. 338ff.

Taylor, Gordon R., *Im Garten der Lüste. Herrschaft und Wandlungen der Sexualität. Mit einer Einleitung von Alexander Mitscherlich*, Frankfurt, 1970. *Kulturgeschichte der Sexualität*, Frankfurt, 1977.

Ussel, J. van, *Sexualunterdrückung. Geschichte der Sexualfeindschaft*, Reinbek, 1970.

(i) MARRIAGE AND DIVORCE

Ankarloo, Bengt, 'Marriage and family formation' in Tamara K. Hareven (ed.), *Transitions: the family and the life course in historical perspective*, New York, 1978, pp. 113ff.

Conrad, Hermann, 'Die Grundlegung der modernen Zivilehe durch die französische Revolution', *Zeitschrift der Savigny-Stiftung für Rechtsgeschichte*, 67 (1950), pp. 336ff.

'Das tridentinische Konzil und die Entwicklung des kirchlichen und weltlichen Eherechts' in Georg Schreiber (ed.), *Das Weltkonzil von Trient*, vol. 1, Freiburg, 1951, pp. 297ff.

Duby, Georges, *Medieval marriage*, Baltimore, 1978.

Friedburg, Emil, *Das Recht der Eheschliessung in seiner geschichtlichen Entwicklung*, Aalen, 1965 (Leipzig, 1865).

Held, Thomas, *Soziologie der ehelichen Machtverhältnisse*, Darmstadt, 1978.

Joyce, G. H., *Christian marriage: an historical and doctrinal study*, 2nd edn, London, 1948.

Kitchin, Shephard B., *A history of divorce*, London, 1912.

König, René, 'Zur Geschichte der Monogamie' in Ruprecht Kurzrock (ed.), *Die Institution der Ehe*, Berlin, 1979, pp. 9ff.

Kurzrock, Ruprecht (ed.), *Die Institution der Ehe (Forschung und Information, Schriftenreihe der RIAS-Funkuniversität 24)*, Berlin, 1979.

Lockock, Herbert Mortimer, *History of marriage: Jewish and Christian in relation to divorce and certain forbidden degrees*, New York, 1894.

Mitterauer, Michael, 'Zur gesellschaftlichen Bewertung von Ehe und Elternschaft' in Ruprecht Kurzrock (ed.), *Die Institution der Ehe*, Berlin, 1979, pp. 17ff.

Schwab, Dieter, *Grundlagen und Gestalt der staatlichen Ehegesetzgebung in der Neuzeit bis zum Beginn des 19. Jahrhunderts*, Bielefeld, 1967.

Shorter, Edward, 'Bäuerliches Heiratsverhalten und Ehebeziehungen in der vorindustriellen Gesellschaft' (excerpts from *Die Geburt der modernen Familie*) in Heidi Rosenbaum (ed.), *Seminar: Familie und Gesellschaftsstruktur*, Frankfurt, 1978, pp. 252ff.

Westermarck, E. A., The history of human marriage, 5th edn, 3 vols., New York, 1922.

Wikman, K. R. V., *Die Einleitung der Ehe: Eine vergleichende Ethno-soziologische Untersuchung über die Vorstufe der Ehe in den Sitten des schwedischen Volkstums (Acta Academiae Aboensis, Humaniora* II), Abo, 1937.

(j) FAMILY LAW AND INHERITANCE

Berkner, Lutz Karl, and Mendels, Franklin, 'Inheritance systems, family structure and demographical patterns in Western Europe 1700–1900' in Charles Tilly (ed.), *Historical studies in changing fertility*, Princeton, 1978, pp. 209ff.

Conrad, Hermann, 'Die Rechtsstellung der Ehefrau in der Privat-rechtsgesetzgebung der Aufklärungszeit' in Josef Engel and Martin Klinkenberg (eds.), *Aus Mittelalter und Neuzeit: Gerhard Kallen zum 70. Geburtstag*, Bonn, 1957, pp. 253ff.

Dörner, A., *Industrialisierung und Familienrecht: Die Auswirkungen des sozialen Wandels, dargestellt an den Familienmodellen des ALR, BGB und des französischen Code civil*, Berlin, 1974.

Goody, Jack, *Death, property and the ancestors*, Stanford, 1962.
'Marriage, prestations, inheritance and descent in pre-industrial societies', *Journal of Comparative Family Studies* 1 (1970), pp. 37ff.
'Strategies of heirship', *Comparative Studies in Society and History* 15 (1973), pp. 3ff.
'Inheritance, property and women: some comparative considerations' in Jack Goody *et al.* (eds.), *Family and inheritance*, Cambridge, 1976, pp. 10ff.

Goody, Jack, and Tambiah, S. J., *Bridewealth and dowry (Cambridge Papers in Social Anthropology* 7), New York, 1974.

Goody, Jack, *et al.* (eds.), *Family and inheritance: rural society in western Europe, 1200–1800*, New York, 1976.

Kierman, V. G., 'Private property in history' in Jack Goody *et al.* (eds.), *Family and inheritance*, Cambridge, 1976, pp. 361ff.

Schwab, Dieter, 'Die Familie als Vertragsgesellschaft im Naturrecht der Aufklärung', *Quaderni Fiorenti per la storia del pensiero giuridico moderno* 1 (1972), pp. 358ff.

Thirsk, Joan, 'The European debate on customs of inheritance, 1500–1700 in Jack Goody *et al.* (eds.), *Family and inheritance*, Cambridge, 1976, pp. 177ff.

Thompson, E. P., 'The grid of inheritance: a comment' in Jack Goody *et al.* (eds.), *Family and Inheritance*, Cambridge, 1976, pp. 328ff.

(k) THE HOME

Chombart de Lauwe, P. H., *Famille et habitation*, 2 vols., Paris, 1959–60.

Gleichmann, P. R., 'Wandel der Wohnverhältnisse, Verhäuslichung der Vitalfunktion, Verstädterung und siedlungsräumliche Gestaltungsmacht', *Zeitschrift für Soziologie* 5 (1976), pp. 319ff.

Rapoport, Amos, *House form and culture* (Foundations of Cultural Geography Series), Englewood Cliffs, N.J., 1969.

Roux, Simone, *La maison dans l'histoire*, Paris, 1976.

Schultz, Alwin, *Das häusliche Leben der europäischen Kulturvölker vom Mittelalter bis zur zweiten Hälfte des 18. Jahrhunderts*, Berlin, 1903.

(l) RELATIVES

Debus, Friedhelm, 'Die deutschen Bezeichnungen für die Heiratsverwandtschaft' in Ludwig Erich Schmidt (ed.), *Deutsche Wortforschung in europäischen Bezügen*, vol. 1, Giessen, 1958, pp. 1 ff.

Fox, Robin, *Kinship and marriage: an anthropological perspective*, Harmondsworth, 1967.

Freeman, J. D., 'On the concept of the kindred', *Journal of the Royal Anthropological Institute* 91 (1961), pp. 192 ff.

Goody, Jack (ed.), *The character of kinship*, London, 1973.

Hareven, Tamara K., 'The dynamics of kin in industrial communities: the historical perspective', *American Journal of Sociology* 84, Supplement (1978), pp. 151 ff.

  'The dynamics of kin in an industrial community' in John Demos and Sarane Spence Boocock (eds.), *Turning Points: Historical and sociological essays on the family* (supplement to *American Journal of Sociology* 84), Chicago/London, 1978, pp. 151 ff.

Meillassoux, Claude, 'The economic basis of kinship', *Journal of Peasant Studies*, 1/1 (1973), pp. 81 ff.

Sabean, David, 'Aspects of kinship behaviour and property in rural western Europe before 1800' in Jack Goody (ed.), *Family and inheritance*, Cambridge, 1976, pp. 96 ff.

Wheaton, Robert, 'Family and kinship in western Europe: the problem of the joint family household', *Journal of Interdisciplinary History* 5 (1975), pp. 601 ff.

Wolf, Eric R., 'Kinship, friendship and patron–client relation in complex societies' in Michael Banton (ed.), *The social anthropology of complex societies*, London, 1966.

Section 4: The medieval family

Arnold, Carl, *Das Kind in der deutschen Literatur des XI.–XV. Jahrhunderts*, Greifswald, 1905.

Barie, Lorraine, 'Kinship in Anglo-Saxon society', *British Journal of Sociology* 9 (1958), pp. 230 ff., 359 ff.

Blaschka, A., 'Die Dienstmagd. Ein realistisches Fragment in einer Handschrift des 15. Jahrhundert', *Wissenschaftliche Zeitschrift der Universität Halle, Gesellschafts- und sprachwissenschaftliche Reihe* 8 (1959), pp. 435 ff.

Borst, Arno, *Lebensformen im Mittelalter*, Berlin, 1973.

Bosl, Karl, 'Die "familia" als Grundstruktur der mittelalterlichen Gesellschaft', *Zeitschrift für bayerische Landesgeschichte 38* (1975), pp. 403ff.; reprinted in Karl Bosl, *Die Gesellschaft in der Geschichte des Mittelalters*, Göttingen, 1975, pp. 84ff.

Brande, Jacob, *Die Familiengemeinschaften der Angelsachsen*, Leipzig, 1932.

Browe, Peter, *Beiträge zur Sexualität des Mittelalters*, (*Breslauer Studien zur historischen Theologie* 23), Breslau, 1932.

Brundage, James A., 'Concubinage and marriage in medieval canon law', *Journal of Medieval History* 1 (1975), pp. 1ff.

Brunner, Heinrich, 'Die fränkisch–romanische dos' in Karl Rauch (ed.), *Abhandlungen zur Rechtsgeschichte*, vol. 2, Weimar, 1931, pp. 78ff.

'Die uneheliche Vaterschaft in den älteren germanischen Rechten' in Karl Rauch (ed.), *Abhandlungen zur Rechtgeschichte*, vol. 2, Weimar, 1931, pp. 165ff.

'Die Geburt eines lebenden Kindes und das eheliche Vermögensrecht' in Karl Rauch (ed.), *Abhandlungen zur Rechtsgeschichte*, vol. 2, Weimar, 1931, pp. 117ff.

'Kritische Bemerkungen zur Geschichte des germanischen Weibererbrechts' in Karl Rauch (ed.), *Abhandlungen zur Rechtsgeschichte*, vol. 2, Weimar, 1931, pp. 198ff.

Bücher, Carl, *Die Frauenfrage im Mittelalter*, 2nd edn, Tübingen, 1910.

Brissaud, V. B., 'L'infanticide à la fin du Moyen Âge, ses motivations psychologiques et sa repression' *Revue historique de droit français et étranger* 50 (1972), pp. 229ff.

Britton, Edward, 'The peasant family in fourteenth century England', *Peasant Studies* 5/2 (1976), pp. 2ff.

Bullough, D. A., 'Early medieval social groupings: the terminology of kinship', *Past and Present* 45 (1969), pp. 3ff.

Cammarosano, Paolo, 'Les structures familiales dans les villes de l'Italie communale (XIIe–XIVe siècles)' in Georges Duby and Jacques Le Goff (eds.), *Famille et parenté dans l'Occident médiéval*, Rome, 1977, pp. 181ff.

Chojnacki, Stanley, 'Dowries and kinsmen in early Renaissance Venice', *Journal of Interdisciplinary History* 5 (1975), pp, 571ff.

Coleman, Emily R., 'Medieval marriage characteristics: a neglected factor in the history of medieval serfdom', *Journal of Interdisciplinary History* 2 (1971), pp. 205ff.

'L'infanticide dans le Haut Moyen Âge', *Annales E. S. C.* 29 (1974), pp. 315ff.

'Infanticide in the early Middle Ages', in Susan M. Stuard (ed.), *Women in medieval society*, Philadelphia, 1976, pp. 47ff.

Donat, Peter, *Haus, Hof und Dorf in Mitteleuropa vom 7. bis 12. Jahrhundert*.

Duby, Georges, 'Structures de parenté et noblesse dans La France du Nord aux IXe et XIIe siècles' in *Miscellanea Mediaevalia in Memoriam Jan Frederik Niermeyr*, Groningen, 1967, pp. 149ff.

Duby, Georges, and Le Goff, Jacques (eds.) *Famille et parenté dans l'Occident médiéval*, Rome, 1977.

Escher, Katherine, 'The Germanic family of the Leges Burgundionum', *Mediaevalia et Humanistica* 15 (1963), pp. 5ff.

Faith, Rosamund Jane, 'Peasant families and inheritance customs in medieval England', *Agricultural History Review* 14 (1966), pp. 77ff.

Faulkner, P. A., 'Domestic planning from the twelfth to the fourteenth centuries', *Archaeological Journal* 115 (1958), pp. 150ff.

Fehr, Hans, *Die Rechtsstellung der Frau und der Kinder in den Weistümern*, Jena, 1912.

Feilzer, Heinrich, *Jugend in der mittelalterlichen Ständegesellschaft. Ein Beitrag zum Problem der Generationen*, Vienna, 1971.

Fröhlich, Karl, 'Die Eheschliessung des deutschen Frühmittelalters im Lichte der neueren rechtsgeschichtlichen Forschung', *Hessische Blätter für Volkskunde* 27 (1928), pp. 144ff.

Ganshof, François, 'Le Statut de la femme dans la monarchie franque', *Recueils de la Société Jean Bodin* 12 (1962), pp. 5ff.

Gieysztor, Alexander, 'Le lignage et la famille nobiliaire en Pologne aux XIe, XIIe et XIIIe siècles' in Georges Duby and Jacques Le Goff (eds.), *Famille et parenté dans l'Occident médiéval*, Rome, 1977, pp. 299ff.

Gransden, Antonia, 'Childhood and youth in medieval England', *Nottingham Medieval Studies* 16 (1972), pp. 3ff.

Haff, Karl, 'Der umstrittene Sippenbegriff und die Siedlungsprobleme', *Zeitschrift für Rechtsgeschichte* 70 (1953), pp. 320ff.

Hammel, Eugene A., 'Some medieval evidence on the Serbian Zadruga: a preliminary analysis of the Chrysobulls of Decani' in Robert F. Byrnes (ed.), *Communal families in the Balkans: the Zadruga*, Notre Dame/ London, 1976, pp. 100ff.

Hanawalt, Barbara A., 'Childrearing among the lower classes of late medieval England', *Journal of Interdisciplinary History* 8 (1972), pp. 1ff.

Hauck, Karl, 'Formes de parenté artificielle dans le Haut Moyen Âge' in Georges Duby and Jacques Le Goff (eds.), *Famille et parenté dans l'Occident médiéval*, Rome, 1977, pp. 43ff.

Hazeltine, Harold Dexter, *Zur Geschichte der Eheschliessung nach angelsächsischem Recht*, Berlin, 1905.

Heers, J., *Le clan familial au Moyen Âge*, Paris, 1974.

Herlihy, David, 'Land, family and women in continental Europe, 701–1200', *Traditio* 18 (1962), pp. 89ff.

'Viellir à Florence au Quattrocento', *Annales E. S. C.* 24 (1969), pp. 1338ff.

'Family solidarity in medieval Italian history' in David Herlihy (ed.), *Economy, society and government in medieval Italy*, Kent, Ohio, 1969, pp. 173ff.

'Mapping households in medieval Italy', *Catholic Historical Review* 58 (1972), pp. 1ff.

'Life expectancies for women in medieval society' in Rosemarie Thee Morewedge (ed.), *The role of woman in the Middle Ages*, Albany, N.Y., 1975, 1ff.

'Deaths, marriages, births and the Tuscan economy (c. 1300–1550)' in Ronald Demos Lee *et al.* (eds.), *Population patterns in the past*, New York, 1977, pp. 135ff.

Holmes, U. T., 'Medieval children: *L'enfant et la vie familiale sous l'ancien régime* by Philippe Ariès', *Journal of Social History* 2 (1968), pp. 164ff.

Homans, George Caspari, *English villagers of the thirteenth century*, Cambridge, 1941.

Hughes, Diane Owen, 'Toward historical ethnography: notarial records and family history in the Middle Ages', *Historical Methods Newsletter* 7 (1974), pp. 61ff.

'Domestic ideals and social behavior: evidence from medieval Genoa' in Charles E. Rosenberg (ed.), *The family in history*, Philadelphia, 1975, pp. 115ff.

'Urban growth and family structure in medieval Genoa', *Past and Present* (1975), pp. 3ff.

Kent, Francis William, *Under the shadow of one will: lineage and family in the Renaissance*, Melbourne, 1972.

Household and lineage in Renaissance Florence: the family life of the Capponi, Ginori and Rucellai, Princeton, 1977.

'A la recherche du clan perdu: Jacques Heers and "family clans" in the Middle Ages', *Journal of Family History* 2 (1977), pp. 77ff.

Klapisch, Christiane, 'Household and family in Tuscany in 1427' in Peter Laslett and Richard Wall (eds.), *Household and family in past time*, Cambridge, 1972, pp. 267ff.

'Déclin démographique et structure du ménage. L'exemple de Prato fin XIVe–fin XVe' in Georges Duby and Jacques Le Goff (eds.), *Famille et parenté dans l'Occident médiéval*, Rome, 1977, pp. 255ff.

Klapisch, Christiane, and Demonet, Michel, ' "A uno pane e uno vino": la famille rurale toscane au début du XVe siècle', *Annales E. S. C.* 27 (1972), pp. 873ff.

Koebner, Richard, 'Die Eheauffassung des ausgehenden deutschen Mittelalters', *Archiv für Kulturgeschichte* 9 (1911), pp. 136ff, 279ff.

Köstler, Rudolf, 'Raub-, Kauf- und Friedelehe bei den Germanen', *Zeitschrift der Savigny-Stiftung für Rechtsgeschichte* 63 (1943), pp. 92ff.

Krause, John, 'The medieval household: large or small?', *Economic History Review* 9 (1957), pp. 420ff.

Kroeschell, Karl, 'Die Sippe im germanischen Recht', *Zeitschrift der Savigny-Stiftung für Rechtsgeschichte* 77 (1960), pp. 1ff.

Haus und Herrschaft im frühen deutschen Recht (Göttinger rechtswissenschaftliche Studien 70), Göttingen, 1968.

Lancaster, Lorraine, 'Kinship in Anglo-Saxon society', *British Journal of Sociology* 9 (1958), pp. 230ff, 359ff.

Lehmann, A., *Le rôle de la femme dans l'histoire de France au Moyen Âge*, Paris, 1952.

Lyon, H. R., 'Kinship in Anglo-Saxon England', *Anglo-Saxon England* 3 (1973), pp. 197ff.

Manselli Raoul, 'Vie familiale et éthique sexuelle dans les pénitentiels' in Georges Duby and Jacques Le Goff (eds.), *Famille et parenté dans l'Occident médiéval*, Rome, 1977, pp. 363ff.

McLaughlin, Mary M., 'Überlebende und Stellvertreter: Kinder und Eltern zwischen dem neunten und dreizehnten Jahrhundert' in Lloyd de Mause (ed.), *Hört ihr die Kinder weinen*, Frankfurt, 1977, pp. 147ff.

McNamara, J.-A., and Wemple, S., 'The power of women through the family in medieval Europe, 500–1100' in Mary Hartman and Lois W. Banner (eds.), *Clio's Consciousness Raised: New Perspectives on the History of Women*, New York, 1974, pp. 103ff.

Meyer, Herbert, 'Friedelehe und Mutterrecht', *Zeitschrift der Savigny-Stiftung für Rechtsgeschichte* 47 (1927), pp. 198ff.

Middleton, Christopher, 'The sexual division of labour in feudal England', *New Left Review* 113–14 (1979), pp. 147ff.

Mitterauer, Michael, 'Haus und Gemeinde in der mittelalterlichen Gesellschaft', *Beiträge zur historischen Sozialkunde* 5 (1975), pp. 21ff.

Morewedge, Rosemarie T. (ed.), *The role of woman in the Middle Ages*, Albany, N.Y., 1975.

Origo, I., 'The domestic enemy: eastern slaves in Tuscany in the 14th and 15th centuries', *Speculum* 30 (1955), pp. 321ff.

Painter, Sidney, 'The family and the feudal system in twelfth century England', *Speculum* 35 (1960), pp. 1ff.

Payen, Jean-Charles, 'La crise du mariage à la fin du XIIIe siècle d'après la littérature française du temps' in Georges Duby and Jacques Le Goff (eds.), *Famille et parenté dans l'Occident médiéval*, Rome, 1977, pp. 413ff.

Phillpotts, Bertha, *Kindred and clan in the Middle Ages and after*, Cambridge, 1913.

Portmann, Marie-Louise, *Die Darstellung der Frau in der Geschichtsschreibung des früheren Mittelalters (Basler Beiträge zur Geschichtswissenschaft 69)*, Basle, 1958.

Power, Eileen, *Medieval women*, Cambridge, 1975.
  'The position of women in the Middle Ages' in C. G. Crumps and E. F. Jacob (eds.), *The legacy of the Middle Ages*, Oxford, 1926.

Ring, Richard R., 'Early medieval peasant households in central Italy', *Journal of Family History* 4 (1979), pp. 2ff.

Ross, James Bruce, 'Das Bürgerkind in den italienischen Stadtkulturen zwischen dem vierzehnten und dem frühen sechzehnten Jahrhundert' in Lloyd de Mause (ed.), *Hört ihr die Kinder weinen*, Frankfurt, 1977, pp. 263ff.

Scammell, Jean, 'Freedom and marriage in medieval England', *Economic History Review* 27 (1974), pp. 532ff.

Schultze, Alfred, 'Die Rechtslage des alternden Bauers nach den altnordischen Rechten', *Zeitschrift der Savigny-Stiftung für Rechtsgeschichte* 51 (1931), pp. 258ff.

Schwarz, Ingeborg, *Die Bedeutung der Sippe für die Öffentlichkeit der Eheschliessung im 15. und 16. Jahrhundert*, Neustadt/Aisch, 1959.

Smith, R. M., 'Some reflections on the origin of the European marriage pattern in England' in C. Harris (ed.), *The sociology of the family*, 1979.

'Kin and neighbours in a thirteenth century Suffolk community', *Journal of Family History* 4 (1979), pp. 219ff.

Stobbe, Otto, 'Miteigentum und gesamte Hand', *Zeitschrift für Rechtsgeschichte* 4 (1864), pp. 207ff.

Stuard, Susan M. (ed.), *Women in medieval society*, Philadelphia, 1976.

Thrupp, John, *The Anglo-Saxon home: a history of the domestic institutions and customs of England from the fifth to the eleventh century*, London, 1862.

Walker, Sue S., 'Widow and ward: the feudal law of child custody in medieval England', *Feminist Studies* 3 (1975), pp. 104ff.; reprinted in Susan M. Stuard (ed.), *Women in medieval society*, Philadelphia, 1976, pp. 159ff.

Weinberger, Stephen, 'Peasant households in Provence: c. 800–1100', *Speculum* (1973), pp. 247ff.

Weinhold, Karl, *Die deutschen Frauen im Mittelalter*, 3rd edn, Vienna, 1897.

Westman, Barbara Hanawalt, 'The peasant family and crime in fourteen century England', *Journal of British Studies* 13 (1974), pp. 1ff.

Wollasch, Joachim, 'Eine adelige Familie des frühen Mittelalters', *Archiv für Kulturgeschichte* 39 (1957), pp. 150ff.

Wood, Margaret, *The English medieval house*, London, 1965.

Section 5: The modern family

(a) THE BRITISH ISLES

Anderson, Michael, 'Household structure and the Industrial Revolution; mid-nineteenth-century Preston in comparative perspective' in Peter Laslett and Richard Wall (eds.), *Household and family in past time*, Cambridge, 1972, pp. 215ff.

Family structure in nineteenth century Lancashire, Cambridge, 1972.

Arensberg, Conrad M., and Kimball, Solon T., *Family and community in Ireland*, 2nd edn, Cambridge, 1968.

Armstrong, W. A., 'A note on the household structure of mid-nineteenth-century York in comparative perspective' in Peter Laslett and Richard Wall (eds.), *Household and family in past time*, Cambridge, 1972, pp. 205ff.

Barley, M. W., *The English farmhouse and cottage*, London, 1961.

Bayne-Powell, Rosamond, *The English child in the eighteenth century*, New York, 1939.

Beales, H. Z., 'The Victorian family' in *Ideal and reliefs of the Victorians: an historic revaluation of the Victorian age*', London, 1947.

Bedford, Jessie, *English children in the older time*, 2nd edn, London, 1907.

Bloch, Iwan, *Sexual life in England past and present*, London, 1938.

Branca, Patricia, *Silent sisterhood: middle class women in the Victorian home*, London, 1975.

Burton, Elizabeth, *The Elizabethans at home*, London, 1958.

  The Jacobeans at home, London, 1962.

  The Georgians at home 1714–1830, London 1967.

  The early Victorians at home 1837–1861, London, 1972.

Collier, Francis, *The family economics of the working classes in the cotton industry 1784–1833*, Manchester, 1965.

Connell, Kenneth Hugh, 'Peasant marriage in Ireland: its structures and development since the famine', *Economic History Review* 14 (1962), pp. 502ff.

Cook, O., *The English country house: an art and way of life*, New York, 1974.

Cunnington, P., and Buck, A., *Children's clothes in England: from the fourteenth to the end of the nineteenth century*, New York, 1965.

Curtis, M. H., 'Education and Apprenticeship' in A. Nicoll (ed.), *Shakespeare Survey*, vol. 17, Cambridge, 1964, pp. 53ff.

Davidoff, Leonore, 'Mastered for life: servant and wife in Victorian and Edwardian England', *Journal of Social History* 7 (1974), pp. 406ff.

Dawes, Frank Edward, *Not in front of the servants: domestic service in England 1850–1939*, London, 1973.

Degler, Carl H., 'What ought to be and what was: women's sexuality in the nineteenth century', *American Historical Review* 79 (1974), pp. 1467ff.

Dyhouse, Carol, 'Working-class mothers and infant mortality in England 1895–1914', *Journal of Social History* 12 (1978), pp. 248ff.

Gibbon, P., and Curtin, C., 'The stem family in Ireland', *Comparative Studies in Society and History* 20 (1978), pp. 429ff.

Giesen, D., *Grundlagen und Entwicklung des englischen Eherechts in der Neuzeit*, Bielefeld, 1973.

Haines, Michael R., 'Fertility, nuptiality and occupation: a study of coal mining populations and regions in England and Wales in the mid-nineteenth-century', *Journal of Interdisciplinary History* 8 (1977), pp. 245ff.

Hair, P. E. H., 'Puritanism and bridal pregnancy: some doubts', *Journal of Interdisciplinary History* 7 (1977), pp. 739ff.

Hecht, J. Jean, *The domestic servant class in eighteenth century England*, London, 1956.

Hewitt, Margaret, *Wives and mothers in Victorian industry*, London, 1958.

Hole, Christina, *The English housewife in the seventeenth century*, London, 1953.

Howell, Cicely, 'Stability and change, 1300–1700: the socio-economic context of the self-perpetuating family farm in England', *Journal of Peasant Studies* 2 (1975), pp. 468ff.

James, T. E., 'The illegitimate and deprived child: legitimation and adoption' in R. H. Graveson and F. R. Crane (eds.), *A century of family law, 1857–1957*, London, 1957.

Karpis, Melvin Roland, 'The Victorian family', *New England Social Science Bulletin* 19 (1961), pp. 20ff.

Kern, Stephen, 'Explosive intimacy: psychodynamics of the Victorian family', *History of Childhood Quarterly* 1 (1974) pp. 437ff.

Langer, William L., 'The origins of the birth control movement in England in the early nineteenth century', *Journal of Interdisciplinary History* 5 (1975), pp. 669ff.

Laslett, Peter, 'New light on the history of the English family', *Listener* 75 (1966), pp. 233ff.

'Size and structure of the household in England over three centuries', *Population Studies* 23 (1969), pp. 199ff.

'The decline of the domestic group in England', *Population Studies* 24 (1970), pp. 449ff.

The world we have lost: England before the industrial age, London, 1971.

'Mean household size in England since the sixteenth century' in Peter Laslett and Richard Wall (eds.), *Household and family in past time*, Cambridge, 1972, pp. 125ff.

Family life and illicit love in earlier generations, Cambridge, 1977.

'Parental deprivation in the past', *Local Population Studies* 13 (1974), pp. 11ff.; reprinted in Peter Laslett, *Family life and illicit love in earlier generations*, Cambridge, 1977, pp. 160ff.

Laslett, Peter, and Oosterveen, Karla, 'Long-term trends in bastardy in England: a study of the illegitimacy figures in the parish registers and in the reports of the Registrar General, 1561–1960', *Population Studies* 27 (1973), pp. 255ff.; reprinted in Peter Laslett, *Family life and illicit love in earlier generations*, Cambridge, 1977, pp. 102ff.

Levine, David, 'The demographic implications of rural industrialization: a family reconstitution study of Shepshed, Leicestershire, 1600–1851', *Social History* 2 (1976), pp. 177ff.

Family formation in an age of nascent capitalism, 1977.

Lochhead, Marion, *The Scots household in the 18th century: a century of Scottish domestic and social life*, Edinburgh, 1948.

The Victorian household, London, 1964.

MacFarlane, Alan, *The family life of Ralph Josselin, a seventeenth-century clergyman: an essay in historical anthropology*, Cambridge, 1970.

Malcolmson, R., 'Infanticide in the eighteenth century' in J. S. Cockburn (ed.), *Crime in England 1550–1800*, London, 1977.

Marshall, D., *The English domestic servant in history*, London, 1949.

McGregor, Oliver Ross, *Divorce in England: a centenary study*, London, 1957.

McLaren, A., *Birth control in nineteenth century England*, London, 1978.

Middleton, Christopher, 'The sexual division of labour in feudal England', *New Left Review* (1979), pp. 147ff.

Mueller, Gerhard Q. W., 'Inquiry into the state of a divorceless society: domestic relations, law and morals in England from 1660–1857', *University of Pittsburgh Law Review* 18 (1957), pp. 545ff.

Nixon, J. W., 'Size and structure of the household in England over three centuries: a comment', *Population Studies* 24 (1970), pp. 445ff.

Oren, Laura, 'The welfare of women in laboring families: England, 1860–1950' in Mary Hartman and Lois Banner (eds.), *Clio's consciousness raised: new perspectives on the history of women*, New York, 1974, pp. 226ff.

Outhwaite, R. B., 'Age at marriage in England from the late seventeenth to the nineteenth century', *Transactions of the Royal Historical Society* 23 (1973), pp. 55ff.

Pinchbeck, Ivy, *Women workers and the Industrial Revolution 1750–1850*, 3rd edn, London, 1977 (1930, 1969).

Pinchbeck, Ivy, and Hewitt, Margaret, *Children in English society: from Tudor times to the eighteenth century*, London, 1969.

   Children in English society: from the eighteenth century to the Children Act, 1948, London, 1973.

   'Kindheit und Familie im vor-restaurativen England' (excerpts from *Children in English society: from Tudor times to the eighteenth century*, London, 1969) in Heidi Rosenbaum (ed.), *Seminar: Familie und Gesellschaftsstruktur*, Frankfurt, 1978, pp. 495ff.

Plant, Marjorie, *The domestic life of Scotland in the eighteenth century*, Edinburgh, 1952.

Plumb, J. H., 'The new world of children in eighteenth century England', *Past and Present* 67 (1975), pp. 64ff.

Richards, Eric, 'Women in the British economy since about 1700: an interpretation', *History* 59 (1974), pp. 337ff.

Roberts, Michael, 'Sickles and scythes: women's work and men's work at harvest time', *History Workshop* 7 (1979), pp. 3ff.

Roe, Frederic Gordon, *The Victorian child*, London, 1959.

   The Georgian child, London, 1961.

Saito, Osamu, 'Who worked when: life-time profiles of labour force participation in Cardington and Corfe Castle in the late eighteenth and mid-nineteenth centuries', *Local Population Studies* 22 (1979), pp. 14ff.

Schochet, G. J., 'Patriarchalism, politics and mass attitudes in Stuart England', *Historical Journal* 12 (1969), pp. 413ff.

Schücking, Levin L., *Die puritanische Familie in literatur-soziologischer Sicht*, 2nd edn, Bonn/Munich, 1964 (1929).

Smelser, Neil, *Social change in the Industrial Revolution: an application of theory to the British cotton industry*, London, 1959.

Smith, Steven R., 'The London apprentices as seventeenth century adolescents', *Past and Present* 61 (1973), pp. 149ff.

   'Growing old in early Stuart England', *Albion* 8 (1976), pp. 132ff.

Stone, Lawrence, 'Marriage among the English nobility in the 16th and 17th centuries', *Comparative Studies in Society and History* 3 (1961), pp. 182ff.

'The educational revolution in England 1560–1640', *Past and Present* 28 (1964), pp. 41ff.

'The rise of the nuclear family in early modern England' in Charles E. Rosenberg (ed.), *The family in history*, Philadelphia, 1975, pp. 13ff.

The family, sex and marriage in England 1500–1800, London, 1977.

Die Familie des englischen Adels' (excerpts from *The crisis of aristocracy 1558–1641*, Oxford, 1965) in Heidi Rosenbaum (ed.), *Seminar: Geschichte und Gesellschaftsstruktur*, Frankfurt, 1978, pp. 437ff.

Tipping, H. A., *English Homes*, 3 vols., London, 1921–29.

Tomes, Nancy, 'A "torrent of abuse": crimes of violence between working–class men and women in London 1840–1875', *Journal of Social History* 11 (1978), pp. 328ff.

Trumbach, Randolph, *The rise of the egalitarian family: aristocratic kinship and domestic relations in eighteenth century England*, New York, 1979.

Tucker, M. J., 'Das Kind als Anfang und Ende: Kindheit in England im fünfzehnten und sechzehnten Jahrhundert' in Lloyd de Mause (ed.), *Hört ihr die Kinder weinen*, Frankfurt, 1977, pp. 326ff.

Vicinus, Martha (ed.), *Suffer and be still: women in the Victorian age*, London, 1972.

(ed.) *A widening sphere: changing roles of Victorian women*, Bloomington, 1977.

Wall, Richard, 'Mean household size in England from printed sources' in Peter Laslett and Richard Wall (eds.), *Household and family in past time*, Cambridge, 1972, pp. 159ff.

'Age at leaving home', *Journal of Family History* 3 (1978), pp. 181ff.

Wohl, Anthony S. (ed.) *The Victorian family*, London, 1978.

Wrigley, Edward A., 'Marriage and fertility in pre–industrial England', *Listener* 75 (1966), pp. 199ff.

'Family limitation in pre–industrial England', *Economic History Review* 19 (1966), pp. 82ff.

(b) FRANCE

Aubenas, R., 'La famille dans l'ancienne Provence', *Annales d'histoire économique et sociale* 8 (1936), pp. 523ff.

Bardet, J. P., *et al.*, *Le bâtiment: enquête d'histoire économique*, vol. 1, *Maisons rurales et urbaines dans la France traditionelle*, Paris, 1971.

Baulant, Micheline, 'La famille en miettes: sur un aspect de la démographie du XVIIIe siècle', *Annales E. S. C.* 27 (1972), pp. 959ff.

Blayo, Yves, 'Size and structure of households in a northern French village between 1836 and 1861' in Peter Laslett and Richard Wall (eds.), *Household and family in past time*, Cambridge, 1972, pp. 255ff.

Bourdieu, Pierre, 'Célibat et condition paysanne', *Études rurales* 5 (1962), pp. 32ff.

'Les stratégies matrimoniales dans le système de reproduction', *Annales E. S. C.* 27 (1972), pp. 1105ff.

Bousquet, G. H., 'Quelques remarques sur l'évolution de l'économie domestique en France depuis Louis-Philippe', *Revue d'histoire économique et social* 45 (1967), pp. 509ff.

Camp, Wesley D., *Marriage and the family in France since the Revolution: an essay in the history of population*, New York, 1961.

Chamoux, A., 'Enfants illégitimes et enfants trouvés', *Annales de démographie historique* (1973), pp. 422ff.

Chamoux, A., and Dauphin, C., 'La contraception avant la Révolution française: l'exemple de Châtillon-sur-Seine', *Annales E. S. C.* 24 (1969), pp. 662ff.

Châtelain, Abel, 'Migrations et domesticité féminine urbaine en France, XVIIIe siècle–XXe siècle', *Revue d'histoire économique et sociale* 47 (1969), pp. 508ff.

Collomp, Alain, 'Famille nucléaire et famille élargie en Provence au XVIIIe siècle', *Annales E. S. C.* 27 (1972), pp. 969ff.

'Ménage et famille: étude comparatives sur la dimension et le structure du groupe domestique', *Annales E. S. C.* 29 (1972), pp. 777ff.

Davis, Natalie Z., 'The reasons of misrule: youth groups and charivaris in sixteenth century France', *Past and Present* 50 (1971), pp. 41ff.

'City women and religious change in sixteenth century France' in Dorothy Gies McGuigan (ed.), *A sampler of women's studies*, Ann Arbor, 1973.

'Women on top' in N. Z. Davis, *Society and culture in early modern France*, Stanford, 1975, pp. 124ff.

'Ghosts, kin and progeny: some features of family life in early modern France', *Daedalus* 106/2 (1977), pp. 82ff.

Depauw, Jacques, 'Amour illégitime et société à Nantes au XVIIIe siècle', *Annales* 27 (1972), pp. 1155ff.

Donzelot, Jacques, *La police des familles*, Paris, 1977.

Dupâquier, J., and Lachiver, M., 'Les débuts de la contraception en France ou les deux malthusianismes', *Annales E. S. C.* 24 (1969), pp. 1391ff.

Duplessis de Grenedan, J., *Histoire de l'autorité paternelle et de la Société familiale en France avant 1789*, Paris, 1900.

Elias, Norbert, 'Wohn- und Lebensformen der höfischen "Familie" im Frankreich des 18. Jahrhunderts' (excerpts from *Die höfische Gesellschaft*, Neuwied, 1969) in Heidi Rosenbaum (ed.), *Seminar, Familie und Gesellschaftsstruktur*, Frankfurt, 1978, pp. 480ff.

Fairchilds, Cissie, 'Female sexual attitudes and the rise of illegitimacy: a case study', *Journal of Interdisciplinary History* 8 (1978), pp. 627ff.

'Masters and servants in eighteenth century Toulouse', *Journal of Social History* 12 (1979), pp. 368ff.

Fine-Souriac, Agnès, 'La famille-souche pyrénéenne au XIXe siècle: quelques réflexions de méthode', *Annales E. S. C.* 32 (1977), pp. 478ff.

Flandrin, Jean-Louis, *Les amours paysannes (XVIe—XIXe siècle)*, Paris, 1975.

Gaillard-Bans, Patricia, 'Maison longue et famille étendue en Bretagne', *Etudes rurales* 62 (1976), pp. 73ff.

Gallet, M., *Paris domestic architecture of the eighteenth century*, London, 1972.

Giesey, Ralph, 'Rules of inheritance and strategies of mobility in pre-revolutionary France', *American Historical Review* 82 (1977), pp. 271ff.

Goubert, Pierre, 'Family and province: a contribution to the knowledge of family structure in early modern France', *Journal of Family History* 2 (1977), pp. 179ff.

Hufton, Olwen, 'Women and the family economy in eighteenth century France', *French Historical Studies* 9 (1975), pp. 1ff.

Hunt, David, *Parents and children in history: the psychology of family life in early modern France*, New York, 1970.

Jeay, Madeleine, 'Sexuality and family in fifteenth-century France', *Journal of Family History* 4 (1979), pp. 328ff.

Lebrun, F., 'Démographie et mentalités: le mouvement de conception sous l'Ancien Régime', *Annales de Démographie Historique* (1974), pp. 45ff.

La vie conjugale sous l'Ancien Régime, Paris, 1975.

Le Roy Ladurie, Emmanuel, *Les paysans de Languedoc*, Paris, 1966.

'Family structures and inheritance customs in sixteenth century France' in Jack Goody *et al.* (eds.), *Family and inheritance*, Cambridge, 1976, pp. 37ff.

Montaillou, village occitan de 1294 à 1324, Paris, 1975.

Maspétiol, Roland, 'Sociologie de la famille rurale de type traditionnel en France' in *Sociologie comparée de la famille contemporaine. Colloques internationaux du Centre National de la Recherche Scientifique*, Paris, 1955, pp. 129ff.

McBride, Theresa Marie, 'Social mobility for the lower class: domestic servants in France', *Journal of Social History* 8 (1974), pp. 63ff.

McLaren, Angus, 'Some secular attitudes toward sexual behavior in France: 1760–1860', *French Historical Studies* 8 (1974), pp. 604ff.

'Abortion in France: women and the regulation of family size 1800–1914', *French Historical Studies* 10 (1978), pp. 461ff.

Paris, William, and Schwartz, Moshe, 'Household complexity in nineteenth century France', *American Sociological Review* 37 (1972), pp. 154ff.

Phillips, Roderick, 'Women and family breakdown in eighteenth century France: Rouen 1780–1800', *Social History* 2 (1976), pp. 197ff.

'Women's emancipation: the family and social change in eighteenth century France', *Journal of Social History* 12 (1979), pp. 553ff.

Sargent, F. L., 'From feudalism to family farm in France', *Agricultural History* 25 (1961), pp. 198ff.

Segalen, Martine, *Nuptialité et alliance: Le choix du conjoint dans une commune de l'Eure aux XVIIIe et XIXe siècles*, Paris, 1972.

Mari et femme dans la France rurale traditionelle, Paris, 1973.

'The family cycle and household structure: five generations in a French village', *Journal of Family History* 2 (1977), pp. 223ff.

Sturmingher, Laura S., 'The artisan family: traditions and transition in nineteenth century Lyon', *Journal of Family History* 2 (1977), pp. 211ff.

Sussman, George D., 'Parisian infants and Norman wet nurses in the early nineteenth century: a statistical study', *Journal of Interdisciplinary History* 7 (1977), pp. 637ff.

Tilly, Louise A., 'Structure de l'emploi, travail des femmes et changements démographiques dans deux villes industrielles, Anzin et Roubaix, 1872–1906', *Le Mouvement Social* 105 (1978), pp. 33ff.

'Individual lives and family strategies in the French proletariat', *Journal of Family History* 4 (1979), pp. 137ff.

The family wage economy in a French textile city: Roubaix 1872–1906' *Journal of Family History* 4 (1979), pp. 381ff.

Walle, Etienne van de, 'Alone in Europe: the French fertility decline until 1850' in Charles Tilly (ed.), *Historical studies in changing fertility*, Princeton, 1978, pp. 257ff.

Wheaton, Robert, 'Bordeaux before the Fronde: a study of family, class and social structure' (dissertation, Harvard University), 1973.

Yver, Jean, *Égalité entre héritiers et exclusion des enfants dotés. Essai de géographie coutumière*, Paris, 1966.

(c) CENTRAL EUROPE

Arnold, Klaus, 'Der Umbruch des generativen Verhaltens in einem Bergbauerngebiet' in Heimold Helczmanovski (ed.), *Beiträge zur Bevölkerungs- und Sozialgeschichte Österreichs*, Vienna, 1973, pp. 404ff.

Baumert, Gerhard, 'Changes in the family and the position of older persons in Germany', *International Journal of Comparative Sociology* 1 (1960), pp. 202ff.

'Einige Beobachtungen zur Wandlung der familialen Stellung des Kindes in Deutschland' in Ludwig von Friedeburg (ed.), *Jugend in der modernen Gesellschaft*, Cologne/Berlin, 1965, pp. 309ff.

Baumert, Gerhard, and Hönninger, E., *Deutsche Familien nach dem Kriege*, Darmstadt, 1954.

Berkner, Lutz Karl, 'The stem family and the developmental cycle of the peasant household: an eighteenth-century Austrian example', *American Historical Review* 77 (1972), pp. 398ff.

'Inheritance, land tenure and peasant family structure: a German regional comparison' in Jack Goody *et al.* (eds.), *Family and inheritance*, Cambridge, 1976, pp. 71ff.

'Peasant household organization and demographic change in Lower Saxony (1689–1766) in R. Lee *et al.* (eds.), *Population patterns in the past*, New York, 1977, pp. 53ff.

Blaschke, Karlheinz, *Bevölkerungsgeschichte von Sachsen bis zur industriellen Revolution*, Weimar, 1967.

Blessing, Werner K., 'Umwelt und Mentalität im ländlichen Bayern. Eine Skizze zum Alltagswandel im 19. Jahrhundert', *Archiv für Sozialgeschichte* 19 (1979), pp. 1ff.

Blochmann, Elisabeth, *Das 'Frauenzimmer' und die 'Gelehrsamkeit'*, Heidelberg, 1966.

Boesch, Hans, *Kinderleben in der deutschen Vergangenheit*, 2nd edn, Jena, 1924, (Leipzig, 1900).

Bolognese–Leuchtenmüller, Birgit, 'Unterversorgung und mangelnde Betreuung der Kleinkinder in den Unterschichten – Familien als soziales Problem des 19. Jahrhunderts' in Herbert Knittler (ed.), *Wirtschafts- und sozialhistorische Beiträge (Festschrift für Alfred Hoffmann zum 75. Geburtstag)*, Vienna, 1979, pp. 410ff.

Braun, Rudolf, *Industrialisierung und Volksleben*, Erlenbach, 1960.

Sozialer und kultureller Wandel in einem ländlichen Industriegebiet (Zürcher Oberland) unter Einwirkung des Maschinen— und Fabrikswesens im 19. und 20. Jahrhundert, Erlenbach, 1969.

Brauneder, Wilhelm, *Die Entwicklung des Ehegüterrechts in Österreich*, Salzburg, 1973.

Bridenthal, Renate, 'Beyond Kinder, Küche, Kirche: Weimar women at work', *Central European History* 6 (1973), pp. 148ff.

Bürgin-Kreis, Hildegard, 'Der Wandel der Familie in Sitte und Recht in den letzten 150 Jahren', *Schweizerisches Archiv für Volkskunde* 49 (1953), pp. 101ff.

Castell, Adelheid Gräfin zu, 'Forschungsergebnisse zum gruppenspezifischen Wandel generativer Strukturen' in Werner Conze (ed.), *Sozialgeschichte der Familie in der Neuzeit Europas*, Stuttgart, 1974, pp. 161ff.

Cohn, 'Gemeinderschaft und Hausgenossenschaft', *Zeitschrift für vergleichende Rechtswissenschaft* 13 (1899), pp. 1ff.

Demeny, Paul, 'Early fertility decline in Austria-Hungary: a lesson in demographic transition', *Daedalus* 97 (1968), pp. 502ff.

Ditt, K., *et al.*, *Familie und soziale Plazierung. Studien zur Sozialgeschichte der Familie in Westfalen im 19. Jahrhundert*, Opladen, 1979.

Duden, Barbara, 'Das schöne Eigentum. Zur Herausbildung des bürgerlichen Frauenbildes an der Wende vom 18. zum 19. Jahrhundert', *Kursbuch* 47 (1977), pp. 125ff.

Ehmer, Josef, 'Wohnen ohne eigene Wohnung. Zur sozialen Stellung von

Untermietern und Bettgehern' in Lutz Niethammer (ed.), *Wohnen im Wandel*, Wuppertal, 1979, pp. 132ff.

Elschenbroich, Donata, *Kinder werden nicht geboren*, Frankfurt, 1977.

Engelsing, Rolf, 'Das häusliche Personal in der Epoche der Industrialisierung', *Jahrbuch für Sozialwissenschaft* 20 (1969), pp. 84ff.; reprinted in Rolf Engelsing, *Zur Sozialgeschichte deutscher Mittel- und Unterschichten*, Göttingen, 1973, pp. 225ff.

'Probleme der Lebenshaltung in Deutschland im 18. und 19. Jahrhundert', *Zeitschrift für die gesamte Staatswissenschaft* 126 (1970), pp. 290ff.; reprinted in Rolf Engelsing, *Zur Sozialgeschichte deutscher Mittel- und Unterschichten*, Göttingen, 1973, pp. 11ff.

'Der Arbeitsmarkt der Dienstboten im 17., 18. und 19. Jahrhundert' in Hermann Kellenbenz (ed.), *Wirtschaftspolitik und Arbeitsmarkt (Sozial- und wirtschaftshistorische Studien)*, 1974, pp. 159ff.

'Zur Stellung der Dienstboten in der bürgerlichen Familie im 18. und 19. Jahrhundert' (excerpts from *Dienstbotenlektüre im 18. und 19. Jahrhundert*) in Heidi Rosenbaum (ed.), *Seminar: Familie und Gesellschaftsstruktur*, Frankfurt, 1978, pp. 413ff.

Feigl, Helmut, 'Bäuerliches Erbrecht und Erbgewohnheiten in Niederösterreich', *Jahrbuch für Landeskunde von Niederösterreich* 37 (1965–67), pp. 161ff.

Fick, Ludwig, *Die bäuerliche Erbfolge im Gebiet des bayrischen Landrechts*, Munich, 1895.

Fliri, Franz, *Bevölkerungsgeographische Untersuchungen im Unterinntal*, Innsbruck, 1948.

Freudenthal, Margarete, 'Strukturelle Merkmale proletarischen Familienlebens zwischen 1880 und 1900' (excerpts from *Gestaltwandel der städtischen bürgerlichen und proletarischen Hauswirtschaft*) in Heidi Rosenbaum (ed.), *Seminar: Familie und Gesellschaftsstruktur*, Frankfurt, 1978, pp. 342ff.

'Bürgerlicher Haushalt und bürgerliche Familie vom Ende des 18. bis zum Ende des 19. Jahrhunderts' (excerpts from *Gestaltwandel der städtischen bürgerlichen und proletarischen Hauswirtschaft*) in Heidi Rosenbaum (ed.), *Seminar: Familie und Gesellschaftsstruktur*, Frankfurt, 1978, pp. 375ff.

Gerhard, Ute, *Verhältnisse und Verhinderungen. Frauenarbeit, Familie und Rechte der Frauen im 19. Jahrhundert*, Frankfurt, 1978.

Griessmair, Johannes, *Knecht und Magd in Südtirol. Dargestellt am Beispiel der bäuerlichen Dienstboten im Pustertal (Volkskundliche Forschungen 1; Veröffentlichungen der Universität Innsbruck 30)*, Innsbruck, 1976.

Hardach-Pinke, I., and Hardach, G. (eds.), *Deutsche Kindheiten. Autobiographische Zeugnisse 1700–1900*, Kronberg, 1978.

Harnisch, Hartmut, 'Bevölkerungsgeschichtliche Probleme der industriellen Revolution in Deutschland' in Karl Lärmer (ed.), *Studien zur Ge-*

schichte der Produktivkräfte. Deutschland zur Zeit der industriellen Revolution, Berlin, 1979, pp. 267ff.

Hartinger, Walter, 'Bayrisches Dienstbotenleben auf dem Land vom 16. bis 18. Jahrhundert', *Zeitschrift für bayrische Landesgeschichte* 38 (1975), pp. 598ff.

Hausen, Karin, 'Mütter zwischen Geschäftsinteressen und kultischer Verehrung. Der "deutsche Muttertag" in der Weimarer Republik' in Gerhard Huck (ed.), *Sozialgeschichte der Freizeit*, Wuppertal, 1980, pp. 249ff.

Haushofer, Heinz, 'Ländliche Dienstboten in Altbayern', *Zeitschrift für Agrarsoziologie und Agrargeschichte* 23 (1975), pp. 47ff.

Hoffmann, Julius, *Die 'Hausväterliteratur und die Predigten über den christlichen Hausstand'. Ein Beitrag zur Geschichte der Lehre vom Haus und der Bildung für das häusliche Leben*, Weinheim, 1959.

Hofmann, E., 'Volkskundliche Betrachtungen zur proletarischen Familie in Chemnitz um 1900', *Wissenschaftliche Zeitschrift der Humboldt Universität Berlin, Gesellschaftliche und sprachwissenschaftliche Reihe* 20 (1971), pp. 65ff.

Hörger, Hermann, 'Familienformen einer ländlichen Industriesiedlung im Verlauf des 19. Jahrhunderts', *Zeitschrift für bayerische Landesgeschichte* 41 (1978), pp. 771ff.

Ilisch, Peter, 'Zum Leben von Knechten und Mägden in vorindustrieller Zeit', *Rheinisch-westfälische Zeitschrift für Volkskunde* 22 (1976), pp. 255ff.

Imhof, Arthur E., *Historische Demographie als Sozialgeschichte. Giessen und Umgebung vom 17. zum 19. Jahrhundert*, 2 vols., Darmstadt, 1975.

'Ländliche Familienstrukturen an einem hessischen Beispiel, Heuchelheim 1690–1900' in Werner Conze (ed.), *Sozialgeschichte der Familie in der Neuzeit Europas*, Stuttgart, 1976, pp. 197ff.

Jurczyk, Karin, *Frauenarbeit und Frauenrolle. Zum Zusammenhang von Familienpolitik und Erwerbsarbeit in Deutschland 1918–1975*, Munich, 1976.

Khera, Sigrid, 'Social stratification and land inheritance among Austrian peasants', *American Anthropologist* 75 (1973), pp. 814ff.

Kirkpatrick, Clifford, *Nazi Germany: its women and family life*, New York, 1938.

Knodel, John, 'Law, marriage and illegitimacy in nineteenth century Germany', *Population Studies* 20 (1967), pp. 279ff.

'Infant mortality and fertility in three Bavarian villages: an analysis of family history from the nineteenth century', *Population Studies* 22 (1968), pp. 297ff.

'Malthus amiss: marriage restrictions in 19th century Germany', *Social Science* 27 (1972), pp. 40ff.

The decline of fertility in Germany, 1871–1939, Princeton, 1974.

Knodel, John, and Maynes, Mary Jo, 'Urban and rural marriage patterns in imperial Germany', *Journal of Family History* 1 (1976), pp. 129ff.

Knodel, John, and Walle, E. van de, 'Breast feeding, fertility and infant mortality: an analysis of some early German data', *Population Studies* 21 (1967), pp. 109ff.

Kocka, Jürgen, 'Family and bureaucracy in German industrial management 1850–1914', *Business History Review* 45 (1971), pp. 133ff.

Köllmann, Wolfgang, *Bevölkerung in der industriellen Revolution. Studien zur Bevölkerungsgeschichte Deutschlands*, Göttingen, 1974.

Könecke, Otto, *Rechtsgeschichte des Gesindes in West- und Süddeutschland*, Marburg, 1912.

Koomen, Willem, 'A note on the authoritarian German family', *Journal of Marriage and the Family* 36 (1974), pp. 634ff.

Kramer, Karl-Sigismund, 'Das Haus als geistiges Kraftfeld im Gefüge der alten Volkskultur', *Rheinland-westfälische Zeitschrift für Volkskunde* 11 (1964), pp. 30ff.

Kraus, Antje, ' "Antizipierter Ehesegen" im 19. Jahrhundert. Zur Beurteilung der Illegitimität unter sozialgeschichtlichem Aspekt', *Vierteljahrschrift für Sozial- und Wirtschaftsgeschichte* 66 (1979), pp. 174ff.

Kretschmer, Ingrid, and Piegler, Josef, 'Ausgedinge'. *Österreichischer Volkskunde-Atlas*, 2/18 Commentary, 1965.

Kuhn, Andrea, *Tugend und Arbeit. Zur Sozialisation durch Kinder- und Jugendliteratur im 18. Jahrhundert*, Berlin, 1975.

Langewiesche, Dieter, 'Politische Orientierung und soziales Verhalten. Familienleben und Wohnverhältnisse im "roten" Wien der Ersten Republik' in Lutz Niethammer (ed.), *Wohnen im Wandel*, Wuppertal, 1979, pp. 171ff.

Lee, W. Robert, 'Bastardy and the socioeconomic structure of south Germany', *Journal of Interdisciplinary History* 7 (1977), pp. 403ff.

'Bastardy in south Germany: a reply', *Journal of Interdisciplinary History* 8 (1978), pp. 471ff.

Lehners, Jean Paul, 'Haus und Familie im Markt Stockerau am Ende des 17. Jahrhunderts', *Unsere Heimat* 4 (1974), pp. 222ff.

Mason, Tim, 'Zur Lage der Frauen in Deutschland 1930–1940, Wohlfahrt, Arbeit und Familie' in *Gesellschaft, Beiträge zur Marxschen Theorie*, vol. 6, Frankfurt, 1976, pp. 118ff.

McLaren, Angus, 'Contraception and its discontents: Sigmund Freud and birth control', *Journal of Social History* 12 (1979), pp. 513ff.

Medick, Hans, 'Spinnstuben auf dem Dorf. Jugendliche Sexualkultur und Feierabendbrauch in der ländlichen Gesellschaft der frühen Neuzeit' in Gerhard Huck (ed.), *Sozialgeschichte der Freizeit*, Wuppertal, 1980, pp. 19ff.

Mendels, Franklin, 'Industry and marriages in Flanders before the Industrial Revolution' in Paul Deprez (ed.), *Population and Economics. Proceedings of Section V of the Fourth Congress of the International Economic History Association 1968*, Winnipeg, 1970, pp. 81ff.

'Agriculture and peasant industry in eighteenth century Flanders' in William N. Parker and Eric L. Jones (eds.), *Economic Issues in European Agrarian History*, Princeton, 1975, pp. 179ff.

Mitterauer, Michael, 'Zur Familienstruktur in ländlichen Gebieten Österreichs im 17. Jahrhundert' in Heimold Helczmanovszky (ed.), *Beiträge zur Bevölkerungs- und Sozialgeschichte Österreichs*, Vienna, 1973, pp. 168ff.

'Zur Frage des Heiratsverhaltens im österreichischen Adel' in Heinrich Fichtenau and Erich Zöllner (eds.), *Beiträge zur neueren Geschichte Österreichs*, Vienna, 1974, pp. 176ff.

'Auswirkungen von Urbanisierung und Frühindustrialisierung auf die Familienverfassung an Beispielen des österreichischen Raums' in Werner Conze (ed.), *Sozialgeschichte der Familie in der Neuzeit Europas*, Stuttgart, 1976, pp. 53ff.

'Gesindeehen in ländlichen Gebieten Kärntens – ein Sonderfall historischer Familienbildung', *Grazer Forschungen zur Wirtschafts und Sozialgeschichte* 3 (1978), pp. 227ff.

'Vorindustrielle Familienformen. Zur Funktionsentlastung des "ganzen Hauses" im 17. und 18. Jahrhundert', *Wiener Beiträge zur Geschichte der Neuzeit* 2 (1975), pp. 123ff.; reprinted in Michael Mitterauer, *Grundtypen alteuropäischer Sozialformen*, vol. 2, Stuttgart, 1979, pp. 35ff.

'Familienformen und Illegitimität in ländlichen Gebieten Österreichs', *Archiv für Sozialgeschichte* XIX (1979), pp. 123ff.

'Zur familienbetrieblichen Struktur im zünftischen Handwerk' in *Wirtschafts und sozialhistorische Beiträge (Festschrift für Alfred Hoffmann)*, Vienna, 1979, pp. 190ff.; reprinted in Michael Mitterauer, *Grundtypen alteuropäischer Sozialformen*, Stuttgart, 1979, pp. 98ff.

Möller, Helmut, *Die kleinbürgerliche Familie im 18. Jahrhundert. Verhalten und Gruppenkultur*, Berlin, 1969.

Monter, William E., 'Historical demography and religious history in sixteenth century Geneva', *Journal of Interdisciplinary History* 9 (1979), pp. 399ff.

Nell, Adelheid von, *Die Entwicklung der generativen Strukturen bürgerlicher und bäuerlicher Familien von 1750 bis zur Gegenwart (Bochumer historische Studien* 1), Bochum, 1973.

Netting, Robert T., 'Household dynamics in a nineteenth century Swiss village', *Journal of Family History* 4 (1979), pp. 39ff.

Neumann, Robert Paul, 'Industrialization and sexual behavior: some aspects of working-class life in imperial Germany' in Robert Bezucha (ed.), *Modern European social history*, Lexington, Mass., 1972, pp. 270ff.

Niethammer, Lutz, 'Wie wohnten die Arbeiter im Kaiserreich?, *Archiv für Sozialgeschichte* 16 (1976), pp. 61ff.

(ed.), *Wohnen in Wandel*, Wuppertal, 1979.

Ottmüller, Uta, *Die Dienstbotenfrage. Zur Sozialgeschichte der doppelten Ausnutzung des Dienstmädchens im deutschen Kaiserreich*, Münster, 1978.

'Mutterschaft und romantische Liebe: Alltagsweltliebe und ihre praktischen Konsequenzen', *Sozialwissenschaftliche Informationen für Unterricht und Studium* 81 (1979), pp. 12ff.

Platzer, Hans, *Geschichte der ländlichen Arbeitsverhältnisse in Bayern*, Munich, 1904.

Plaul, Hainer, *Landarbeiterleben im 19. Jahrhundert*, Berlin, 1979.

Rach, Hans-Jürgen, *Bauernhaus, Landarbeiterkaten und Schnitterkasernen*, Berlin, 1974.

Reulecke, Jürgen, and Weber, Wolfhard (eds.), *Fabrik, Familie, Feierabend*, Wuppertal, 1979.

Roller, Otto Konrad, *Die Einwohnerschaft der Stadt Durlach im 18. Jahrhundert*, Karlsruhe, 1907.

Rümelin, E., 'Heiratsalter und Fruchtbarkeit der Ehen und ihre Entwicklung seit 1500', *Württembergische Jahrbücher für Statistik und Landeskunde* (1923–24), pp. 9ff.

Sabean, David Warren, 'Household formation and geographical mobility: a family register study for a Württemberg village, 1760–1900', *Annales de Démographie Historique* (1970), pp. 275ff.

'Famille et tenure paysanne: aux origines de la Guerre des Paysans en Allemagne', *Annales E. S. C.* 27 (1972), pp. 903ff.

'Family and land tenure: a case study of conflict in the German Peasants' War (1525)', *Peasant Studies Newsletter* 3 (1974), pp. 1ff.

'Verwandtschaft und Familie in einem württembergischen Dorf 1500–1870: einige methodische Überlegungen' in Werner Conze (ed.), *Sozialgeschichte der Familie in der Neuzeit Europas*, Stuttgart, 1976, pp. 231ff.

Sandgruber, Roman, 'Gesindestuben, Kleinhäuser und Arbeiterkasernen. Ländliche Wohnverhältnisse im 18. und 19. Jahrhundert in Österreich' in Lutz Niethammer (ed.), *Wohnen im Wandel*, Wuppertal, 1979, pp. 107ff.

Sauermann, Dietmar (ed.), *Knechte und Mägde in Westfalen um 1900*, Münster, 1972.

Schaub, Walter, 'Städtische Familienformen in sozialgenealogischer Sicht (Oldenburg 1743–1870)' in Werner Conze (ed.), *Sozialgeschichte der Familie in der Neuzeit Europas*, Stuttgart, 1976, pp. 292ff.

Schlumbohm, Jürgen, 'Strasse und Familie. Kollektive und individualisierende Formen der Sozialisation im kleinen und gehobenen Bürgertum Deutschlands um 1800', *Zeitschrift für Pädagogik* 25 (1979), pp. 697ff.

Schmidt, Karl, *Gutsübergabe und Ausgedinge. Eine agrarpolitische Untersuchung mit besonderer Berücksichtigung der Alpen- und Sudetenländer*, Vienna/Leipzig, 1930.

Schneider, Lothar, *Der Arbeiterhaushalt im 18. und 19. Jahrhundert, dargestellt am Beispiel des Heim- und Fabrikarbeiters (Beiträge zur Ökonomie von Haushalt und Verbrauch* 4), Berlin, 1967.

Schomerus, Heilwig, 'Die Wohnung als unmittelbare Umwelt. Unternehmer, Handwerker und Arbeiterschaft einer württembergischen Industriestadt 1850–1890' in Lutz Niethammer (ed.), *Wohnen im Wandel*, Wuppertal, 1979, pp. 211ff.

Schulte, Regina, 'Dienstmädchen im herrschaftlichen Haushalt. Zur Genese ihrer Sozialpsychologie', *Zeitschrift für bayerische Landesgeschichte* 41 (1978), pp. 879ff.

Sering, Max. (ed.), *Die Vererbung des ländlichen Grundbesitzes im Königreich Preussen*, 4 vols., Berlin, 1899–1910.

Shorter, Edward, 'Bastardy in south Germany: a comment', *Journal of Interdisciplinary History* 8 (1978), pp. 459ff.

Sieder, Reinhard, 'Strukturprobleme ländlicher Familien im 19. Jahrhundert', *Zeitschrift für bayerische Landesgeschichte* 41 (1978), pp. 173ff.

Spree, Reinhard, 'Die Entstehung der differentiellen Säuglingssterblichkeit in Deutschland seit der Mitte des 19. Jahrhunderts (Ein Versuch zur Mentalitätsgeschichte)' in Arthur E. Imhof (ed.), *Mensch und Gesundheit in der Geschichte (Abhandlungen zur Geschichte der Medizin und Naturwissenschaften* 39), Husum, 1980.

'Strukturierte soziale Ungleichheit im Reproduktionsbereich. Zur historischen Analyse ihrer Erscheinungsformen in Deutschland, 1870–1913' in Jürgen Bergmann (ed.), *Geschichte als politische Wissenschaft (Geschichte und Theorie der Politik* 1), Stuttgart, 1979, pp. 55ff.

Stekl, Hannes, 'Häusliches Personal und "soziale Frage"', *Jahrbuch des Vereins für Geschichte der Stadt Wien* 34 (1978), pp. 342ff.

Tenfelde, Klaus, 'Arbeiterhaushalt und Arbeiterbewegung 1850–1914', *Sozialwissenschaftliche Informationen für Unterricht und Studium* 6/4 (1977), pp. 160ff.

'Ländliches Gesinde in Preussen. Gesinderecht und Gesindestatistik 1810–1861', *Archiv für Sozialgeschichte* 19 (1979), pp. 189ff.

Teuteberg, Hans-Jürgen, 'Die häuslichen Daseinsformen der Arbeiterfamilie', *Beiträge zur historischen Sozialkunde* 5 (1975), pp. 75ff.

Treue, Wilhelm, 'Haus und Wohnung im 19. Jahrhundert' in Walter Artelt *et al.* (eds.), *Städte-, Wohnungs- und Kleidungshygiene des 19. Jahrhunderts in Deutschland*, Stuttgart, 1969, pp. 34ff.

Walle, Etienne van de, 'Household dynamics in a Belgian village, 1847–1866', *Journal of Family History* 1 (1976), pp. 80ff.

Weber, Helmut, *Der deutsche bäuerliche Übergabevertrag als vorweggenommene Erbfolge in den Hof. Ein Beitrag zur Geschichte der bäuerlichen Hofübergabe*, Berlin, 1941.

Weber-Kellermann, Ingeborg, 'Die Familie auf dem Lande in der Zeit zwischen Bauernbefreiung und Industrialisierung', *Zeitschrift für Agrargeschichte und Agrarsoziologie* 26 (1978), pp. 66ff.

'Die gute Kinderstube. Zur Geschichte des Wohnens von Bürgerkindern' in Lutz Niethammer (ed.), *Wohnen im Wandel*, Wuppertal, 1979, pp. 44ff.

Weiland, Hans Georg, *Die geschichtliche Entwicklung des bäuerlichen Altenteils und seine Regelung nach dem Reichserbhofgesetz*, Emsdetten, 1939.

Weinzierl, Erika, and Stadler, Karl (eds.), *Geschichte der Familienrechtsgesetzgebung in Österreich (Justiz und Zeitgeschichte 3)*, Vienna, 1978.

Wesener, Gunter, *Geschichte des Erbrechts in Österreich seit der Rezeption*, Graz/Cologne, 1957.

Wopfner, Hermann, *Bergbauernbuch. Von Arbeit und Leben des Tiroler Bergbauern in Vergangenheit und Gegenwart*, 3 vols., Innsbruck, 1951–60.

Woude, A. M. van der, 'Variations in the size and structure of the household in the United Provinces of the Netherlands in the seventeenth and eighteenth centuries' in Peter Laslett and Richard Wall (eds.), *Household and family in past time*, Cambridge, 1972, pp. 299ff.

Wurzbacher, Gerhard, *Leitbilder gegenwärtigen deutschen Familienlebens. Methoden, Ergebnisse und sozialpädagogische Forderungen einer soziologischen Analyse von 164 Familienmonographien. (Mit einem einführenden Vergleich über die bundesdeutsche Familie 1950–1968)*, 4th edn, Stuttgart, 1969.

(d) SCANDINAVIA

Agren, Kurt, et al. (eds.), *Aristocrats, farmers, proletarians: essays in Swedish demographic history*, Uppsala, 1973.

Akerman, Sune, et al. (eds.), *Chance and change: social and economic studies in historical demography in the Baltic area*, Odense, 1978.

Brox, Ottar, 'Natural conditions, inheritance and marriage in a north Norwegian fjord', *Folk* 6 (1964), pp. 35ff.

Drake, Michael, *Population and Society in Norway, 1735–1865*, Cambridge, 1969.

Eriksson, Ingrid, and Rogers, John, *Rural labor and population change. Social and demographic developments in east-central Sweden during the nineteenth century (Studia Historica Upsaliensia 100)*, Uppsala, 1978.

Gaunt, David, 'Familie, Haushalt und Arbeitsintensität' in Arthut E. Imhof (ed.), *Biologie des Menschen in der Geschichte*, Stuttgart, 1978, pp. 219ff.

'Family planning and the preindustrial society: some Swedish evidence' in Kurt Agren et al. (eds.), *Aristocrats, farmers, proletarians: essays in Swedish demographic history*, Uppsala, 1973, pp. 28ff.

'Pre-industrial economy and population structure. The elements of variance in early modern Sweden', *Scandinavian Journal of History* (1977), pp. 183ff.

Hojrup, Ole, 'Die Arbeitsteilung zwischen Männern und Frauen in der bäuerlichen Kultur Dänemarks', *Ethnologia Scandinavica* (1975), pp. 23ff.

Löfgren, Orvar, 'Family and household among Scandinavian peasants: an exploratory essay', *Ethnologia Scandinavica* (1974), pp. 17ff.

'Arbeitsteilung und Geschlechterrollen in Schweden', *Ethnologia Scandinavica* (1975), pp. 49ff.

Pederson, Ragnar, 'Die Arbeitsteilung zwischen Frauen und Männern in einem marginalen Ackerbaugebiet – Das Beispiel Norwegen', *Ethnologia Scandinavica* (1975), pp. 37ff.

Rich, G. W., 'Changing Icelandic kinship', *Ethnology* 15 (1976), pp. 1ff.

Sheild, Betty, 'Women in Norway: their position in family life, in Employment and Society'. Oslo, 1970.

Sjovall, Hjalmar 'Abortion and contraception in Sweden 1870–1970', *Zeitschrift für Rechtsmedizin* 70 (1972), pp. 197ff.

Sweetser, D. A., 'Urbanization and the patrilineal transmissions of farms in Finland', *Acta Sociologica* 7 (1964), pp. 215ff.

Tomasson, Richard F., 'A millennium of sexual permissiveness in the north', *American Scandinavian Review* 62 (1974), pp. 370ff.

'Premarital sexual permissiveness and illegitimacy in the Nordic countries', *Comparative Studies in Society and History* 18 (1976), pp. 252ff.

(e) EASTERN AND SOUTH-EAST EUROPE

Andorka, Rudolf, 'Un exemple de la faible fécondité légitime dans une région de la Hongrie. L'Ormànsag à la fin du XVIIIe siècle et au début du XIXe: contrôle, des naissances ou faux-semblants?', *Annales de Démographie Historique* (1972), pp. 25ff.

'The peasant family structure in the eighteenth and nineteenth centuries', *Acta Ethnographica Academiae Scientiarum Hungariae* 25 (1975), pp. 321ff.

Atkinson, Dorothy, 'Society and the sexes in the Russian past' in Dorothy Atkinson et al. (eds.), *Women in Russia*, Stanford, 1977.

Atkinson, Dorothy et al. (eds.), *Women in Russia*, Stanford, 1977.

Bardach, Julius, 'L'indivision familiale dans les pays du Centre-Est européen' in Georges Duby and Jacques Le Goff (eds.), *Famille et parenté dans l'Occident médiéval*, Rome, 1977, pp. 335ff.

Benet, Sula, 'Some changes in family structure and personality among peasants of Great Russia', *Transactions of the New York Academy of Sciences* 32 (1970), pp. 51ff.

Burié, Olivera, 'The Zadruga and the contemporary family in Yugoslavia' in Robert F. Byrnes (ed.), *Communal Families in the Balkans: the Zadruga*, Notre Dame/London, 1976, pp. 117ff.

Byrnes, Robert F. (ed.), *Communal families in the Balkans: the Zadruga essays by Philip E. Mosely and essays in his honor*, Notre Dame, 1976.

Czap, Peter Jr, 'Marriage and the peasant joint family in the era of serfdom' in David L. Ransel (ed.), *The family in imperial Russia*, Urbana, 1978, pp. 103ff.

Denich, Bette S., 'Sex and power in the Balkans' in M. Z. Rosaldo and L. Lamphere (eds.), *Women, culture and society*, Stanford, 1974, pp. 243ff.

Dopsch, Alfons, 'Die slavischen Hauskommunionen', *Osterreichische Rundschau* 19/2 (1909).

Dunn, Patrick P., ' "Der Feind ist das Kind": Kindheit im zaristischen Russland' in Lloyd de Mause (ed.), *Hört ihr die Kinder weinen*, Frankfurt, 1977, pp. 535ff.

Dunn, Stephen P., 'The family as reflected in Russian folklore' in David L. Ransel (ed.), *The family in imperial Russia*, Urbana, 1978, pp. 153ff.

Elnett, Elaine Pasvolsky, *Historic origins and social development of family life in Russia*, New York, 1927.

Erlich, Vera, 'The southern Slav patriarchal family', *Sociological Review* 32 (1940), pp. 224ff.

'Phases in the evolution of family life in Yugoslavia', *Sociological Review* 37 (1945), pp. 50ff.

Family in transition, Princeton, 1966.

'The last big Zadrugas: Albanian extended families in the Kosovo region' in R. F. Byrnes (ed.), *Communal families in the Balkans: the Zadruga*, Notre Dame/London, 1976, pp. 244ff.

Fel, Edit, and Hofer, Tamas, *Proper peasants: traditional life in a Hungarian village*, Chicago, 1969.

Freeze, Gregory L., 'Caste and emancipation: the changing status of clerical families in the great reforms' in David L. Ransel (ed.), *The family in imperial Russia*, Urbana, 1978, pp. 124ff.

Grossmith, C. J., 'The cultural ecology of Albanian extended family household in Yugoslav Macedonia' in Robert F. Byrnes (ed.), *Communal families in the Balkans: the Zadruga*, Notre Dame/London, 1976, pp. 232ff.

Halpern, Joel M., 'Town and countryside in Serbia in the nineteenth century. Social and household structure as reflected in the census of 1863' in Peter Laslett and Richard Wall (eds.), *Household and Family in Past Time*, Cambridge, 1972, pp. 401ff.

'Individual life cycles and family cycle: a comparison of perspectives' in J. Cuisenier (ed.), *The family life in European societies*, The Hague, 1977, pp. 353ff.

Halpern, Joel M., and Anderson, David, 'The Zadruga: a century of change', *Anthropologica* 12 (1970), pp. 83ff.

Halpern, Joel M., and Halpern, Barbara K., *A Serbian village in historical perspective*, New York, 1972.

Hammel, Eugene A., *Alternative social structures and ritual relations in the Balkan*, Englewood Cliffs, N.J., 1968.

'Social mobility, economic change and kinship in Serbia', *Southwestern Journal of Anthropology* 25 (1969), pp. 188ff.

'The Zadruga as process' in Peter Laslett and Richard Wall (eds.), *Household and family in past time*, Cambridge, 1972, pp. 335ff.

'Reflections on the Zadruga', *Ethnologia Slavica* 7 (1977), pp. 141ff.

Hauptmann, Ludmil, *Hauskommunionen der Südslaven. Historisch-politische Blätter*, Munich, 1883.

Ilieva, N., and Oshavkova, Vera, 'Changes in the Bulgarian family cycle from the end of the 19th century to the present day' in Jean Cuisenier (ed.), *The family life cycle in European societies*, The Hague, 1977, pp. 382ff.

Johnson, Robert Eugene, 'Family relations and the rural–urban nexus: patterns in the hinterland of Moscow, 1880–1900' in David L. Ransel (ed.), *The family in imperial Russia*, Urbana, 1978, pp. 263ff.

Jovanovič, *Die historische Entwicklung der serbischen Hauskommunionen*, Belgrade, 1896.

Koenker, Diane, 'Urban families, working–class youth groups, and the 1917 Revolution in Moscow' in David L. Ransel (ed.), *The family in imperial Russia*, Urbana, 1978, pp. 280ff.

Konsulova, N. D., *Die Grossfamilie in Bulgarien*, Erlangen, 1915.

Kriukov, M. V., 'Types of kinship systems and their historical interpretation', *Soviet Anthropology and Archeology* 11 (1972), pp. 107ff.

Kula, Witold, 'La seigneurie et la famille paysanne en Pologne au XVIII siècle', *Annales E. S. C.* 27 (1972), pp. 949ff.

Laslett, Peter, and Clarke, Marilyn, 'Houseful and household in an eighteenth–century Balkan city. A tabular analysis of the listing of the Serbian sector of Belgrade' in Peter Laslett and Richard Wall (eds.), *Household and family in past time*, Cambridge, 1972, pp. 375ff.

Moryay, Judit, 'The joint family in Hungary' in *Europa et Hungaria, Congressus Ethnographiv in Hungaria 1963*, Budapest, 1965, pp. 231ff.

Moseley, P. E., *The distribution of the Zadruga within southeastern Europe. The Joshua Starr memorial volume, Jewish Social Studies* 5, 1953, pp. 219ff.; reprinted in Robert F. Byrnes (ed.), *Communal families in the Balkan: the Zadruga*, Notre Dame/London, 1976, pp. 58ff.

'The peasant family: the Zadruga, or communal joint-family in the Balkans, and its recent evolution' in Caroline Farrar Ware (ed.), *The cultural approach to history*, New York, 1940, pp. 95ff.; reprinted in Robert F. Byrnes (ed.), *Communal families in the Balkan: the Zadruga*, Notre Dame/London, 1976, pp. 19ff.

'The Russian family: old style and new' in Ruth Nanda Anshen (ed.), *The family: its function and destiny*, New York, 1959, pp. 104ff.; reprinted in Robert F. Byrnes (ed.), *Communal families in the Balkans: the Zadruga*, Notre Dame/London, 1976, pp. 70ff.

'Adaption for survival: the Varžić Zadruga', *Slavonic East and European Review* 21 (1943), pp. 147ff.; reprinted in Robert F. Byrnes (ed.), *Communal families in the Balkans: the Zadruga*, Notre Dame/London, 1976, pp. 31ff.

Palli, Heldur, 'Parish registers, revisions of land and souls, family reconstitution and household' in Sune Akerman (ed.), *Chance and change: social and economic studies in historical demography in the Baltic area*, Odense, 1978, pp. 143ff.

Peisker, J., 'Die serbische Zadruga', *Zeitschrift für Sozial- und Wirtschaftsgeschichte* 7 (1899), pp. 211ff.

Plakans, Andrejs, 'Seigneurial authority and peasant family life: the Baltic area in the eighteenth century', *Journal of Interdisciplinary History* 5 (1975), pp. 629ff.

   'Peasant farmsteads and households in the Baltic littoral 1797', *Comparative Studies in Society and History* 17 (1975), pp. 2ff.

   'Familial structure in the Russian Baltic provinces: the nineteenth century' in Werner Conze (ed.), *Sozialgeschichte der Familie in der Neuzeit Europas*, Stuttgart, 1976, pp. 346ff.

   'Identifying kinfolk beyond the household', *Journal of Family History* 2 (1977), pp. 3ff.

   'Parentless children in the soul revisions: a study of methodology and social fact' in David L. Ransel (ed.), *The family in imperial Russia*, Urbana, pp. 77ff.

Ransel, David L. (ed.), *The family in imperial Russia*, Urbana, 1978.

Rheubottom, David B., 'Time and form: contemporary Macedonian households and the Zadruga controversy' in Robert F. Byrnes (eds.), *Communal families in the Balkans: the Zadruga*, Notre Dame/London, 1976, pp. 215ff.

Shanin, Theodor, 'A Russian peasant household at the turn of the century' in Theodor Shanin (ed.), *Peasants and peasant societies*, 1971, pp. 30ff.

Shinn, William T., 'The law of the Russian peasant household', *Slavic Review* 20 (1961), pp. 601ff.

Sicard, Emile, *La Zadruga sud-slave dans l'évolution de groupe domestique*, Paris, 1943.

   La Zadruga dans la littérature Serbe (1850–1912), Paris, 1943.

   Problèmes familiaux chez les slaves du sud, Paris, 1947.

   'The Zadruga community: a phase in the evolution of property and family in an agrarian milieu' in Robert F. Byrnes (ed.), *Communal families in the Balkans: the Zadruga*, Notre Dame/London, 1976, pp. 252ff.

Sklar, June L., 'The role of marriage behavior in the demographic transition: the case of eastern Europe around 1900', *Population Studies* 28 (1974), pp. 231ff.

Strohal, J., *Die Entwicklung der Hauskommunionengesetzgebung in Kroatien und Slavonien*, 1907.

Thomas, W. J., and Znaniecki, F., *The Polish peasant in Europe and America*, Chicago, 1918–20.

Tovrov, Jessica, 'Mother–child relationship among the Russian nobility' in David L. Ransel (ed.), *The family in imperial Russia*, Urbana, 1978, pp. 15ff.

Vinski, Z., *Die südslavische Grossfamilie in ihrer Beziehung zum asiatischen Grossraum*, Zagreb, 1938.

Volin, Lazar, 'The peasant household under the Mir and the Kolkhoz in modern Russian history' in Caroline Ware (ed.), *Cultural approaches to history*, New York, 1940, 125ff.

Zarnowska, Anna, 'La famille et le statut familial des ouvriers et des domestiques dans le royaume de Pologne au déclin du XIXe siècle', *Acta Poloniae Historica* 35 (1977), pp. 113ff.

(f) THE MEDITERRANEAN REGION

Bardis, Panos D., 'The changing family in modern Greece', *Sociology and Social Research* 40 (1955), pp. 19ff.

Bell, Rudolph, *Fate and honor, family and village. Demographic and cultural change in rural Italy since 1800*, Chicago, 1979.

Campbell, J. K., *Honour, family and patronage: a study of institutions and moral values in a Greek mountain community*, Oxford, 1964.

Davis, J., *Land and family in Pisticci*, London, 1973.

A Venetian family and its fortune, 1500–1900, Philadelphia, 1975.

Dupâquier, Jacques, and Jadin, Louis, 'Structure of household and family in Corsica, 1769–1771' in Peter Laslett and Richard Wall (eds.), *Household and family in past time*, Cambridge, 1972, pp. 283ff.

Fitzmaurice-Kelly, Julia, 'Women in sixteenth-century Spain', *Revue Hispanique* 70 (1927), pp. 557ff.

Friedl, Ernestine, 'The role of kinship in the transmission of national culture to rural villages in mainland Greece', *American Anthropologist* 61 (1959), pp. 30ff.

'Dowry, inheritance and land tenure' in Jack Goody (ed.), *Kinship*, Harmondsworth, 1971.

Goldthwaite, Richard A., *Private wealth in Renaissance Florence: a study of four families*, Princeton, 1968.

'The Florentine palace as domestic architecture', *American Historical Review* 77 (1972), pp. 977ff.

Kertzer, David, 'European peasant household structure: some implications from a nineteenth century Italian community', *Journal of Family History* 2 (1977), pp. 333ff.

Lisón-Tolosana, Carmelo, 'The ethics of inheritance' in G. J. Peristiany (ed.), *Mediterranean family structures*, Cambridge, 1976, pp. 305ff.

Litchfield, R. Burr, 'Demographic characteristics of Florentine patrician families, sixteenth to nineteenth centuries', *Journal of Economic History* 29 (1969), pp. 191ff.

Livi-Bacci, Massimo, 'Fertility and nuptiality changes in Spain from the late eighteenth to the early twentieth century', *Population Studies* 22 (1968), pp. 83ff.

Peristiany, J. G. (ed.), *Mediterranean family structures*, Cambridge, 1976.

Pitt-Rivers, Julian, 'Ritual kinship in the Mediterranean: Spain and the Balkans' in J. G. Peristiany (ed.), *Mediterranean family structures*, Cambridge, 1976, pp. 317ff.

The fate of Shechem, or the politics of sex: essays in the anthropology of the Mediterranean, Cambridge, 1977.

Tentori, Tullio, 'Social classes and family in a southern Italian town: Matera' in J. G. Peristiany (ed.), *Mediterranean family structures*, Cambridge, 1976, pp. 273ff.

Whitaker, Jan, 'Familial roles in the extended patrilineal kin-group in northern Albania' in J. G. Peristiany (ed.), *Mediterranean family structures*, Cambridge, 1976, pp. 195ff.

Index

absolutism, 4, 9, 80, 81, 123, 131
accommodation: for the elderly, 154,
161–2, 163, 169; living, 151;
non-familial, 96; public, 77
adaptation, social, 90
adolescence, 93–117; age of, 95–6, 110,
115; alienation of, 94; as cheap labour,
107–9, 126; commercialization of,
117; conditions of work, 97, 103, 105,
107–8; culture, 94, 111, 112, 115–17;
emancipation, 113, 114, 115–17, 132;
in the family household, 97–117,
150–3; in the family cycle, 49–52,
53–5, 62, 66–9, 83, 109–10, 137–8;
fostered, 99; 'in service', 98–9, 100,
101, 103–9; independence of, 96, 102,
109–17, 152, 166, 174; influence on,
94, 100, 111–13, 115–17; interactions
of, 94, 95, 98, 111–13; job
qualifications, *see* work training;
maltreatment of, 108; marriage, 96,
114; maturity, 95–6; mortality, 35;
occupational choice, 109–17 *passim*;
peer groups, 3, 88, 94, 111–12,
115–17; sex life, 114; social class and,
110; social status of, 97, 101;
socialization, 94, 95, 98, 100–2, 104,
106, 112–13, 115–17
adoption, 10, 16
adulthood, 96

age, 34–5, 88, 94–5; of adolescence,
95–6, 110, 115; at death, 34–5; and
family composition, 64–9; and family
cycle, 50–2, 55, 64–9, 144, 146–53
passim; at inheritance, 34; of marital
partner, 126–7, 148–9; 151, 167; at
marriage, 34, 36–9, 50, 57, 58, 62, 65,
66, 96, 114, 144–51, 167; patterns,
64–5, 144; of physical maturity, 95;
'working', 51–3, 61, 93–117 *passim*,
166, 174
ageing, 142–55, 157–76; concept of, 155;
description of, 143; and family
structure, 142–55; gender and,
148–50, 153, 162, 169, 170–1, 172–5;
and historical change, 142–55;
morbidity and, 147–8; occupation
and, 159–76; post-parental
comradeship, 152–3; and poverty,
170; psychological problems of, 157,
166–7, 174–6; social meaning of,
144–55
agnatic relationships, *see* descent
agrarian society, 26, 37–44, 57, 77,
100–1, 145, 148, 152, 157–60, 165–70,
173–6 *passim*; developments in, 38,
125; protection in, 77; *see also* farm
communities, peasantry
alienation, 71, 94, 107
Altenteiler, 15, 17, 162